AFRICAN WRITERS

FOUNDING EDITOR

TOM MBOYA

The Challenge of Nationhood

A COLLECTION OF
SPEECHES AND
WRITINGS

HEINEMANN EDUCATIONAL BOOKS
LONDON · IBADAN · NAIROBI

Heinemann Educational Books Ltd
22 Bedford Square London WC1B 3HH
P.M.B. 5205 Ibadan · P.O. Box 45314 Nairobi
EDINBURGH MELBOURNE AUCKLAND EXETER (NH)
NEW DELHI HONG KONG SINGAPORE KUALA LUMPUR
KINGSTON PORT OF SPAIN

ISBN 0 435 90081 1

© The Estate of Tom Mboya 1970
First published by André Deutsch 1970
First published in *African Writers Series* 1970
Reprinted 1972, 1975, 1979

Printed and bound in Great Britain by
Fakenham Press Limited, Fakenham, Norfolk

CONTENTS

DEDICATION

For those who seek fulfilment, the challenge of development offers the most exciting and rewarding experience. With independence a new phase in the struggle for nationhood begins. The search for unity must continue. The urgent needs of the people cannot wait for there is no probationary period for a newly independent state. International power politics and competition in world trade pay no regard to the fact that emergent nations face a demanding and precarious period of transition.

In this setting the developing countries face the challenge of development. There is no alternative but to prosecute the task of development with resolution in the knowledge that independence would be reduced to a mere slogan if this challenge is not met boldly.

The youth, the leaders, the women, the intellectuals, the workers and the people of the new nations accept the opportunity and challenge of nation building in the spirit of *Harambee* and self help.

'Some people see things and ask why? I dream of things and say why not?' — *Robert F. Kennedy*

FOREWORD
BY H. E. MZEE JOMO KENYATTA
President of the Republic of Kenya

It is with profound respect that I write a foreword to this selection of writings and speeches by the late Tom Mboya. It was his intention that this work, which he was preparing at the time of his assassination, should stand as a record of some of his ideas and ideals which have been of great importance in the shaping of independent Kenya. Instead, because of his untimely and tragic death, this book must be part of his memorial. It is a tangible form of his work whose greater but less tangible form exists in so many spheres of our modern economic, social and political development.

In the dark and difficult days of the Emergency he emerged as an uncompromising champion of the struggle for Kenya's independence and freedom and indeed for the freedom of the whole of Africa. In so doing he was adamantly, ceaselessly and courageously re-inforcing the efforts of those who had started the struggle for the emancipation of the people of Kenya. Tom Mboya was one of the most effective and progressive Ministers of my Government. He was a mature political leader who never involved himself in petty and parochial matters. The part he played in the task of building the Kenya nation is invaluable and will remain an inspiration to all of us. Tom was always prepared to devote much of his time and energy to the service of his nation and to the welfare of mankind. On many occasions he has ably represented Kenya in important world councils and has been instrumental in bringing about rapid economic and social transformation in Kenya. Those of us who were privileged to work with Tom knew at first hand of his brilliance and restless energy. These talents he devoted to the betterment of our country, our continent and the world. Those who will know him through the writings on the pages which follow will not fail to become aware that here was indeed a man of true greatness.

Jomo Kenyatta

14th September 1969

ACKNOWLEDGMENTS

I am indebted to Professor Ogot who inspired the idea of a book on my speeches and who did most of the research and selection of the original set of speeches to be considered for publication as well as the sections to be considered. Tony Hughes read through all the speeches advising on the choice of speeches and arrangement of the book and read through the manuscript. I am grateful to him for this help. Mr. Philip Ndegwa, Permanent Secretary in the Ministry of Economic Planning and Development, read the speeches and advised on the subject matter as well as assisting with some of the footnotes; Miss Olga Marlin, Principal of the Kianda College with a team of girls did the final typing of the manuscript; my Secretary Miss Sheila Campbell typed many of the corrections and revisions of the manuscript; I owe a special debt of gratitude to all these people and to Mr. Otieno Nundu my private secretary who is responsible for the safekeeping of all my old documents.

My wife Pamela and my children Rosemary, Maureen, Peter, Susan and Lucas had to bear many hours and evenings when I locked myself in my study to read the manuscripts and re-read the speeches. I am glad for their love and encouragement.

There are others who contributed in many ways including those who inspired me such as the officials in my Ministry, the Members of Parliament, the many members of self-help groups, the teachers and students, the leaders and members of women's groups and the people of our country whose aspirations, hopes, expectations and problems are the subject of this book. Last but not least K.A.N.U. the party of which I have been Secretary General since it was founded and our President, His Excellency Mzee Jomo Kenyatta who gave me the opportunity of responsibility to learn at close quarters the issues discussed in this book together with the privilege to make my contribution towards their solutions. To one and all I express my deep gratitude and express the hope that God will give us the life and strength to see the work started carried to fulfilment.

Introduction

CRISIS OF CONFIDENCE

going through multiple transitions — all
...nialism to independence; from illiteracy to
...ence agriculture to a monetary modern economy;
...tribal rural life to a new urban cosmopolitan life; from traditional
tribal custom to Christianity and new attitudes to our women and youth.
Wage employment has also brought about its own changes. All these
transitions have placed maximum pressures on our people and institutions. In less than a decade of independence our enemies have too often
been given the opportunity to point a finger at our tragedies; our
friends have sadly drawn attention to our shortcomings and we ourselves
must often feel frustrated at the non-realisation of our dreams and
aspirations. We have found ourselves in a critical and hostile world
which insists on perfection where Africa is concerned — despite the
fact that none of the older nations have themselves achieved such
perfection!

If we are wise we shall not despair at our difficulties and disappoint-
ments. Unless we are foolish we shall not declare with shrill and
unconvincing propaganda that everything is perfect. Rather our task
should be to examine and to analyse our experience in order to plan a
better path for the future. If such a study leads us to abandon cherished
notions and to depart from what we once thought necessary, so be it.
Only the most searching analysis, perhaps resulting in startling and
radical conclusions, will be sufficient. For the few years of freedom from
colonial rule have led us to the point where Africa faces a crisis — a
crisis of confidence. This crisis of confidence is the result of new realisa-
tions in a large number of areas where we had been accustomed to
provide over-simple answers. Now we are being forced to acknowledge
that simple answers do not exist in practice; and the danger is that we
shall lose our nerve in the face of this realisation, or try to replace old
slogans by new ones. This would be disastrous. Our task is to think, and
to act on that thinking. We know our goals; in the light of our African
experience we must think again about the realities underlying our
problems.

In the field of international relations there is a crisis concerning our
policy of non-alignment. Most of the developing world, most of the

countries which have achieved independence since the Second World War, have declared themselves to be non-aligned. Yet all of them have found it difficult to implement this policy in practice. International relations is not a subject in which absolute right and absolute wrong are clearly defined. This is a lesson which the nations of Africa have quickly learned during their few years of independence. For example, there is no such thing as bilateral aid without strings. Nations need friends and friendship is a two-way relationship. Some nations rejected association with France and tried Russia yet found that this new ally was equally demanding. The countries of East Africa were glad enough to look to Britain's friendship to help them out during their army mutinies of 1964. Egypt has had reason to draw closer to the Soviet Union for help in re-arming following her defeat by Israel. Now the Nigerians and the Biafrans have found it necessary to go looking for allies — and they have sometimes discovered friendship in the strangest places and in the most unusual combinations.

It would be impossible to deny that such alliances have their dangers. Aid of any kind, and especially military assistance, has a way of bending the attitudes and policies of the recipient, however much he may protest to the contrary. Furthermore, it is only to be expected that the big powers will attempt to export their ideologies to other nations. One reason they fail is that they try to impose not only the fundamentals and principles of their beliefs, but also the superficial details and practices which have become part of their ideology simply because of their own national experience. Thus, it is obvious that the communism practiced in the Soviet Union is something very different from that which was envisaged by Marx or Lenin. It has been modified in practice to suit Russian conditions; it is hardly likely therefore that exactly the same system will suit Cuba, the whole of Africa or Czechoslovakia. Similarly, capitalism in Europe and America has been modified, in some cases almost out of recognition.

In general it can be said that any economic or political system must be flexible if it is to survive and be of benefit to society. It should never be forgotten that systems are established to serve the society: they are not totem poles to be worshipped. Further, it would be unrealistic to think that established systems in one part of the world can, without modification be transplanted in other parts of the world. Ideologies may provide general signposts through the complexities of social living; they do not and cannot provide easy answers to all the daily problems which confront us.

Thus it is that since independence African countries have come to realise that certain practical realities of life make it impossible to order our external affairs in purely ideological terms. Take the extreme case of countries such as Lesotho and Botswana which for geographic reasons find themselves compelled to build trade and other contacts with South Africa. These two countries cannot boycott South Africa and survive: the matter is as simple as that.

Our new nations seek to establish themselves in the world community as free, sovereign and independent states. They want to have influence on world affairs. They want to establish an identity and image of their own. They need to be objective and to establish a reputation for independence and a sense of justice. They want to be taken seriously and refuse to agree that issues such as world peace, disarmament, etc. should be a monopoly of the super powers. They do not want to be subject to the gravitational pull of any one of the power blocs.

National self-interest is the basic motivation of any country's external relations. Such consideration led Britain to seek to hold a balance of power in Europe in the eighteenth and nineteenth centuries. It is self-interest which has caused modern France to ease itself away from the American-dominated western alliance. For all the slogans and diatribes it is essentially this rather than ideology which has split communist China from the Soviet bloc. The nations of Africa, I am glad to say, have quickly learned what international affairs are all about.

I am not suggesting that our foreign policies have become, or should in the future become, purely Machiavellian, without reference to principle. It is simply that we have learned to live with the world as it is and set out from there to remould it in a practical manner. Take the question of pan-Africanism, for example. When the first few states in Africa became independent some people thought that continent-wide unity could be achieved overnight. It was naïve to think that Africa could escape the internal squabbles over boundaries and loyalties of a kind which have existed since nation states were first created. Experience has shown us that unity will only come slowly and through careful planning. It seems, for example, that economic co-operation provides a more lasting basis for unity than hastily conceived political federations.

There are so many fields in which the principles of speculative theory have been modified by harsh experience. It was quite understandable that at independence we should start with a brave rush to create our own political, social and economic institutions and attitudes. Our desire was laudable; the difficulties we have experienced mean that we must adjust our tactics of change. Certainly there is no point in change for its own sake. Only if some special institution has meaning for our people or has utility within our special circumstances is it justified.

Look at the political institutions. In most cases we have started off with those bequeathed to us by the former colonial powers. This is the system we have been used to working within. We may introduce certain superficial innovations but the principles and so much of the machinery remain the same. It is difficult to break away entirely, to steer a new course, to create institutions which are African yet which are appropriate for modern society. Ease of communication is drawing the people of the world closer together. While we have every right to safeguard our identity it would be foolish and indeed against our own interest to keep ourselves apart just to be different.

There are facts which we have to bear in mind while properly seeking *African* ways. We must not reject the experience of others while devising means of incorporating traditional African attitudes of mutual social responsibility and grassroots democracy in our modern institutions.

Around the time of independence there was much talk of Africa's need for one-party states — not that the idea is exclusively African. Recent events have shown that one-party systems are not necessarily as strong as or as efficacious as some people thought. They are not a protection for the masses against tyranny, nor do they provide a sure protection for any group to maintain its entrenched position in the face of popular dissatisfaction and revolution. At the time of independence few people talked about the role of the armed forces. Yet it is probably true to say that the army has been more significant in post-independence politics in Africa than any other group or institution. It has been more significant than, say, the trade unions, the churches, teachers, or even perhaps than political parties. Various answers have been found to the problems posed by the existence of armed forces. Some countries have deliberately divided their forces, carefully separating the army, the police, armed youth brigades and other services. Some countries bring military leaders into partnership in the political hierarchy. Others think the best way is to integrate the whole of the armed services into the political fabric of the state by making all of them members of the ruling party. Thus there is a search for an arrangement in this new power structure. It is too early to say if these various experiments will succeed. Tensions between social, economic and other interest groups exist in any state. Certainly by bringing all groups into the party you have a framework within which to resolve potential conflicts. But it could be argued too that if the party and the government are one and the same thing you have not solved the problem, merely shifted it. For the time being however, the important thing is that the problem has been recognised and efforts to find a solution are being made and must continue to be made.

All the same I believe that any system is preferable to the no-party state. The party provides a forum where people can be assisted to understand and to participate in the formulation of policy. It is the meeting place for supporters of the government and those who run the government. It is here that the development and creation of new institutions and new policies must be thrashed out.

Where the party is weak the danger arises that the leadership will become increasingly isolated from the people. Instead of the two-way communication channel which a well organised party provides, governments may come to rely increasingly on officials, administrators and even secret police for their knowledge of their own citizens.

A feeling of 'them' versus 'us' arises among the people and the government falls — by democratic means if relatively free elections take place, otherwise by some more violent process.

Nor is the exercise of power at the centre the only problem. At the time of independence we promised 'Government of the people, by the people and for the people'. The idea is that the people will participate through their elected representatives — who are expected to speak for them and to keep them in contact with the government — in parliament. Soon after independence new problems come to the surface. First comes the problem of contact between the elected representatives and their electors. Many electors begin to complain about the representatives whom they no longer can approach — or even see! Then there comes the problem of relations between the elected members, i.e. back-benchers and the ministers of the cabinet. Many back-benchers suspect the ministers and even accuse them of betraying the people! The fact that they belong to the same party is soon forgotten and only the ministers are left to defend government policies. Sometimes policies are discarded and personalities become the main bone of contention in parliament! Party discipline is another problem. No satisfactory system seems to have really emerged. The party wants to assert itself while the members of parliament resent what they consider to be interference with their right to speak for their electors freely. In many cases the organisers of coups in Africa have used apparent confusion and bickering in parliament as the excuse for their action.

So far no African state has satisfactorily solved the question of local authorities. Obviously there is no universal ideal for the correct division of powers and functions between central and local government. In Africa the tendency has generally been towards a consolidation of power at the centre. In some cases this has been done peacefully and without bloodshed. In other cases secessionist movements have asserted themselves, normally on the basis of allegations of ethnic domination, as in the Sudan and Nigeria. Provided that the state is not too large the more centralised systems seem to be most appropriate, in view of our scarce resources of human skills and the relatively clear-cut needs in social services and similar fields where local government normally operates. The efforts to find a solution to this problem have often been made difficult by the search for national stability through national unity after independence. The people recognise national leadership and do not often even appreciate the functions of the local authorities. They expect the national leaders to be responsible for all matters affecting their welfare. Any attempt by the new central government to lay blame on local governments for failure to provide services is regarded as a political manœuvre to avoid responsibility. Where a multi-party situation exists opposition parties can use local authorities to fight the party in power. But perhaps the most crucial question is still how to create local authorities that can respond positively to the urgent task of development.

Another crisis to which various solutions have been proposed is that of the position of civil servants. Some countries have brought civil servants right into politics, making many appointments subject to political control and bringing politically appointed officials into parliament itself. Others have opted for a civil service insulated from politics, although even here it should be pointed out that officials such as those in the administration and information services have clear political functions and commitments. The difficulty is that while the government wishes to use civil servants for political purposes it fears that if they become too active they may usurp its own functions. The problem is rendered more acute because the civil service has attracted most of the best educated people in the nation to its ranks. The administrators are generally better educated and have a broader view of the world than local leaders and councillors, or for that matter than most members of parliament.

This is in fact one of the arguments used by those countries who have chosen to draw civil servants into politics and to allow them active political roles. This in turn leads to a problem which is indeed fundamental to the concept of mobilising a one-party state: it assumes that everyone in the country will agree with at least the basic policies of the government and ruling party. Even where a national concensus exists on ideological matters such a system does not necessarily provide for the working out of genuine conflicts between different interests; between producers and consumers, between wage-earners and peasants; between urban and different regions of the country; between those who have adequate land and those who do not; between those who own or control property and those who do not.

The two-party system and even the multi-party system do not provide completely adequate solutions to these conflicts but they do provide a framework within which interests can project their needs. Yet the single-party state can also provide a unified scheme within which differences can be accommodated, especially during times of crisis. What really matters is whether the political system established allows and facilitates effective discussion of various views before final policy is formulated. Without such a practical possibility suppressed pressures eventually and inevitably lead to revolution.

In any state a balance must be struck between individual liberty and coercion. The choices are often much more difficult for a developing country. A country which is economically and socially advanced can more readily tolerate its 'drop-outs', tramps, 'hippies'. For us the man who, generally through ignorance, is wasteful of national resources is much more clearly a liability. How justified are we in enforcing agricultural modernisation, in making people take anti-mosquito measures, in preventing them from using third-rate bulls for breeding? Are we right in forcing young people into youth organisations, or bare-buttocked members of society into trousers?

It is all very well in theory to say that our state of under-development and the existence of a national concensus justify more authoritarian measures. But a government does not operate according to theories. Practical decisions have to be taken every day of the week. A busy minister or official has to take snap decisions on issues where liberty, freedom and individual rights are at stake. Politically speaking it can be argued that we are in such a state of crisis that authoritarian rule is justified. It is said that opposition is a luxury we cannot afford, since it will divert us from the progress whose general direction is widely agreed within the nation.

Yet the danger is that where opposition is given no institutional framework it may find expression in unconstitutional forms. The absence of a formal opposition party in most parts of Kenya during the preparations for local government elections did not prevent anxieties arising from disputes within K.A.N.U. — the ruling party!

And so the debate goes on and experiments continue in the effort to establish the right political institutions and to find the proper role and place for the political parties. But perhaps the most crucial factor during this period is the role and personality of the men at the top — those who head the governments of the new states. In most cases the head of the government is also the head of the party in power. He is also regarded as the political philosopher for the new nation. It is also true to say that most African states are still under the first generation leadership, i.e. the leadership of the same persons who led these countries during the struggle for independence into freedom. The momentum that brought them to power is still strong. Their record of struggle and sacrifice is still fresh in the minds of the people who continue to have the same faith and confidence in them as they did when they called them to unite against colonial rule. Such is their position of influence with the people that they are in most cases unchallengeable. In this position they can be the architects and initiators of the changes needed to establish the new institutions for the future. So much depends on their individual foresight, imagination and personal commitment. It is also true that their personality can be a force for stability and progress even though no practical party organisation or development of new institutions may be taking place at the same time. In such a case the second generation leadership would inherit a framework that is so dependent on personality that it cannot survive the person on whom it depended. This could bring with it a phase of deep political problems — tribalism, personality cult, foreign intervention and even military coups. There is no blueprint or text-book formula that can be handed over to our new countries to help ease the problems of establishing new institutions. Each country will have to go through its own experiences in order to find the appropriate answer. The first generation leaders hold the key here and shoulder a very heavy responsibility to our future generations. A good start now can mean so much in terms of development and progress. A bad start could undo all the efforts made even in achieving independence itself. This is the time also for the education of the people to see the need for stability and its relation to the pace of progress. It is at this stage that we can remove the threats of tribalism and other divisions. The influence of our leaders and the respect they enjoy as a result of their past contribution should be used to introduce to the people new procedures and methods in our society so that these can with the passage of time become part of our new tradition, in fact a new way of life. If they fail, then revolution and governments based on the law of the jungle may very well take over the freedom and independence for which our people have sacrificed so much! This may seem too black a picture to paint but I feel we need to be aroused about the need for deliberate study and efforts to find practical institutions before it is too late. Our concern with urgent economic problems, our trust in present leaders and our involvement in international affairs may leave us with too little time and manpower to attend to this task of foundation building.

Perhaps the greatest crisis facing Africa today is the economic one. We face a situation in which millions are undernourished, uneducated, living narrow lives in poor conditions. This alone would be bad enough. What makes it all the more critical is that these same people, our citizens, had high hopes that independence will change everything.

The fact that these ultimate goals become the immediate demand of the people brings very real problems to our societies. Let us take a concrete example. The Kenya Government intends that the country should move towards universal primary education. Its supporters — and its critics — demand implementation *today*. We know that we need first to train our teachers, to have the necessary buildings. We know we must choose between scarce resources. One more teacher means one less social worker (or builder or administrator). Cement used for schools cannot be used for hospitals or roads or better homes or factories. Money invested in education is so much less available for agricultural development or power stations. The man diverted to teaching primary school entrants cannot at the same time teach the increased secondary school classes whose matriculants are so desperately needed for national development.

Agonising choices must be made. However impartially a government may seek to make the choices its motives will be suspected. Under such conditions it is all too easy for a government to become defensive and to fall back upon catch-phrases. Worse still, the government, especially if it is a weak one, could try to respond to the demands of various groups in an unco-ordinated fashion. This leads to mismanagement of the economy.

Slogans can be a useful way of explaining policies. But sometimes they are used instead of policies, and then — sooner or later — the leaders are in serious trouble with the people who feel they have been misled or cheated. For example you can tell the ordinary man he must develop through self-reliance; that he must pull himself up by his own bootstraps. This isn't much good for the man who doesn't even have any boots! It's really no good telling the peasant scratching away at the soil to be self-reliant. He's been self-reliant since he was born — that's why he's still scratching away. Nor can we ask a peasant to tighten his belt in the spirit of *Harambee** and self-help if he does not at the same time see positive policies and measures aimed to assist him get over the immediate obstacles. If the slogan is to mean anything that peasant must be *helped* to become self-reliant.

All the same discussion about self-reliance and self-help does serve a useful purpose in reminding us that with independence our fate and future must now be in our own hands. We cannot depend entirely upon external sources of capital, technical assistance, training or whatever it might be. In the final analysis everything which we receive from outside should supplement and facilitate our own efforts. If this is to be the case then it is apparent that agricultural developments must be the basis of our development, for it is here that our under-used human resources can be utilised. We must make sure that our people do not think that development means merely one or two big factories. Nor should they be left with the idea that development is entirely the responsibility of the government. The people's role in development needs

* Harambee is the motto on the National Coat of Arms and means 'Let us pull together'.

to be emphasised at every stage. There are psychological and sociological aspects of development which need further study if we are fully to make use of the vast human potential of our countries. Self-help and self-reliance are noble ideas yet paradoxically guidance and planning are just as necessary here as anywhere else if they are to be effective. Indeed, lack of direction from above may lead to wasted effort and quickly to disenchantment. With leadership self-help is a means of rallying the people and creating enthusiasm to face the challenges of development. Without effective leadership the concepts themselves will be discredited — to our future embarrassment.

When they speak of the community, members of the African élite too often think primarily in terms of the urban minority, and judge issues according to the attitude of townspeople instead of thinking of the majority who still live in the rural areas. Unlike the developed countries, hardly any African country can claim that more than 15 per cent of its population live in the urban areas. Since the urban dwellers are themselves more articulate than their country cousins and in a better position to push their own interests, the gap between town and country-side has grown greater and the seeds of another crisis are sown.

In the case of Kenya, we must remember the needs of the 92 per cent of our people who live in the countryside. This does not merely mean that we should concentrate upon agricultural development. Our manu-facturers must be making items needed in the rural areas. We must see to it that the whole quality of life in the countryside is changed. The Government has gone a long way towards spreading social services throughout the country but there are still gaps when it comes to facilities such as social halls, mobile cinemas, communal radios and similar facilities which are necessary for human development and for the effective mobilisation of the people for development.

Furthermore steps must be taken to reduce under-employment in these areas. Redundant labour must be freed for useful economic activities such as road and bridge construction, commercial activities, and rural industries.

This brings me to what is one of the most difficult of the issues facing some of the developing countries in this time of crisis: the land. Land use and land reform present us with manifold problems. In Kenya we had the problem of deciding whether foreigners should continue to have areas exclusively reserved for them and, indeed, whether foreigners should continue to hold land at all. Few will deny that the whole idea of reserving land on a racial basis, above all for foreigners, is totally unacceptable in an independent country.

Should one go further and stop foreigners acquiring agricultural land? Certain projects which are of economic value to the country do require the setting aside of land if they are to go ahead. The establishment of a sugar industry, for example, may require a plantation-style nucleus-estate round the factory, at least for a considerable period until the local people can supply enough cane to make the factory economic. Similar considerations may apply in the cases of creating horticultural, fruit and vegetable farming to support a canning enterprise.

Apart from a few exceptions of this kind, it is my view that agricultural land must be reserved primarily for citizens.

A related aspect of this problem is to decide which citizens should have the chance to use the land. Under a policy of willing-buyer/willing-seller transactions, certain people with particular initial advantages may acquire land out of all proportion to their needs.

They may start off with some spare capital, some special skills and training, better access to information, loans and services. Up to a point it is right that such people should be encouraged to farm land, for they are the ones who will make the best use of it. Yet other aspects must also be considered. Land is a national asset which must be utilised for the good of the country. The masses who are not fortunate enough to have capital and skills may find themselves landless. Governments in Africa need to watch any tendency towards land accumulation very carefully or they may find themselves in very serious trouble with the people. Many countries already have landlessness and unemployment. Policies which look only to immediate economic ends without considering social and political aspects could be very short-sighted.

Governments should ensure that means are found of spreading loans, extension services and agricultural education much more widely. Unless a conscious effort is made to spread skills and opportunities more widely, a growing mass of citizens will find themselves cut off from any opportunity to better themselves through farming, with disastrous human and political results. It is obvious that there is need for clear policies of land use and reform in order to lay a firm foundation for a socialist society in our countries.

An even more sensitive question arises when one considers tribal claims to land. There are many areas in the former White Highlands in Kenya which certain people claim should be reserved for that tribe based on the concept of tribal spheres of influence. But the government has a responsibility to all the people and must find a rational policy for the productive use of the land available.

This leads to the most sensitive question of all, namely land in former tribal reserves. In spite of land consolidation and the granting of title, traditional attitudes still prevail in this sector. Although there is no legal impediment, for a number of reasons land transactions in these areas are generally within the tribe. Sale or disposal of land is in the hands of Local Land Boards. Government attempts to replace such boards with impartial national bodies would I am sure be suspect.

But as modernisation, especially the granting of title, becomes more widespread this question will become increasingly important. The issue will also be raised in respect of land lying within a tribal area but which is not being used in the best national interest.

Under the circumstances should people from other areas be encouraged or discouraged from acquiring such land? What form of title should they receive? What should be their relationship with the original tribal claimants? I do not presume to have all the answers to all these questions. I do believe the time has come for us to ask such questions and discuss them frankly. It is only by tackling these questions that we can eventually arrive at a practical policy for the country.

Another area which should be looked into is that of trade unions. Compared with the peasantry which forms the mass of the population, organised labour in Africa is a relatively small, privileged minority. At the same time its potential strength within a country is just as great at that of trade unions in countries where organised workers are numerically significant. That is why so many African countries have found it necessary to curb the unions. Often this has been done by bringing them into the party or governmental structure. Some governments have merely introduced legislation governing the procedures for dealing with industrial relations and disputes.

Nor should it be forgotten that if workers in paid employment make use of their bargaining power in a ruthless manner they may well reduce employment opportunities for their brothers. Spiralling wages and benefits will naturally lead employers to keep their labour force at a minimum. Any policy dealing with trade unions must involve a study of prices, rents, profits, etc. In other words there is need for an incomes policy very soon after independence.

Unemployment is one of the greatest crises which confronts some newly independent states. The rising expectations which accompany independence cause an accelerated drift to the towns in search of paid employment. Education policies produce an ever-growing number of school-leavers. Stern measures formerly used by the colonial authorities are no longer appropriate or politically acceptable in a democratic society.

Urgent and practical policies must be implemented to solve this explosive crisis. Many African countries see part of the answer in rural development. It is in the rural areas that the majority of the population will live for a long time to come. Industrialisation, which it is hoped will cope with the problem of unemployment and school-leavers more efficiently, is a slow process. The success of rural development in absorbing the unemployed, and in particular unemployed school-leavers, requires a radical overhaul of the educational system, designed to teach people the skills required for their economic and human development in rural areas. Obviously the emphasis will be upon farming but attention needs to be paid to the encouragement of ancillary and servicing skills.

I have already touched on one of the crises which we face on the economic side. This concerns the choices we have to make when allocating our scarce resources. Above all, this is a question of choosing between consumption and investment, and it is perhaps the most difficult problem facing African countries in their planning efforts. Our people, whose living conditions are so unbearable, expect quick and dramatic improvements in their welfare soon after independence. Further, during the struggle for independence, many African politicians promised such things as free medical service, unemployment compensation, free and universal primary education. An impression was created that all that was needed to establish a welfare state was independence! The task before us now is to convince the people that the welfare state is not the cause, but the effect of development. More consumption now means fewer resources available for investment, and therefore makes it harder to raise future incomes and create employment. On the other hand the living standards of the masses of our people are so low that it would be both politically and economically unwise to ignore present needs. A balance must be struck. Fortunately, given proper planning, a determination to implement plans, and regional co-operation, it is possible for steady progress to be made towards more consumption at the same time as increasing the proportion of resources spent on investment. But that kind of balance is not likely to materialise unless the people themselves are actively involved in both planning and plan implementation.

Another point of crisis in Africa is related to some of the issues we have already considered. This is economic aid. In the modern world no nation is completely self-reliant and certainly none are self-sufficient. There are constant movements of capital and consumer goods, of skilled and unskilled manpower. There is a continuing interchange of knowledge and techniques.

These exchanges of goods, of personnel or of ideas take place mainly on the basis of *mutual* profit. Certainly there is some degree of altruism but it is of marginal significance. I think that the developed countries have been partly to blame for present misunderstandings and cynicisms because they have used the language of altruism to conceal their real motives in providing aid as a weapon in their international affairs.

We must remember that the developed countries are nevertheless developing and that their own economies are not always strong. When such countries come up against a balance of payments crisis or run into monetary difficulties, foreign aid is one of the first items of expenditure to suffer.

The unjustified emphasis placed upon altruism in the discussion of international economic dealings was one of the main causes for the failure of the U.N.C.T.A.D. negotiations. We must now recognise national self-interest as the basic fact of international economic dealings and go on from there. One part of the answer — but it is only one part — lies in the developing countries making themselves more acceptable as trading partners or as areas of investment for developed countries.

Another way in which the developing countries can improve their own trading and capital investment terms is by uniting. It is in the realm of economic co-operation that the principles of pan-Africanism have the greatest prospect of beneficial implementation. Above all, it is here that national self-interest and continent-wide unity come together. There is wide scope for African producer nations to club together more effectively. The results of disunity can be seen in the way the Western financial, trading, and investment groups — and even the European Economic Community — play off African states one against the other. There is enormous scope too for regional development within Africa. Genuine regional common markets will enable more rapid development. Not only will they allow for specialisation and industries of optimum size; these very factors will be a great inducement to investment from outside.

I do not ignore the political problems involved here. Many countries in Africa hold back from closer association with their neighbours because they fear they may be swallowed by a bigger or more dynamic partner. This feeling is particularly strong in Africa because the peoples' awareness of their national identity is still fairly superficial. Between the strongly entrenched tribal sentiments and proposed inter-African groupings many leaders at the national level may fear that their own roles and those of their nation may be reduced.

These fears are quite often well-founded and must not, in any case, be ignored when making efforts to promote regional co-operation. Among other things this means that the forms of economic co-operation established must take into account the need to ensure that each participating country benefits from that co-operation. Definite measures will have to be taken: experience shows that a policy of *laissez-faire* will produce inequitable benefits.

Africa's current crisis of confidence also manifests itself in a social and pyschological manner. It is here that the problem becomes most personal. How do you accept modernity and at the same time fulfil nationalist aspirations ? At the time of Ghana's independence there was much talk of 'the African personality'. We hear less of this today, although the ideas which were born of that discussion are still very much part of our thinking.

It is understandable that new countries should wish to create systems in which aspects of their own culture have a place. Since the world is going through tremendous social changes this is all the more important and yet all the more difficult. Countries which have years of nationhood behind them can face with equanimity the wave of worldwide unrest among their youth. Technological advance and economic interdependence will still leave them with their national identities clearly defined. For us it is more difficult. To grasp at superficialities will not help.

Is a man promoting African culture because he wears an ostrich feather or a beaded cap and sandals? Is it particularly African to wear fabrics which a designer in Hong Kong thinks suitable for this market; or to put a piece of animal skin over a Western suit or to wear some Muslim attire with your European clothes? Or, to put it the other way round, is an African not an African because his wife chooses some Western fashion, because he prefers modern plumbing or Western furniture in his home? What we need to do is to develop a culture based on the African traditions, yet not shunning international contacts and developments. We must not confuse poverty with culture for there is no point in clinging to practices and habits which arose merely from a lack of something better.

I believe it would be entirely wrong to seek to create an inward-looking, isolated African society. What we need are African writers and artists who can express and interpret our lives, our traditions, our culture in the deepest sense — *and in a universal way.* We must promote our music, our singing and our musical instruments. We must progress, too, and acknowledge the value of the synthesis where our traditional culture mixes with world culture — be it in music, literature or any other art. I do believe there is room for our schools and colleges to pay more attention to this subject.

It must be remembered in this regard, however, that our educational institutions are part of a universal culture. Our universities naturally wish to be in the same league as universities throughout the world. They want to be part of the world with regard to science, technology and learning. They want to explore space, split the atom, tame the deserts and rivers and conquer disease. Will they achieve this by turning inwards and searching for the Africa that was?

Mention of education should remind us that half of our population in Kenya consists of young people. While we are doing all we can to widen the economic and social horizons of those who are already adult, obviously our main education efforts, in the widest sense, are directed towards this young half of the society who will lead tomorrow.

In the world today there is something of a crisis of confidence between the generations. In many older countries young people are questioning the values of their elders and their own cultures. They are questioning the relevance and even the validity of institutions and alliances established over the years before and during the last world war. Science and technology have revolutionised relations and contacts between man and nations. They have opened up new areas of interest to the younger generation — areas never dreamed of by their parents and elders. Revolution in education systems, the lowering of the age at which children can enter school, vote or start work have all bred an impatience in young people which it is necessary to understand. And in developing countries the transition from tribal to urban and modern society presents new and additional problems.

These youthful attitudes of impatience and modernity can be healthy and can lead to progress and necessary change. Yet while well-established societies can easily contain student revolts, similar outbursts in a developing country could have more serious consequences — perhaps undermining the very structure of the state. Not only are the young relatively more numerous: much more than in the more developed states, they are the leaders of tomorrow, for the result of the efforts and sacrifices which their parents have made is that they will be much better educated than their elders. All this makes it essential that the youth of our nations be thoroughly inculcated with a strong sense of service.

Some countries have made an approach to this problem through their system of national service. In Ethiopia and India, to take just two examples, college students have to spend a certain time working in the villages. Kenya does have a National Youth Service but this does not bring the educated face to face with the day to day and mundane problems of nation-building. We must be careful to avoid bringing up different classes among our young people. Whatever their differences of academic achievement we must make sure that they are brought up to appreciate the principles which guide our young nation. They must all be made to feel part of what we are striving for, involved in the traditions we are building, instead of becoming alien from their own traditions as the youth of Europe seem to be.

The principles upon which we are building our new nations need to adapt and adopt from the experience of others. Equally, they must be rooted in our own past, in such traditions as mutual social responsibility which was an important concept in African society. It is from their parents and in their younger years, especially from their mothers, that the next generation will learn their basic values.

This is an additional reason for looking again to the needs of our womenfolk. After all, they too make up half of our nation! Economically they play a most important part in national life, especially in the traditional agricultural sectors which are rapidly being modernised. Nor should their social and political potential be under-estimated. It should not be forgotten that during the struggle for independence the women were most active, not so much at the spectacular levels of leadership, but more in the mundane but essential roles of canvassing support, organisation and assistance at public meetings.

I have a feeling that this question of preventing class antagonism is even more of a problem between women than between men. It is essential that our educated women should make greater efforts to understand the problems of their less fortunate sisters, and should take more active steps to help us all to solve these problems of living together and creating a harmonious society.

All our womenfolk, educated or not, need to be more closely involved at every level in the political and social life of the nation.

We face a challenge here. It is for the women to make greater efforts to enter into public life, social work, economic development, professional activities; it is for the men to ensure that they meet these efforts not with hostility but with encouragement and assistance. We cannot, through ignorant prejudice, afford to under-use the talents and potential of half of our citizens, merely because they are women.

In these introductory words I have tried to bring together some of the strands of the problems which together create for us in Africa an enormous challenge. I have deliberately ranged widely from matters of international affairs, and the nature of the state, to more intimate social and psychological problems, such as those of women and youth, which developing countries such as Kenya face in an acute form.

All these challenges, and others which are considered in the material which comprises the body of this book, represent for us in Africa a crisis of confidence. There is one solution to the crisis of confidence to which I would like to draw special attention. I refer to the force for good which nationalism can provide. We have already seen how nationalist feelings were aroused and harnessed by political leaders during our struggle for independence. Many of us have had experience of this, one of the most powerful of emotions which can grip people and inspire them to action. Of course, nationalism can be a negative and destructive force, as Europe has seen in National Socialism and as we in Africa have seen in the racist nationalism of South Africa's Afrikaners.

We, on the contrary, need to mobilise this force of nationalism against racialism and against tribalism. More than that, our efforts for economic, political and social progress can draw inspiration from national pride. The emblems, the symbols, the banners of any nation; the pride of the people in their institutions and their achievements, all these can and must be harnessed if we are to achieve the progress which the citizens expect.

National pride and self-respect can help the leaders of a country to reject the blandishments of those foreign interests who would bend them to their own attitudes and interests.

Nationalism can give an extra impetus to the self-reliant efforts of peasants and workers. It can help the better-off to make sacrifices in support of our efforts to build a just and equitable society.

As long as there is preparedness on the part of African leaders and thinkers to face these problems squarely, then there is hope. There must be serenity in knowing what cannot be solved immediately; there must be courage in deciding what can and must be changed; there must be wisdom to know the difference. There are those who look at this crisis of confidence and merely see in it the chance to promote personal ambitions through reckless attacks on the efforts of the governments and others easily interpret the crisis as a sign that independence has not yet come. Then there is the danger that others will look for an easy way out by falling victims of foreign manipulators who seek to exploit the crisis. All such people must be rejected. They do not only betray the cause of African freedom, they betray themselves. This crisis calls for the deepest commitment among African leaders; those who will not be easily swayed or diverted from their commitment to Mother Africa.

This selection of speeches represents an attempt to study, to analyse and to answer some of the challenges and problems, the prospects and opportunities before our great continent. I offer them for what they are. A humble and sincere and frank contribution to a field in which so much remains to be done and where every true son of the soil must feel compelled to express concern and be involved.

I dedicate this work to the many people of Africa who go to bed each night dreaming of the promise of Africa.

T. J. Mboya
Nairobi, March 1969

Keynote Address

TENSIONS IN AFRICAN DEVELOPMENT

TENSIONS IN AFRICAN DEVELOPMENT

Address at Conference on Tensions in Development
New College, Oxford, 1961

In 1961 the Council on World Tensions invited Tom Mboya to deliver a paper at a conference on Tensions in Development. The Conference was held at New College, Oxford and Tom Mboya's paper was subsequently edited together with other speeches. Tom Mboya was no stranger to Oxford having studied at Ruskin College in 1955/56. His paper brings together so many threads of the problems facing Africa today that it is placed here at the beginning of these texts as a keynote document for the whole book.

One of the most significant facts of the contemporary world situation is the emergence of Africa and the African people from the prison cells of colonial rule and from the obscurity imposed by foreign domination. The emergence of Africa and the impact of Africa on the world and on international institutions such as the United Nations are indisputable facts. Even the most retrograde conservative finds it difficult to deny that the Africa of today presents a new fact to the world, infused with new aspirations and aims, calling for recognition and a right to be admitted into the community of nations of the world. Africa is awake and is on the march to the tune of nationalism, while nationalism is dictating the tempo and rhythm of the march of the people of Africa to independence, freedom, order, justice, and economic dignity. A recognition of this new African dynamism and a grasp of the elements and forces motivating it are vital to the understanding of tensions inherent in the current developments in Africa. I think it is worth emphasising that these forces are already playing an important role in laying the foundations of the future institutions of Africa in terms of politics, economics, and social orientation.

I will point out the areas in Africa where there are tensions and I will, where I can, try to analyse the causes and consequences of the tensions.

Africa is a vast continent; the immensity of its size and the massiveness of its problems, alone, make it difficult for anybody to write with accuracy on any aspects of its rapid and kaleidoscopic changes. The best one can do is to generalise here and there and make specific suggestions or propositions only where one has enough facts to warrant them. Another limitation is that people involved in movements such as ours cannot always achieve a perspective view. As a politician I believe in action and results. I hardly find the time to analyse and categorise the many problems which I am involved in solving.

Today Africa is in a tense mood. The most dominant social and political force is, in contemporary Africa, nationalism. The intensity of nationalistic feeling among the people explains much of the tension we experience throughout the continent, and that feeling justifies the many rapid changes now taking place in Africa. I do not need to define what nationalism is, for it is a familiar historical phenomenon. The only explanation I feel called upon to make is the exposition of the particular aims and goals of African nationalism.

Africa, as we all know, came under European colonial domination during the last quarter of the nineteenth century. From that time until the early part of the present century, practically all parts of Africa were brought under colonial rule. The European colonial powers portioned out various parts of Africa as their spheres of influence and began ruling and exercising power in accordance with the dictates of their laws, culture, political traditions, and economic demands. This process of colonisation set in motion the economic and political orientation which explains why Africa is what it is today. Under colonial rule, Africa has been transformed, but the indigenous people have played very little part in shaping their own future. Economic structures and political institutions favourable to the colonising powers were imposed on the millions of dominated and silent African masses. Unbridled economic and human exploitation proceeded unchecked; and socially, the African people found themselves uprooted and placed outside the age-old values and beliefs on which their communities had thrived for centuries.

As time went on, the African people rediscovered themselves. They became conscious of their own identity, yet found themselves robbed of authority. They recognised the fact that the European ruler could not be regarded as an honest friend while he exercised his power and violence at the expense of the subject masses. This realisation brought about the subjective self-promotion we now call African nationalism. Deep down in the mind of every African nationalist there are echoes of the past. On the one hand, there is the echo of the past African world with its ideals, values, and cosmological ideas — the past that the African has lost touch with due to the interposition of colonial rule. We are seeking an integration with all that is good and constructive about this past in order to salvage our personality and to find a foundation on which to build our own institutions. On the other hand, there is the recent past of colonial rule, littered with memories of colonial suppression, but also with modern scientific methods of production, education, and so on. We want to harness fully the advantages of this colonial past and to use it as an instrument of contact with the rest of the world.

Africa is one of the underdeveloped continents of the world. Socially, Africa is underdeveloped in the sense that its tribal components have not yet found a proven basis for collective action. It is still possible for tribal differences to provoke inter-country tension, especially because the boundaries were drawn up artificially without regard to ethnic groupings. On the basis of tribe alone, the bulk of Africa can wrap itself in all sorts of claims and counter-claims, struggles and convulsions. Whether or not tribalism is going to be a cause of widespread tensions in Africa will depend on the honesty and quality of African leadership.

Further, Africa is socially underdeveloped because there is almost no social and cultural traffic between English- and French-speaking Africa. The culture imposed on us sticks like burrs. English-speaking Africans, formerly subjects of Britain, are most familiar with the etiquette, language, economics, and politics of Great Britain. They constantly listen to the B.B.C. and the local English programmes. They might listen to the Voice of America, Russia, or India if their outlook is wide. But most of them are uninformed when it comes to the events, news, and institutions of the Portuguese or ex-French territory next door. Similarly, the French-speaking Africans, formerly French subjects, know more about France — its politics, economics, literature, and philosophy — than they know about the English-speaking countries surrounding their own. This lack of communication is a definite source of tension in this continent. Education, and teaching of both the French and English languages on both sides, concerted efforts to revive the old cultural links, communication at economic and commercial levels are some of the ways in which these barriers can be broken. Again, these undertakings call for very honest leadership. Trade unions can provide the links to start with, but the extent to which they can be used as links in the chain is dependent on whether they all agree to function with some measure of freedom from their own governments.

Economically, Africa is underdeveloped in the sense that mass poverty is universal. This poverty is not entirely due to poor natural resources, and could be lessened by methods already proved successful in other parts of the world. It is reflected in deficiencies like the shortage of schools, social services, hospitals, universities, and technical institutions. It is further reflected in the number of our women who die in childbirth, the universality of malnutrition, the high incidence of various diseases, low wages, and in the contrast between the wealth of Europe and North America on the one hand, and the poverty prevailing in Africa on the other. The continent as a whole is underdeveloped. Poverty is a threat because our people have already learned that they are entitled to a better life. It is difficult to restrain the surging expectations on the part of our people for more education, more health facilities, higher wages, and all the other conditions of a better life.

A very fertile source of tension exists in the realisation that the colonial powers who have hitherto been responsible for the economic development of Africa have either not done their best in developing the continent or have taken so much out of it as to render the Africans poor. It is not mere propaganda to say that, under colonial rule, economic, human and social development in Africa has been unduly subordinated and subjected to the profit motive. Capital from the metropolitan countries sought profits for the benefit of the owners and their countries. African countries have been developed to supply the demands of the metropolitan economies, and in this process deliberate efforts to combat poverty in Africa were forgotten. Arising from the way our economies have been developed are numerous frictions and tensions which most African leaders have already recognised and are doing their best to minimise. It is a fact, that because of the 'colonial' nature of our economies, a unique economic isolation has been forced on various parts of our continent. Our African currencies, now pegged to the currencies of present or ex-metropolitan countries, are exchanged with a great deal of difficulty. Our transport and communication systems have been designed for political rather than economic convenience. Inter-African trade is hampered by exchange difficulties, transport bottle-necks, and unfair tariffs — all instituted by colonial rule.

Africa is still largely dependent on Europe. This fact is, in itself, another source of tension because dependence is not consistent with our national pride and makes a sham of the independence we are supposed to have won. If one studies the direction of African international trade and the balance of trade of the various African countries, one cannot avoid arriving at the conclusion that the present arrangements are inequitable. Better arrangements must be made so that the prices of our primary commodities exported from Africa are in line with the ever-increasing import propensity of the African economies. The economies of African countries are adversely affected by fluctuations in world prices of the commodities they export and these fluctuations have political repercussions. The solution for this kind of problem is partly political and partly economic.

There are other sources of friction in the development of Africa. One of them concerns the relationship between our people and industry. Under colonial rule, some economic structures have emerged in our countries which are not suitable and which must either be changed or considerably modified. I think the system of relations between workers and employers in Africa is one of these. Wage-earning in Africa is already a strongly based institution; there are millions of Africans who have no other means of livelihood. Like other workers, these Africans expect that wage-earning will prove human and gratifying. As workers and citizens they expect the same respect accorded to other citizens. They want to feel that they are an integral part of industry, doing something meaningful and valuable for the country; they want security in employment, and above all they want dignity accorded to their labour. They want to be consulted on all matters which affect them.

It is unfortunate that these very natural expectations are far from realisation in practically all parts of Africa. The main explanation for this sad state of affairs is the fact that the employer-employee relationship, as developed in colonial Africa, has lacked mutual respect and goodwill. First of all, it has been poisoned by racialism, because the bulk of the employers of African labour have been, and even at this time still are, governments which, even after independence, still exercise the colonial vice of regimenting and suppressing workers. Also, most private employers are non-Africans whose relations with their employees are capitalistic. They regard African workers in terms of colonial stereo-types such as 'they are lazy', 'their needs are few', and so on, and consequently pay them very low wages and order them about as in the heyday of colonial rule.

It is true that illiteracy, lack of trained trade union officials, and a narrow base of industrial development are still impeding the growth of strong and independent democratic trade unions to protect the interests of the African working classes. But a start towards improvement has already been made, and tension between the African worker and his employer will assume vital significance unless the whole system of industrial relations is given an immediate democratic and African orientation. The same goes for the whole development we now call 'Africanisation'. We support it because we believe that it is a necessary concomitant to political independence. But if it is attempted without raising the whole base of living of the working masses, then a gambit will be open. There will be a lot of friction between the African sub-stitutes for colonial administrators (who will be in a new ivory tower) and the working people (whose lot will not have changed). This situation would be dynamite. Unless the rate of developing skills and of capital formation is accelerated, Africanisation, though good and logical, will be a source of tension. In this, as in other respects, the search for the capital and the know-how for the promotion of quick economic and social development is a very important consideration.

In connexion with this problem of capital and skill shortage, I would like to point out an aspect which I regard as very serious. This is the lack of education. This deficiency is actually the main source of tension in Africa. Because of the lack of trained men and women, even independent African countries have to depend on outside experts to help them run the countries. We then have a situation in which the ministers are Africans but the technicians are Russians, Poles, or Yugoslavs in country A; French, Swedes, and Americans in country B; British, Canadian, and American in country C; American, British, Swiss, Yugoslav, and Russian in country D. This is a bad situation: first, because it helps to perpetuate the political and economic Balkani-sation of Africa; second, because it increases the cost of development projects, since the foreign staff employed have to be paid the high salaries they are used to in their own countries; and lastly, because it increases the dangers of neo-colonialism.

Following independence — or even before — all African countries are faced with the problem of what kind of political structure to adopt in order to ensure internal peace, order, and continuity of economic activities. The leaders must establish and maintain order to enable the government to promote economic and social development. The responsibility for virtually all types of development becomes the concern of the government; for the indigenous people are poor and they still lack business and commercial skill. On its part, government finds itself with many projects in hand, but without capital or technical know-how to sustain development. Added to these difficulties is the fact of the autocratic background of colonial rule dressed up in institutions such as the judiciary, civil service, municipalities, police, etc. — all copied from the metropolitan country but put to very little democratic use all along.

Will democracy survive in Africa? To those who think that democracy will survive only if the colonial institutions are preserved, I have this to say: 'You will be disappointed'. To those willing to understand the difficulties we face in fulfilling the aims of African nationalism outlined above, viz., increasing the wealth and power of our countries to enable us to preserve the freedom and dignity of every individual citizen, I would say that the whole aim must be fulfilled simultaneously. The problem of deciding what constitutes democracy and what institutions are best for its realisation can be a mere academic exercise. What is necessary is that force must be minimised and persuasion substituted for it as a tool of governmental action. A government sometimes needs unusual powers to implement some decisions, and it must be recognised that the use of this kind of power will be much more frequent in the emerging countries, with unproven foreign institutions grafted on, than in the politically and economically stable countries, with numerous conventions or generally accepted codes of political conduct.

There are two other internal factors I consider necessary to democracy: free association of all the people of the country with the control and the functioning of the government at all levels; and the existence of various democratic voluntary bodies, such as free trade unions, cultural and professional associations, and a large body of people with independent thinking and outlook to help influence the activities of those in power. Whether there will be two or more political parties is not a *sine qua non* of democracy. External structures and institutions must be judged by their effects on the people. The challenge we face in Africa will lead to the emergence of new political institutions, and some of the colonial political structures will either be discarded deliberately or will die a natural death. But the good or suitable ones will remain. In bending these institutions to the services of the peoples they have hitherto been by-passing, there will be necessary modifications all over. Even the judiciary will have to be modified. The administration of the civil service will also have to undergo a complete metamorphosis.

I envisage a complete revolution in the structure and functioning of the civil service of a country like Kenya when it is shorn of European domination and the 'colonial mentality'. The vital question here is, what will be the relations between the civil servants and the politicians? This is not a difficult thing. So far, our civil service has served the colonial purposes of preserving order — to enable the colonial governments to collect taxes and to enable colonial capital investments to pay dividends. For the advancement of independent African countries, the purposes of the civil service must range far wider. They will be expected to work for order and security of the person and property of everybody; they will be expected to deal justly with everybody. They will be expected to work under and to carry out much more extensive and egalitarian economic and social policies, unlike those of the colonial regime. Colonial administration hardly trains for this kind of work; there is always tension in the civil service in the transitional period following independence. The civil service must assume its independence of politicians and political parties, for this is the only way to ensure its continuity.

Colonial administrations have a habit of exercising the policy of 'divide and rule', even if this is not in the long-term interests of the country under its jurisdiction. They recruit police from specified tribes, certain grades of labour from others, clerks from elsewhere. This makes the civil service unrepresentative and provides the basis for tribal conflict. Allied to this is the question of the imbalance in the economic and social development in the various regions of colonial Africa. This fact is a source of very serious tension.

I have said a lot about tensions in the development of Africa and about changing relations between African countries and the former or present colonial powers. What of the future relationship? What I have to say on this matter is not new; it has been said again and again by African leaders and others. Our relations with former metropolitan powers must be reviewed, and new relations both economic and political, must be based on genuine equality. We all agree that this is the next step. And let this equality be carried to its logical conclusion. If we are equal, only help us where we need help; stop being paternalistic. We need a continuing flow of technical, specialist, financial, and other types of aid. We will take it from you, and from any other nations ready to offer aid with no strings attached. Do not grumble when we take it. We take it because we need it, and we take it because it is given free. Remember, we are also capable of gauging the ulterior motives of all those who offer to help us. This ability is not the monopoly of the rich and developed people alone. We need technical and financial aid, both private and public. Improved relations with former metropolitan countries can be achieved if existing inequitable economic relations are put on new levels of equality; if on both sides every effort is made to heal the scars of colonial association; if our associations with ex-metropolitan countries such as the Commonwealth, Common Market, etc., are shorn of the difficulties involved in the economic and political relations between the African countries. There is a lot we can do to get along together, I think.

Our relations with the two leading world powers, the United States and the Soviet Union, must be brought under the same reckoning. They have vast wealth; they are squandering millions on nuclear armament to 'protect' us, while they fail to protect us from poverty, ill-health, illiteracy, and our other basic enemies. We have made it clear to them that we shall never accept the role they are trying to devise for us, namely, that of pawns in their power game. No, this we shall never accept. Our internal and external policies will consistently be governed by what is best for our people, for our development and our future.

Lastly, we have the concept of African unity and solidarity and the realisation of the 'African personality'. In the effort to break away from the colonial past, with its artificial divisions, its psychological and economic enslavement, its misrepresentation overseas and within Africa, African nationalism faces the challenge of creating trust, confidence, leadership, and effective regional economic and political co-operation. Neo-colonialism, attempts at Balkanisation, and outright

Cold War manœuvres have to be watched, in addition to the challenge of personal ambitions, tribalism, lack of communication, and certain language difficulties which must be checked in the interest of a given region, and of pan-Africanism in general.

Part One

KENYA

When a full and complete history of nationalism in Kenya comes to be written,* it will be necessary to re-assess the roles of violent and non-violent methods in the struggle for Kenya's independence.

It has become fashionable to equate the nationalist movement in Kenya with the Mau Mau revolt of 1952/55. Such an equation ignores the first sixty-six years of British colonial rule in Kenya as well as the last ten, the revolutionary decade from 1953 to 1963. Moreover, to regard those who were actively involved in Mau Mau as the only 'freedom fighters' is to overrate their contributions to the nationalists' cause at the expense of other freedom fighters.

Such an explanation also ignores the important fact that even within the Mau Mau movement there were different groups, e.g. detainees, forest fighters, political refugees who fled the country, etc., all of whom made different contributions.

In this book, one of the basic problems facing an independent Kenya — the challenge of development — is discussed through the speeches and writings of one of the constitutional freedom fighters, who has also played a key role in the new Kenya.

Born on 15th August, 1930, and brought up away from his home area, Tom Mboya was one of the most detribalised African politicians. This was the source of his strength during the struggle for political independence when the emphasis was upon national unity against the imperialists; and latterly the source of his weakness because the attainment of political independence has resulted in the consolidation of ethnic loyalties in Kenya.

Mboya's peculiar combination of shyness and self-assurance masked a strong personality that inspired many Kenyans to action. To understand his role in the nationalists' struggle as well as in the reconstruction programmes which have been mounted since independence, one must understand the unholy combination of high

---

* Some of the chief actors in the Kenya drama have already given us glimpses of this history: Kenyatta, J., *Suffering Without Bitterness*, E.A.P.H. Nairobi, 1968; Mboya, T. J., *Freedom and After*, André Deutsch, London, 1963; Odinga, O., *Not Yet Uhuru*, Heinemann, London, 1967. See also *The Myth of 'Mau Mau': Nationalism in Kenya*, by C. G. Rosberg and J. Nottingham, Fredrick A. Praeger, New York, 1966. The authors discuss nationalism in Kenya largely as a background to Mau Mau. This tends to give a distorted picture of the nationalist struggle.

ideals and low intrigue which characterise Kenya politics. In other words, it is essential for a proper assessment of his contribution, that we should understand the bitter and ruthless political world in which he operated since 1952, when he first joined politics. After a brief term as a sanitary inspector with the Nairobi City Council which he joined in 1951, he resigned from his job to devote himself full time to trade union activities. He became the General Secretary of the Local Government Workers' Union. In 1952, Mboya joined the Kenya African Union. And in the vacuum of leadership that occurred as a result of the arrest and detention of top K.A.U. leaders, he became the Director of Information and the Acting Treasurer of the party before it was banned. In September, 1953, he became the General Secretary of the Kenya Federation of Registered Trade Unions (later Kenya Federation of Labour) and turned his attention to the creation of a strong and united labour movement. And throughout the Emergency, the K.F.L. functioned as a nationalist movement. The labour movement provided him with a springboard which allowed him within a few years to become widely known as an African leader.

In 1955, Mboya achieved considerable fame when he settled a long strike of 4,000 dock workers at the port of Mombasa. He persuaded the strikers to return to work, then pleaded their cause before a tribunal, delivering a masterful eight and a half hour speech in support of their cause. A European lawyer represented the employers. Mboya won, however, and the workers got a 33⅓ per cent wage increase. It was the first time in Kenya's history that an African had performed such a feat. Later in the same year, he successfully represented his former fellow workers with Nairobi City Council.

From the first African elections in 1957 to the Lancaster House constitutional conference of 1960, Mboya and Oginga Odinga dominated Kenya politics; and their contribution in the fight for independence during these three difficult years cannot be over-emphasised.

By December 1955, Mau Mau as a military force had been almost crushed, but the future of the colony still remained unsettled. 'Settler Rule' had been discredited, and separate development had failed. The important question was: 'What next in Kenya?' Between 1955 and 1960 Kenya was therefore the scene of a vigorous triangular struggle — extreme Europeans wanting to maintain the *status quo*; the radical

Africans preaching the doctrine of 'Africa for the Africans'; and in between the so-called moderates of all races. Out of this struggle, in which Mboya played a crucial role, there developed by 1960, a new situation.

The basic problem facing the African leaders was how to produce a workable African government for a racially mixed country; and the fight for such a workable African government had to be carried out under emergency regulations. In an article published in the London *Observer* of 14th December, 1958, entitled *Kenya: A Grave Decision*, Mboya portrayed vividly the dilemma which faced constitutional freedom fighters:

'The dilemma facing an African leader committed to peaceful negotiations is a difficult one. What is the right policy to follow? We have tried to work through the Legislature without success. We have sought round-table negotiations, and been refused. We have petitioned, counselled, appealed and warned. All these efforts have got us nowhere.

'Meanwhile, our constituents become more frustrated, restless and militant. On our flanks we see arising irresponsible, would-be leaders willing to exploit these difficulties. Owing to the Emergency Regulations, maintaining discipline among our supporters is extremely difficult since our rights to hold meetings and make organisations are severely restricted.

'Yet we know that if one set of leaders does not give the people what they want, the people will demand either a change of policy or a change of leadership.'

The release of Kenyatta and the return of the 'Old Guard' represented a testing time for Mboya and the younger leaders. It was alleged that Mboya was not loyal to Kenyatta and that he was working to become the first prime minister of an independent Kenya. His political opponents even suggested without attempting to substantiate the charge, that he had sold Kenya to America and Britain. But Jomo Kenyatta quickly recognised Mboya's talents and was not prepared to sacrifice him to tribal or personality squabbles within the Kenya African National Union, of which Mboya had become the Secretary-General.

From April 1962, Mboya held several portfolios in the Kenya Government. Starting as Minister for Labour in the Coalition (K.A.N.U.-K.A.D.U.) cabinet, during which he initiated discussions which led to the signing of the Industrial Relations Charter in October 1962, he became Minister for Justice and Constitutional Affairs on the attainment of internal self-government on 1st June, 1963. During the following year, he was chiefly concerned with constitutional developments which culminated in the abolition of the *Majimbo* Constitution and the introduction of the Republican Constitution on 12th December, 1964. He was then appointed to the new Ministry of Economic Planning and Development.

In his new position, he was responsible for the formation of the Sessional Paper No. 10 on *African Socialism and its application to Plannining Kenya* (see pp. 73–105) and the drawing up of the first Development Plan of Kenya.

In the different ministerial positions as well as in his role as the Secretary-General of the ruling party, Kenya African National Union, Mboya was deeply involved in the shaping of government policies. Many of his critics held him responsible for the middle-of-the-road policies Kenya has adopted and which the Opposition regard as a sell-out to Western finance.

The fact that he became the scapegoat for all the sins of the Kenya Government gives added significance to his speeches and writings. They reflect in a large measure the thinking and policies of the Kenya government during the post-independence period.

KENYA AS A NATION

Address to members of the Kenya National Farmers' Union at Eldoret, 23rd July, 1962

In the years before independence a fancy franchise, gerrymandering, racially reserved seats, nominated members, constitutional restrictions and other devices were used by the colonial authorities to frustrate nationalist government. In spite of the dangers of compromising their position, the leaders of the majority party, Kenya African National Union, agreed in 1962 to serve in a Coalition Government containing representatives of other political and racial organisations, in order to hasten political advance. Tom Mboya, it may be remembered, was not only an elected member of the Legislative Council, but also Secretary-General both of K.A.N.U. and the Kenya Federation of Labour. He took the particularly brave step, in the circumstances of accepting the portfolio of Labour.

This speech was made when he was Minister for Labour in the Coalition Government to the members of the Kenya National Farmers' Union at Eldoret, 23rd July, 1962. With the approach of Independence, hundreds of Europeans began planning their exodus from the country. Many farms were allowed to fall into ruin. This speech challenges the European settlers in their stronghold of Eldoret and questions their sincerity of purpose and their loyalty to Kenya.

While many European settlers chose to leave after Independence it is interesting that a considerable number of them, including some who had been politically active, chose to stay on. A number of Europeans, Sir Michael Blundell, Lord Delamere, Sir Wilfred Havelock among them, have become citizens of the country; Mr. Humphrey Slade the present Speaker of the Kenya Parliament, unanimously elected to the position by the Members, was a settler representative in the Legislative Council before independence.

I want to talk to you today about Kenya as a nation. Some of the things I shall have to say may not please you. But as farmers, you have grown used to a harsh environment, and everything you do or attempt is governed by the physical facts of life. I believe that if we are going to co-operate in the task of nation-building we must shed the fears and suspicions which have existed between our various communities for so long.

It is suggested by some people that there is no such thing as a Kenya nation. All kinds of arguments and recriminations are thrown up to try to prove that any nationalist ambitions for Kenya must encounter more difficulties than could ever be overcome. Noisy minorities in all walks of life, both here and in their contact with overseas interests, keep plugging away at their 'no confidence' theme. Some people say that Kenya is heading for economic disaster and political chaos and tribal war.

Such people are not thinking from their heart or from their mind, but from their emotions and fears. Such people are not nation-builders; they are afraid and refuse to see their real duty in Kenya.

When I talk now about a 'Kenya nation', I am not speaking as a political romantic, but as a realist. Any sincere politician or leader must have some vision in front of him. There must be something much more than notoriety to attract him towards unceasing work, the bitterness of struggle, the temptations and the pressures. There must be a factor of dedication, an undeniable impulse to build and to serve. In this he must satisfy himself. There are very few other rewards.

It is not only the vision of the leaders that dictates our struggle. There are the deep-rooted aspirations of our people. These people may appear simple and uneducated; they may not be articulate but they are human beings and not stones. They have an inborn pride and a genuine desire for self-improvement and self-fulfilment. These are facts which may have dodged many people in the past but with which we all must reckon in the future. To ignore this force would be to lead to frustrations and explosions — indeed we have already had such an experience in Kenya.

It is not, however, the fear of this force that should dictate our decisions. There is the positive side of this force, namely, its ability to face the challenge of nation-building. We have to release this force of our people for new and constructive purposes. We have to harness the enthusiasm for self-improvement to form the spearhead in our efforts for nation-building.

What, after all, does it mean when people talk about 'the position of the Europeans' or 'the problem of farmers'? To me it only suggests one thing: that over the past few years, for some reason, the Europeans shut themselves inside a kind of thorn *boma* of traditional thinking, hoping either that this would insulate them from events outside, or, more recently, that somebody would produce large sums of money to move them safely and profitably out of Kenya. Despite wishful thinking and pious hopes Kenya has not stood still. History has caught up with many of our people and the fact of a Kenya nation has aroused varying degrees of outrage, or criticism, or patronising commentary, or enthusiasm and practical support. But, maybe because so much has happened so quickly, the fact of Kenya has not yet achieved widespread understanding.

Broadly speaking, it has been the tradition of some people, even some in Africa, to think of Africa in terms of Rider Haggard situations or *Sanders of the River*. If you expect me to be honest with you, you must be honest in return. And so you must admit that people — over the years — have set out to persuade themselves and others, that the Africans 'were perfectly happy' with their mud huts and *posho* and whatever work could be dragged out of them for pittance wages, until 'political agitators' started to stir them up with talk about 'education' and 'trade unions' and 'democracy'.

This attitude, expressed in this way, is written in the pages of our modern history. And on the foundation of this attitude had been built the view, which many must have encountered and shared, that the impudent emergence of African leadership — in this African country — was first rooted in desire for power, or wealth, or revenge. I've even heard it argued that the motive force was desire to be invited overseas, for social entertainment.

The real motive force was quite simple. Any phase of evolution must have its milestones of increasing maturity. Thus, a few years ago, and quite suddenly in the eyes of many Europeans, Kenya produced from the ranks of her people, African leaders equipped with sophistication and talent and national — as distinct from patriarchal — ambition. Their first objective, their first approach, was quite simply *equality*. That was the first moment of truth. It was a moment that called for goodwill, but instead it was generally greeted with rebuff. The ideas of race bedevilled Kenya then — the ideas of superiority and domination and privilege. There was no point of contact between black and white. There was not allowed to be any mingling of philosophies, any mutual exploration of background or purpose, any pooling of resources, any kind of common ground.

The missing link was the wisdom and foresight needed in these early days. Constructive ambition was turned into conflict. Racial attitude was matched by racial attitude. Many Europeans expected 'gratitude'.

In the period leading up to 1960, the daily and weekly press of Kenya was not of much help in bringing wisdom and foresight to bear. The principles and policies that were given at least their rough shape by a Lancaster House Conference of early 1960 came to many as a tremendous shock, from which some have never really recovered. Why was this ? Because to a large extent the 'Wind of Change' had blown through Kenya unnoticed.

Relying on the local press many Europeans had been ill-prepared for Mr. Macleod's statements at Lancaster House. Their vision of Kenya was that of a marriage between South African apartheid policies and Sir Roy Welensky's policies. Perhaps this was the most revealing moment of our history. How so much can happen before our very eyes without our being able to comprehend it! It is this that explains the attitude and panic of those who ten years ago clamoured for independence for Kenya, but who are now preparing to desert Kenya on the eve of independence.

Think what has happened, despite this lesson of 1960. A fortnight ago Mr. Maudling was here, on a visit that proved very useful in many ways. Work has now started on constitutional drafting in the back-rooms of Westminster, and on papers flying to and fro between London and Nairobi. This simple fact represents the wide measure of genuine agreement that exists in the country about one of the twin pillars of Kenya's independence: the constitution. We shall have elections in roughly six months' time, from which there will emerge a government of the people, to carry Kenya into independence in 1963.

The other twin pillar is that long-standing practical and emotional issue in Kenya, the land. We have come a long way here too, in terms of common sense, justice and national thinking, since the days when all political speeches on one side spoke of 'the anachronism' and on the other side of 'the sanctity' of the White Highlands.

One of the interpretations of the Colonial Secretary's recent announcement that Britain would finance as a first step a million-acre resettlement project, and then consider going further — is this: although the scale and the speed of this project have been criticised, it is going to mean that those European mixed farmers who want to leave, will be enabled to do so. And to anyone determined to leave I would say merely — in that historic House of Commons phrase — 'in the name of God, go'. Kenya can do without anybody who has to be persuaded or cajoled to stay.

From this point that we've reached, the building of Kenya as a nation is going to be the biggest pioneering job in the history of Africa. You can't take up any compromise position now. Either you're going to play your part wholeheartedly in the challenge of the future, or you're going to run away from it all.

We understand full well that almost all the productive capacity of Kenya has to spring from conservation and wise use of the land. We understand the critical importance of agriculture, in its influence on living-standards and external trade, on urban growth and industrial development, on economic well-being and social contentment.

I see this, and want you to see it as well, as a national contribution. And I also see this every achievement of the land, the agriculture, as the combined effort of ownership and management and labour. With my background, and in my particular present job, I am very conscious that our agriculture as a whole — the mixed farms and ranches and plantations — employ a labour force of something like a quarter of a million.

Sometimes, you, know, I get it thrown at me by people who say that when all the Europeans have 'scrammed out of Africa'* these farm-workers will simply join the queue of unemployed and how do I like that? If we're going to be honest with each other, now and in the future, let us not shirk bringing out into the open all such attitudes and accusations.

People who say this kind of thing seem to me to combine vicious

---

* In a much-quoted phrase Mr. Mboya, when Chairman of the All African Peoples' Conference's first gathering in Accra in 1958 had said to the white man to 'scram out of Africa'. A glance at the text of that speech indicates that he was not referring to the Europeans as individuals but to their colonial or racial rule.

irresponsibility with a peculiar kind of despair. They can have no feeling for humanity, and no sense of national duty at all.

It is an odd moral outlook that would use unemployment as the currency in a game of politics. But Kenya now needs moral strength, and people of this kind are beyond the reach of any sympathy from me. Others tell their discharged workers, on occasion, to 'go and get a job from Kenyatta or Mboya . . .' Such people are not only untrue to Kenya, they do great harm to the Europeans who seriously wish to stay.

There is little I can add to all I've said before, in public here or in private discussions in London, about the festering sore of unemployment. I don't know whether some of you realise, even today, what unemployment means, in terms of loss of self-respect and human degradation, bitterness, and the seeds of subversion. To meet this unemployment, in a country with so much crying out to be done, calls for national outlook and dedication. We must transform the sense of our greatest peril into the sense that here is our greatest task.

Those who have decided to stay have got to create or discover human relationships, to bring into account things that you've hardly ever looked for: sensibilities and ambitions and loyalties and needs. You've got to understand that we all share human functions and frailties, and we're all in the same Kenya boat.

So often we talk of fears about personal security. The only way to dissolve fears is to remove their cause. Crime, of the kind that worries us, is rooted partly in economics, and partly in the psychology of this day and age, when the country has advanced so swiftly that sections of all communities could hardly keep in step. We need a fund of economic understanding and psychological resilience. Under both these headings it is up to each of us to give a lead.

We are all involved now in the business of building a nation. Your security fears will disappear when the people can see that you are working like everybody else, towards a goal that everybody wants to reach, for rewards that we all can share.

If you accept this, you are with us, not on sufferance but unaffectedly as colleagues and friends, important components of Kenya as a nation. Your Member, Mr. Welwood, told us in Legislative Council a fortnight ago, that many of you would feel unable to accept the consequences of independence, or some such phrase. Why should this be? There will be a Bill of Rights for all Kenya citizens which we — the political leaders

— have designed and will defend. All who accept this will no longer be 'members of the immigrant community', but full members of a new community which will demand all our dedication, all our attachment to morality, all our strength.

Let me emphasise one thing, while talking to you today. On the attainment of our independence all who were formerly 'non-Africans' must become full citizens of Kenya. As soon as you do so, any kind of discrimination in your status or your rights will disappear. Your interests will be as defensible in law, and of as great concern to the Government, as the interests of anybody else. But if you are not prepared to be citizens of Kenya, there will be no place for you here, except as aliens.

As a young nation Kenya cannot afford the luxury of squabbles with people who do not intend to stay. We have a tremendous economic and vocational struggle ahead. Either you are with us or you are not even on the field of play. We cannot let ourselves be weighted down by people who might cling to Kenya for a while, because they like 'the way of life', or because they're making money, or — so people often put it — 'to see how things turn out'. We cannot give *carte blanche* to benefits, of these or other kinds, gained without national investment of dedication, sacrifice and strength.

I told you earlier about the first moment of truth. I tell you now that, in Kenya's history, this is the second and critical moment of truth.

With mutual trust, and a sharing of faith, and a pooling of all our talents and resources, we can meet together this challenge of building a nation, irrespective of background or creed. This is what we want. It is what Kenya needs: the dedicated contribution of every race, every tribe, every worker, every farmer, every civil servant, every business-man, every teacher, every doctor, every family.

People ask me then how I can talk about a nation amid all the surface differences between K.A.N.U. and K.A.D.U., amid the clamours for Somali seccession and *mwambao* and the claims of the Masai.* This is

---

* At this time the minority party, Kenya African Democratic Union tended to represent the conservative, less advanced and pastoral Africans. The Somalis in the North East of the country were still pressing their claims for secession. Some elements at the coast wanted a separate existence (*mwambao*). The Masai, divided by the Kenya-Tanganyika border, were unsure of their future position in the new states.

superficial thinking. Inevitably, the birth-pangs of a nation must be attended by different party outlook, different bargaining position, different viewpoint or approach. To date, our people have been dragged through history. Henceforth we will write our own history. And this is the point at which outlooks and loyalties will coalesce.

True, we have tribal differences and sensitivities. So often people point at the Congo and warn that Kenya is doomed to become another Congo. I do not share this view. We have passed the stage when this could have happened. We have passed through more trials than most African countries and I believe we have come to appreciate freedom to a point where we would be prepared to defend it with our lives. We do not intend to exchange British colonialism for either local dictatorship or Soviet and American economic colonialism.

Out of all the emergencies and instabilities, the economic recession of the past decade, the immediate challenge before us is that of recovery. And on this we must build. I've been frank with you throughout this speech. I've dealt with many of the bitter comments that got hurled at me and other African leaders. Let us forget the mistakes and the weaknesses of the past, on all and every side. Our duty now is to the future.

THE ROLE OF THE PARTY IN INDEPENDENT KENYA

An article published in Pan Africa, *Nairobi, 1964 and written by Tom Mboya in his capacity as Secretary-General of K.A.N.U.*

We have not had much party activity since the elections in May last year. It is possible that some of our supporters think that because we won the elections and formed the Government, the party is no longer really important or necessary. Such thought would be most misleading and would convey ignorance of the real function of the party even after independence. However, we the leaders must accept some responsibility for this slackness in the party activities in the months following the elections. I hope that our members and supporters will understand the pressures under which we have had to work. Following the elections, we had the task of negotiating the date for Independence and the Independence Constitution itself. By concentrating on this, we were able to fulfil our election pledge to give Kenya independence in 1963. In addition, we spent many months planning and preparing for the Independence Celebrations.

The purpose of this article is not to look back and explain our recent weaknesses in party organisation, but to look into the future and discuss our party in the context of the new situation: the role of the party in independent Kenya.

Before independence our party was rightly geared to the struggle against colonialism. Its structure, organisation and slogans — and even mood — were conceived to ensure it could be an effective weapon against the colonialists. Now that we are free, we have to reconstruct the party for the new task of nation-building, economic freedom and the creation of a pan-African as well as an international personality. In the old days, the party was used to arouse the people against the colonialists. Today it has to be used to arouse them for the national effort — for work in the villages and on national schemes as part of our effort in nation-building. In the old days the party agitated against the Government and taught the people to doubt and suspect and even hate the Government and any of its administrators. Today the party is the Government and must teach the people to accept, respect and trust the

Government and its officers. In the old days the member of parliament was the spokesman of his people, but had nothing to do with the Government. He was an agitator. In fact to have been identified as a spokesman of the Government implied betrayal of the nationalist cause. Today the member of parliament must both belong to his constituents as well as ensure that the Government's intentions and policies are understood and implemented as the only way through which progress can take place. The member of parliament can no longer remain merely an agitator gallivanting all over the world or spending all his time in Nairobi making speeches. He needs to be closer to the people and to-gether with county councillors and regional assembly members in his area give leadership at the local level without which efforts at self-help schemes, co-operatives, etc. may very well fail. The member of parlia-ment should in fact be functionally associated with both the party and the Government, to ensure the ordinary man is fully aware of his asso-ciation with and voice in the Government. It is on this basis then that we should look at certain aspects of our party organisation for the future.

Perhaps the first question that we shall have to decide upon is the structure of the party. In this regard there are a number of important points requiring careful study. These include:

(a) whether party branches should continue to be based on the admini-strative district unit as in the past or changed to constituency units;

(b) whether we need to continue with all the various committees i.e. National Secretariat, National Executive Committee, National Governing Council or do away with one or two of these and have a new properly representative National Executive responsible for party policy, discipline and liaison with the Prime Minister and the Cabinet. In this regard we have to study the relations between the party and the Government and determine the point at which formal relations ought to be established to ensure smooth trans-lation of party policies into Government programme — and the translation of Government decisions and programmes into schemes and work projects;

(c) the relations between the back-benches and the Cabinet as well as the party executives;

(d) the position of the party youth and women's wings in the light of new developments such as the National Youth Service, the National Community Development Schemes, etc.;

(e) the party and external relations after independence;

(f) the party and other organisations in Kenya, i.e. trade unions, co-operatives, farmers' organisations, social bodies, etc.

There may be other questions, but these appear to me to be of immediate importance and it might be useful to discuss them here briefly.

In the days of the Kenya African Union, branches were organised only on the basis of convenience. In some cases it was the administrative district unit, in others it was just the township unit and yet in some cases there were several branches of the union within one administrative district. The approach was based on a practical determination of organisation arrangement. After the banning of K.A.U., the imperialist Government refused to allow the formation of a new nationwide African political organisation. Instead, in 1956, the Government introduced legislation limiting organisation of political parties to administrative district units — this was to coincide with Government's own administrative convenience. It had nothing to do with convenience of organisation. When K.A.N.U. was formed it was decided to dissolve the district parties as separate societies and the district organisation became the branch unit of the party. This was a convenient move as it eliminated complications as regards transfer of assets, and elections of delegates to the K.A.N.U. inaugural conference as well as the election of new branch officials. It should also be noted that at the time members of the Legislative Council represented vast areas often including more than one administrative district. The Legislative Council member was therefore the umbrella bringing together a number of district associations.

Looking into the future, we have to take into account the new role of the member of parliament as the spokesman for his constituency and the fact that we have now more than one such member in each administrative district and even in the larger towns. We have to ensure the structure of the party facilitates the functions of the member of parliament and enables him to work with, and is answerable to the party. It should ensure there is no room for friction between the member and the chairman of the party branch and between members who happen to come from the same district. Above all, the party structure should ensure that in the event of a snap election the selection of candidates in each constituency and the running of the election campaign can be done smoothly with the full co-operation of the voters in the constituency. We should ensure further that the branch unit is one in which the elected representatives of the people can demonstrate the meaning of a people's government by generating local initiative and sense of responsibility. Lastly, we need a structure which provides for effective discipline in the party emanating from a feeling of full participation by all party members at the local level. People have a tendency to resent any control coming from outside.

Having regard to all these considerations, it becomes imperative that the new structure must give formal recognition to the constituency within which the member of parliament would function. This could be done in several ways. One way is to have the constituency become the branch unit of the party. The second way is to have the constituency become the sub-branch unit in place of the administrative locations and divisions in a district. If this second alternative is followed, we would have to work on the assumption that there would be no direct contact between the constituency and the head office of the party except through the district branch. We must consider the merits or demerits of such arrangement.

I know that this could be a very sensitive and hotly debated subject but I feel that if we study closely structures of parties in other countries and consider only the need for the smooth working and effectiveness of our party instead of individuals who may lose or gain positions within the party we should be able to arrive at a sound decision. But whatever we do, we must not lose sight of the role which the party has to play in the future, i.e. as a vehicle for development.

Coming now to the component parts of the party, it would appear that here too we need to decide on a new structure. There is a need for a powerful national executive committee which meets regularly and ensures liaison with the Prime Minister and the Cabinet. The National Governing Council would become superfluous if such an executive committee were created. The present National Executive Committee is in fact a committee of the National Governing Council and has no final authority. Such national executive committee would include representatives of the constituencies, the backbenchers, party regional assembly members and the Cabinet.

It would ensure that party policies approved by the delegates' Annual Conference are translated effectively into Government, regional authority, and county council programmes throughout the country. It would further ensure that the party machine was used all over the

country to give the leadership necessary to promote Government programmes. Through the constituency organisation, the members of
parliament, the regional assembly members and the county and municipal councillors would have the dual responsibility of promoting party
as well as Government programmes. This would bring the Government
and its servants closer to the ordinary people and create in the country
the enthusiasm and excitement needed in the effort for nation-building.
The party and the Government must work together in every village
whether it is to educate the masses in securing a change in attitudes or
to ensure respect for law and order and create confidence in the new
regime. The remoteness of the Government during colonial days must
be replaced by the involvement of the masses in Government decisions
and programmes during independence.

The party may have to create a new committee at the regional level to
ensure that party activities and policies are uniform throughout the
regions. Such committee would also ensure that party members in the
Assembly work together and carry out party policies. This could be
called 'K.A.N.U. Regional Governing Council'.* It would report
regularly to the National Executive, but should not take away the right
of constituency branches to have direct access to headquarters and
national executive committee. Thus this Council would not be involved
in such things as membership drives or the administration and running
of the constituency branches.

To ensure effective working of the party, the delegates' conference
must be organised to provide real and serious debates on policy. It must
not be just a contest for factions and personalities. The party Head Office
should have a small committee to prepare carefully thought-out papers
on the different subjects. These should be circulated to the constituencies and the national executive and form the background for discussion
at the delegates' conference.

I have already referred to the role of the members of parliament in
the party, but the member of parliament has an additional and very
important part to play in the parliamentary system. From among them,
the Prime Minister picks his Cabinet and on them he relies for the

* Now Provincial Committees. Regional Assemblies were abolished by a Constitutional Amendment in 1964.

necessary support to get measures passed through parliament. The back-benchers can make or wreck their Government and it is necessary that their relations with the Cabinet and the party are clearly understood. It is necessary that the party ensures that the Cabinet and the back-benchers work harmoniously together. Both must in the first place owe their complete loyalty to the party and abide by the policies and directions issued by the national executive. The Cabinet has the task of translating such policies into legislation and programmes. It must be allowed the full scope and authority to exercise Governmental powers. Its actions can be questioned or even challenged in the national executive. Whereas healthy debate should be allowed in the parliament, the party whip must be respected at all times. Members of parliament rightly demand to be taken into confidence and consulted or informed as fully as possible on measures before they come on the floor of the house for debate. This should be done through briefing sessions between the Prime Minister and the Ministers and members of parliament. The back-benchers' committee on different subjects should also meet regularly with Ministers concerned. It is necessary at the same time to recognise that Cabinet secrecy and collective responsibility must be preserved; otherwise the Government itself may face serious internal problems. The back-benchers should accept this position and refrain from converting back-bench meetings into Cabinet sessions.

It is therefore necessary to ensure that members of parliament recognise that the party is supreme and that all of them serve their party. They must make the habit of going back to their constituencies to help explain Government measures and to collect the genuine reactions and views of their constituents to put before the Prime Minister and Ministers when they meet. The constituency must not be left to guess and the member must not develop the attitude or habit of thinking whatever he feels or says represents the views of his constituency without giving them the chance to discuss matters with him. It is not my intention at this stage to discuss the merits and demerits of a one-party state. The fact, however, is that K.A.N.U.'s strength has increased so much that K.A.D.U. can no longer be regarded as a threat to the K.A.N.U. Government. In parliament today the only threat or embarrassment could come from our own party members. This places a heavy responsibility on each of our members. Provided the component parts of the party work effectively and the relations between the back-benchers and the Cabinet are conducted on the basis I have described, there should be no cause for frustration or excuse for defying the party whip.

In the days of the struggle for independence, we created a youth and women's wing for the party. The party is grateful for the work and sacrifices which the youth and women's wings made for the party and for Kenya. Looking back today one comes to the conclusion that the establishment of the youth-wing was done haphazardly and without planning for the future. At first the youth-wing members were to help raise the membership of the party, but although they were employed on this, no proper arrangements were made for their subsistence. As time went on, this part of their function was given up. Many of them worked full-time or just stayed at party offices throughout the day without specific work. It was not uncommon to find youth-wingers begging for money and food from different leaders. This part of our party's history was its biggest weakness. It led to a demoralisation of the youth-wingers and it cheapened their position. It got them a bad name and even the good ones were lumped together with the bad. When factions broke down the youth-wingers were left without support and even leaders got tired of their begging. The relations between the youth-wing and the party got out of hand. This situation was especially bad in the urban areas.

The youth-wingers often played a decisive part in the organisation of rallies, the election campaigns and the public processions. They successfully reduced the threat of K.A.D.U. and other opposition parties. But our reports and records show that the party has never thought out the youth-wing problem sufficiently. For example, several party conferences discussed this matter and ended up with different decisions. There was the question of the age limit which was never fully resolved. Then there was the argument as to whether youth-wingers should be nationally organised or left to be organised only at the branch level. When it was decided to organise youth at the branch level, there was no effective machinery to co-ordinate their activities at the national level or to ensure their discipline at the branch level.

The youth are not only important to the party, they are also important to the nation. Their enthusiasm and daring adventurous spirit is just what we need. But their energies must be channelled to useful and productive purposes. The Government's National Youth Service plan is one way of doing this. But it will be necessary to supplement it with other youth programmes: they could play a part in the national community development schemes. The educated youth could be used, for example, in adult literacy campaigns.

As far as the party is concerned, certain decisions must now be taken; we must avoid having idle, unemployable and hungry youths whose services can be bought for a two-shilling tip. We must insist that the party youth-wing is not a full-time or a full day's job. Apart from those who join the National Youth Service, the party youth-winger should be a part-time activist who works for the party after office hours on a voluntary basis. There should be an age limit for the youth-wing and there should be a national council for the party youth-wing — this is not to be confused with a separate youth-wing party organisation. Any youth employed on full-time party work must be paid a wage to avoid the embarrassments of the past few years. It appears to me that the party will need to create a new atmosphere in which members of the youth and women's wings become the trusted friends of the people in the villages. Violence or indiscipline by any member of the youth-wing should be severely punished. The youth and women's wing members should help to promote self-help schemes in addition to their work in organising the party. They should help organise sports and recreational functions and especially in the development of our African cultures — dances, playes, etc. The party youth-wing leaders should be given opportunity for training in leadership and group organisation in some of the countries that have developed these techniques. They should also be assisted to make proper contact with international youth organisations — through the party. Such an approach should not be in conflict with the Government's Youth programme. These two approaches should in fact be complementary. We will rely heavily on youth to help propagate the new ideas and policies of the Government and the philosophy of our new society. The party must develop a youth training programme of its own within Kenya where party policy and philosophy can be properly passed on to the party youth-wing leaders.

Speaking about our women's wing, one is bound to acknowledge the great contribution the women have made in the development and victory of our party. The remarks I have made about the reform of the youth wing should apply to the women's wing. The members of the women's wing should be encouraged to continue to give voluntary help to the party. Young girls or women should, of course, be recruited into the National Youth Service, in addition to their playing an important role in community development schemes. What has disturbed most of us is the absence of political or nationalist awareness among the educated African women. With a few exceptions, most educated African women seem to have stayed away from the active support of the party. Yet this is the class which could be elected to various bodies including the County Councils, the Regional Assemblies and Parliament. It is true that these women need assistance, but assistance is more useful where there is initiative and a spirit to belong and contribute. Once in a while, a woman has come to apply for parliamentary or Central Legislative Assembly seat. In every case this is the first time such applicants have shown real interest in the party and when such applications fail, they are not heard of again. The new Kenya will require the enthusiastic support and participation of these women. In the past, Europeans who were responsible for *Maendeleo ya Wanawake* and Community Development gave too much emphasis to women's development on the lines of acquiring only European behaviour, standards and status. This approach is negative and has been responsible for the apparent gap in the social contact between the educated and illiterate African women. In fact one notices what appears to be an exclusive African women's club seeking contact with other races, and not with their own womenfolk. There are a number of active African Women's organisations in the country, but none of these have made any impact in terms of typical African social and community development. Although they have various conferences and activities, they have little or no activity in the villages or in the areas where Africans live in towns. It is not enough to lecture, to write, to make speeches about the standards to be achieved by African women. There is great scope for the party to enlist the active support of the educated African women; we should, seek them out and bring them into the party. In this regard, I feel a women-leaders' training programme should be introduced within the party on the same lines as the one proposed for the youth-wing.

Apart from the internal and structural aspects of the party's machine and organisation, we have to look at the question of the party's external relations. Before independence the party had some offices and representatives abroad. It was also common to find party officials visiting various countries and speaking in the name of the party or Kenya. We are not only now free but our party forms the Government of Kenya. There is no need therefore for party offices or representatives stationed abroad. Kenya's diplomatic representatives should be left free to speak for the people of Kenya abroad. This is one area in which confusion and embarrassment could be created if the party tried to work its own external relations in competition with the Government. Of course, the party will continue to maintain friendly relations with other political parties outside Kenya and we may even have exchanges of friendly visits with other parties, but we must not create the situation where the individual or the party as such continues direct relations with foreign Governments. This is a function of our Government. There are international institutions with which we can establish relations as a party but here too we must be careful not to embarrass the Government in its foreign policies.

The question of scholarships and receiving aid from abroad in the name of the party is one which must also be watched. Our party having formed the Government has the responsibility of helping the Government show the people that it is able to work for the welfare of all the people. In this way we ensure K.A.N.U.'s victory at the next elections. We should not therefore interfere with the Government in formulating educational and foreign aid programmes for Kenya. The party's friends abroad should in fact be persuaded to assist the K.A.N.U. party in power within the machinery of the Government. There are genuine areas such as political tours and training abroad which the party could still carry out, but this must be done in consultation with the Government. All along one assumes that the Government for its part will implement fully and positively the party's foreign policy.

Within Kenya there are other organisations that constitute the various groups of forces with which Government needs to co-operate in the task of nation building. Until now we have not established any formal or informal relations with these organisations. The actual form of relationships that a political party should establish say with trade unions, farmers, co-operatives, chambers of commerce, etc., is a very much debated subject but there can be no question as to the need for effective consultation as between these bodies and the party. Somewhere along the line there must be the harmonisation of policies and even co-operation between these bodies and the party. Suspicion and misunderstanding between these bodies could build unnecessary resistance and even frustrations that may hamper urgently needed progress in the country. The recent agreement signed between the Government, the

Federation of Kenya Employers and the Kenya Federation of Labour clearly shows that there is goodwill and a readiness to sacrifice in the interests of the nation.* If there is to be co-operation with the Government in planning effective self-help schemes, then the party must discuss some of its plans with these other bodies. Such co-operation and consultation will ensure that the party, the peasants, the trade unions, the co-operatives and the chambers of commerce speak with one voice, giving the country a clear sense of direction. This will remove the possibility of different policies that may confuse the people and slow down progress. This is not just a question of having trade unions, and other bodies to affiliate to the party formally, but I am confident that a practical formula can be found to ensure effective and harmonious relations even without such formal affiliation.

Lastly, we will have to review the position of our finances. Too often our members and even branch officials have come to expect financial assistance either from the head office of the party or even from individual national leaders. Apart from funds received from membership fees the party has not in the past established an effective countrywide fund-raising programme. Such a programme would include youth and women's wings activities, sports, athletics, football, cultural dances, plays, etc., organised in public halls, stadiums, etc. The party cannot exist on the funds derived from membership fees alone.

In the past the party has been able to appeal for assistance from sympathetic groups, countries and persons outside Kenya. This was during our fight against colonialism. Now that we are independent such assistance must come to an end. Our friends expect us to stand on our own feet and to build our party out of local effort. This is as it should be. Continued receipts of funds for party work could lead to complications or pressures in foreign and economic policies. We could find our position compromised or embarrassed by people who may expect that because they continue to assist our party we should accept

* The Tripartite Agreement was a pact between the Government, the Kenya Federation of Labour and the Federation of Kenya Employers. It was drawn up with Tom Mboya as principle inspirer and spokesman for the Government in the negotiations. It provided for a standstill in wage demands and strike action by the unions and an undertaking by the Government and employers to increase their labour forces by certain proportions.

their policies for Kenya. This must be avoided. Apart from this there are still a number of countries in Africa under colonial rule and European domination. All assistance available from African states and African friends must be concentrated on these countries. What is more, we too must begin making our contribution towards the freedom struggle of these countries. In other words, instead of our party expecting assistance from outside, our party and Government are expected to give assistance to others. Already we have had a number of refugees and organisations from these countries coming to Kenya in expectation of sympathy and help. It is not enough that we sympathise with these freedom fighters. We must give them the tools with which to carry on their fight. This is what was done for us and we must now do the same for others. All this points to the need for us to have a much stronger and financially stable party organisation.

The political situation and the constitutional structure of Kenya have changed considerably since this article was written. Nevertheless the principles it enunciates remain valid and some of the proposals have been incorporated in new arrangements. In 1964 the Kenya African Democratic Union dissolved itself to merge with the Kenya African National Union. In 1966 a new party, the Kenya Peoples' Union was formed by Mr. Oginga Odinga, formerly Vice-President of K.A.N.U. and the Republic of Kenya.

The most important developments related to matters dealt with in the above article have been:

(1) *The Limuru Conference*, 1966, at which the K.A.N.U. party structure was changed to implement proposals for seven Vice-Presidents (one for each Province). This move was intended to remove fears that K.A.N.U. was dominated by two Provinces — Central and Nyanza, by ensuring that all areas had a voice in the party's inner councils. It was a means of integrating the former K.A.D.U. leadership more closely into K.A.N.U. It placed the office of the President of the party in an undisputed position and removed some of the speculation about the succession. The Conference also removed the bar on dual party and government office holding for the post of General Secretary. Until then Mr. Mboya's holding of Ministerial office and the

party office of Secretary-General had been against the party's constitution. The Conference also strengthened the responsibility of the Secretary-General with regard to the party headquarters.

(2) Regular caucus meetings of K.A.N.U. members of parliament are now held with Ministers present and are normally chaired by the President.

(3) *Development Advisory Committees*. These were created in 1965 to ensure that co-ordination of and participation in development matters at the District and Provincial levels are fully effective. Membership of these committees at the District levels:

- (a) All the members of the Development Committee of officials only — (officials of the Central Government and Local Authorities). These are officials whose functions in the field are of economic nature of Education, Health, Roads, etc.
- (b) All members of Parliament from a District or Province for the District and Provisional Development Advisory Committees, respectively.
- (c) The chairman of the County Council. (This is now being revised to include the chairman of Municipalities and smaller urban areas).
- (d) Two or three leading citizens to be nominated by the Provincial Commissioner or District Commissioner in consultation with the District Development Committee.

The District Commissioners and Provincial Commissioners are the chairmen of the Committees and the Provincial Planning officers are the secretaries.

(4) A Constitutional Amendment Act of 1966 provided for the compulsory resignation from parliament of any member who changed from the party on whose ticket he was elected to parliament or local authority.

(5) *K.A.N.U. Provincial Committees*. It has been suggested that such committees should be formed within the party structure, corresponding with the same level in the country's administrative organisation. The absence of party bodies at this level leaves the party Vice-Presidents without organisational backing or channels for consultation.

(6) *The K.A.N.U. Conference, State House, Nairobi.* This Conference came at a time when there was a need for reviving party activity. It brought party functionaries at branch level together with national party leaders and from the gathering came a new spirit and activity which continued until the local government elections later the same year. It was at this meeting that the party decided that there should be legislation to prevent independent, non-party candidates from standing in local government elections. The Government subsequently introduced the necessary amending legislation into Parliament and this became law, as the Constitutional Amendment Act of 1968, after receiving the approval of the National Assembly. An associated Act made similar provisions with regard to Local Government contests. This necessitated a tightening of the regulations controlling nominations by parties.

(7) *The 1968 State House Conference, Mombasa.* At this meeting new party rules were adopted relating to the selection of candidates for parliamentary and local government elections. The meeting also changed the basis of representation at party national conventions. Until that time each District sent an equal number of delegates but the new arrangement gives equal representation to each National Assembly constituency. The constituencies' delimitation on the other hand takes into account a number of factors such as population, communications and other geographic considerations so that in future party representation will equally reflect this basis.

(8) *The K.A.N.U.-Administration Conference, Nakuru, 1968.* The purpose of this meeting was to bring together Provincial and District Commissioners on the one hand and K.A.N.U. chairmen and National Executive Committee members on the other. There had been some uneasiness in their relations. The administration felt that local party officials did not appreciate government problems and that this was responsible for fostering negative attitudes towards the Government in the countryside. The party chairmen, for their part, felt that the officials did not give them due respect and that they were ignored. The meeting discussed ways in which they could work more closely together with consultation and co-operation in the field.

A number of issues are still not settled. No satisfactory structure has been found for youth within politics although this problem has become less acute because energies have been absorbed in the National Youth Service, for improved education and better economic and social opportunities for the party youth supporters. Nor have structures and attitudes changed yet to give to women a voice in the party, the government and in society generally commensurate with their comprising at least half of the country's population. For a discussion of the role of the Civil Service see another of the speeches published in this book (pp. 162–167).

(9) *Selection of Party candidates for election to parliament.* In his speech to the nation on 12th December, 1968, H.E. The President, announced a proposal of new electoral rules that would require political parties to hold primaries in which all party members would vote to select their party candidates for election to parliament. This announcement followed on criticism against selection of candidates by party branch committees for the Local Government elections in August. It was felt that the committee system was open to abuse and that it was possible for the true feelings of party members to be ignored. It was also felt that the decision to stop independents from standing could only be justified if selection machinery within the parties was truly democratic.

THE ROLE OF TRADE UNIONS IN DEVELOPMENT

Extracts from a speech delivered at the Conference of the Railway African Union, 1965

This book would be incomplete if it did not include one of Mr. Mboya's many speeches on the trade union movement and the place of organised labour in the task of nation building. Tom Mboya was among the many young African leaders who came into politics through the trade unions. In 1952 he joined the Nairobi African Staff Association becoming its Secretary almost immediately. Later that year he helped form the Kenya Local Government Workers' union and became its first National General Secretary — a post he held for ten years till 1962 when he was appointed Minister of Labour in the Coalition Government. In 1953 Mr. Mboya was elected General Secretary of the Kenya Federation of Labour — a post he held until he resigned ten years later in 1963.

The idea of consultation between management and workers has now been accepted by many industries as a necessary provision for the prevention and settlement of disputes. But this method cannot be relied on wholly as now and again differences might arise such that the machinery fails to provide a solution. In case of such a deadlock then some provision has to be arranged whereby the disputes can be settled.

It is here the Government has to come in not because it is in itself a big employer but because it will be for the good of all parties concerned. Industrial disputes if they affect essential services of the country are bound to threaten the internal peace and so it is in the interest of the community in general and the workers and the employers in particular that industrial conflict be minimised as far as possible. No government worth its name would stand and watch the tug-of-war between the employers and the workers go on indefinitely. While strikes and lock-outs are sometimes inevitable weapons for the parties they are luxuries which developing countries of Africa cannot afford. It is for this reason that the Government has the obligation to undertake measures for the prevention and settlement of industrial disputes.

In Kenya the present machinery for settling disputes is embodied in the Trade Disputes Act. This Act makes provision for the settlement of trade disputes by establishing Arbitration Tribunals, Boards of Inquiry and the Industrial Court.

Let me make a passing reference to the Industrial Court. For many years the need for an industrial court in Kenya has been felt and expressed by employers, unions and Government alike. The setting up of the Industrial Court this year is a milestone in the industrial relations policy pursued by the Kenya Government. It will offer to both sides of industry a channel for settling their disputes privately and without involving the statutory machinery of arbitration or board of inquiry. It is our hope that the Court will standardise awards, wages policy and conditions of employment and thus bring about a steady but progressive improvement in the conditions of the workers. It will also improve the prospects of good industrial relations. In the past we have relied on *ad hoc* tribunals appointed as and when disputes occurred.

The promotion of co-operation between the employers, workers and Government underlies our national policy in labour relations and this is the objective of our labour legislation and administration. There is a very close relation between the Government and both employers and unions. We have in Kenya a well-established pattern of consultation through the Labour Advisory Board.

In 1962 when I was Minister for Labour I decided to demonstrate the Government's faith and goodwill towards the labour movement by putting into practice the idea that instead of compulsory legislation we would work out a voluntary system — an Industrial Relations Charter to embody in it all the obligations expected of the employers and unions in a free Kenya. The Industrial Relations Charter which was signed in October 1962 covered issues such as recognition of unions, check-off system, dispute procedure and demarcation. In this document the employers and the unions acknowledge that they recognise consultation and co-operation on a basis of mutual understanding as an essential contribution to efficiency and productivity, and that progress can only be made on a foundation of good conditions of service. It is the Government's policy that as far as possible the industries should be self-governing in industrial relations.

The recent Tripartite Agreement signed in March 1964 for the Relief of Unemployment is another vivid example of this same approach. Under this agreement Government, trade unions and employers agreed to work together in the relief of unemployment. It provided that:

(a) The Government and public services would increase their establishment by 15 per cent.

(b) All private employers would increase their labour force by 10 per cent.

(c) There would be no redundancy declared for a period of 12 months.

(d) No new wage claims would be made by unions for at least 12 months.

(e) No strikes or lock-outs would be called for the 12 month period.

(f) Government would if necessary legislate to enforce the check-off system.

The voluntary sacrifices which the scheme requires from all sides of industry is clear proof of the strides already made in Kenya.

While the primary purpose of a trade union movement is to strive to improve the wages and condition of living of the workers, if it is to develop freely on the basis of freedom and democracy political freedom must first of all be acquired in each colonial territory. This is why the trade union and the national movement are almost invariably linked in independent territories. The desire to improve industrial relations must be intimately associated with the desire for national independence. In Kenya where the employers were themselves foreigners associated with the ruling power the struggle against the employer involved the unions in political activities. The two movements are more fused together when the same trade union leaders are at the same time the driving force of nationalism. This was the position I found myself in. I was for a long time both the General Secretary of the Kenya Federation of Labour and of the African National Union. I have since given up the former.

It is very often asked as to how we can make the distinction between politics and trade unionism. The first problem facing the unions is to decide about the type of political activities that could be promoted within the trade unions without losing its character. It must also be realised that no trade union would like to transform itself into a political party. The unions must be free to express their opinions on political issues that have a direct influence on the economic and social conditions of their members. I personally feel very strongly that this role should be played by the trade union federation rather than individual unions. It was the avowed policy of the colonial governments to disassociate the trade unions completely from politics not only through legal restriction but through constant threats of cancellation of their registration as societies.

The trade unions having played their part in the national movement to achieve political independence must now play their part in consolidating independence and helping in the task of economic reconstruction. The new governments are not prepared to allow any obstruction in the economic development either from trade unions or any other group of persons. It is for these reasons that certain governments have taken decisions to pass legislation denying workers the right to strike. These laws are meant to ensure that the government programmes are not obstructed. It is the greatest challenge to the trade union movement to create the atmosphere in which its various rights can continue to be recognised but in which at the same time people feel that the unions are participating fully in the cause of nation building. The Kenya Government recognises that trade unions form an important part of our social structure today and encourages sound and healthy trade unions. We consider them an essential aspect of economic and social progress. To this end it endeavours to develop and promote good labour relations rather than rely on repressive legislation.

The Kenya Federation of Labour which is the central trade union body is affiliated to the International Confederation of Free Trade Unions. I have myself been a member of the I.C.F.T.U. executive board, and Chairman of the East, Central and Southern Africa area committee. The attachment to I.C.F.T.U. was a great help to Kenya particularly during the state of emergency when for the fear of the international labour movement the colonial government refrained from banning the K.F.L. During my visit to Israel in 1962 I studied the Israel pattern and as a result of my visit a joint enterprise was launched between Hisdardut of Israel and the K.F.L. The initial scheme was one of consumer co-operatives. The aim of the scheme was to attempt to establish the trade union movement as a definite partner in the whole effort of economic development.

With the coming of independence and the fact that our foreign policy is based on the idea of positive non-alignment international affiliation has become a very sensitive issue in Africa. The I.C.F.T.U. is anti-communist and is essentially an organisation of trade unions from the Western bloc. This is a fact which is bound to affect future relations in Africa. The Organisation of African Unity has now asked its Commission for Labour to examine this matter. Attempts have been made to establish independent trade union centres and although for the moment there is conflict on this point in Africa, I believe that very soon the African states will be able to reach agreement on a pattern which will apply throughout the continent. Although I retain the most friendly relations with the I.C.F.T.U. and will never forget their help during our hour of need, I feel they must begin to face some of the realities of Africa.*

The Kenya Federation of Labour registered in 1955 is still the authoritative central body of employee trade unions and has about 30 affiliates. It has no direct affiliation with our party K.A.N.U. but works closely with it and with the Government.†

* The Kenya Government ruled against affiliation by the central organisation of trade unions and this brought to an end affiliation with the I.C.F.T.U., W.F.T.U. and A.A.T.U. in 1965.

Latterly Mr. Mboya discussed the possible setting-up of a central organisation of trade unions in Africa. He expressed the view that in the political and economic circumstances such a continent-wide organisation would find it difficult to function and could in fact be a weapon to be used by some people to subvert development efforts in a state whose policies some African leaders may not approve of. He suggests instead an I.L.O.-type organisation for Africa where the trade unions, the employers' associations and the Ministers of Labour from each African state can meet regularly to exchange views and consult on technical, legislative, educational and other problems. The recommendations would then be subject to ratifacation by each Government as it sees fit. Standing Committees of Workers could be established within this set-up to facilitate continental consultation.

Mr. Mboya has also expressed the view that individual trade unions could be allowed to affiliate with international technical and professional bodies to facilitate education and exchange of experience.

† The Kenya Federation of Labour together with a rival group — the Workers Congress were wound up following a Presidential Ministerial Commission on which Mr. Mboya was a member in 1965. A new central body was established — the Central Organisation of Trade Unions (C.O.T.U.) with Mr. Clement Lubembe. M.P., former Secretary General of K.F.L. as Secretary.

SOME ASPECTS OF LABOUR PROBLEMS IN ECONOMIC DEVELOPMENT

An Address by Hon. T. J. Mboya — 1965

Every government faces the problem of reconciling the self-interest of the individual with the welfare of society. In the labour field we must find a way to reconcile the self-interest of the employed with the need to increase employment. Our Sessional Paper No. 10 of 1965 has given an important role to the concept of mutual social responsibility. We are now seeking ways of making that concept a reality. The labour field is a particularly fruitful place in which to explore possible ways of achieving mutual social responsibility.

The principal objective of the Kenya Government is to promote the welfare of the people of Kenya. Economic development and growth rates are only short-hand ways of talking about the goal. Apparent success according to these measures may camouflage some very real problems that must be solved if our people are to share equitably in development. A high growth rate, a high investment rate, and increasing wages must not blind us to high levels of unemployment and under-employment. It is these levels that will be our major labour and man-power problems for many years to come.

We are all experienced enough with statistics to know that while the man with one foot in the cooker and one foot in the fridge usually feels fine, he is not in good shape. From the labour-manpower viewpoint, despite our average favourable situation, major problems exist. These include:

(1) The number of Africans who have the education and experience to occupy high level positions is limited.

(2) Expatriates occupy a relatively large proportion of high-level positions.

(3) A large proportion of our resources is being invested in education but the output is not yet in balance with our manpower requirements.

(4) Many Africans are unemployed or less than fully employed.

(5) Many school leavers cannot find useful employment and others have job aspirations beyond their capabilities and training.

(6) A large proportion of our labour force is engaged in agriculture at low levels of productivity.

(7) Wages in urban areas are being determined on the basis of power which, at times, does not coincide with economic requirements, and which is magnifying the difference between urban and rural income.

Several of these problems are difficult to handle because those who 'have' in a society are articulate, relatively powerful, and often well organised to present their case forcefully. Too often they get more, and those who 'have not', get less. The worker who is employed in the monetary economy in Kenya is fortunate. He has a wage; he has the provident fund; there is a health centre in his area; his union may organise and present his views.

The 'have-nots' in society normally are not well organised and must rely on government and political parties to represent their interests. For example high wages in urban areas are fine for the employed union members, but the Government must also be aware that they can increase the prices those less fortunate must pay or decrease returns on investment to the extent that a job for his younger brother will not be created.

Our primary goal must be to share on a widespread basis the benefits of more rapid growth. Indeed, this is a fundamental objective of African socialism, and our Sessional Paper No. 10 of 1965 notes three major instruments for progressing toward this objective — the tax structure, the backward areas programme, and incomes policy. Changes in tax structure must be conditioned by social as well as revenue needs. In particular, those fortunate enough to have incomes above the average must share their incomes with the very poor through the tax system so that Government can provide education and training, health services, and other forms of assistance to the needy and under-privileged. The backward areas programme is expected to follow similar principles on a geographic basis in order to ensure that progress is not limited to major municipalities.

Incomes policy, therefore, does not stand alone and isolated as our only attack on problems of income distribution, but it must play an extremely vital role. We must do more than provide welfare services and subsidies to the poor. We must create job opportunities for them and provide the training necessary for them to fill those jobs.

Keeping wage levels at reasonable levels is a basic contribution that we can make toward attracting investors who will create jobs. Reasonable and stable wages, responsible unions and productive, reliable works will also stimulate investors to rely more substantially on labour input as a means of production. This should create even more employment. But these are matters that none of us can pretend to understand fully.

I would suggest that we must give more attention to the function of wages in developing countries. Are wage increases a fair mechanism for redistributing income or distributing gains in wealth when so few are participating in this monetary economy? Would it be better to keep wages reasonable enough to encourage employment and maintain a reasonable cost of living for those who are unemployed or unable to increase their incomes much above the subsistence level?

Without being doctrinaire on this issue, it seems evident that with a large subsistence agricultural sector and high levels of unemployment and under-employment, wage increases for the few employed are an inadequate means of distributing economic gains. At our present stage it is more important for wages to be set which stimulate employment. Gains from productivity must be shared with the unemployed and through price reductions with consumers generally.

Let me suggest that we ask ourselves about every wage issue: Is this the wage that will produce and retain the work force that is needed to do this job? As for profits, we might ask: Do we require this level of profits to encourage the level of investment needed to produce the jobs we want?

If we ask, is this wage fair to the worker, let us not forget to ask, is this wage fair to the man who needs a job created for him or fair to the subsistence farmer who needs a pipe with some clean water?

It takes many institutions to run a country and I regard trade unions as one that is indispensable. The natural power of employers needs this counter-balance. But large-scale private wars between labour and management cannot be permitted in poor developing countries. The cost of strikes may be bearable to labour and management, but the social costs are unbearable. Stability and productivity are essential to development. Unions must assist in developing a work force that acts responsibly on policy matters and produces profitably at the workbench. On policy matters, a responsible position is to represent not only those who are union members but those who wish they were lucky enough to have a job so they could become union members.

The Government has many obligations that are related to these private policies. It must hold down the cost of living. It must help protect the very life of trade unions that risk their popularity by being responsible. It must assume that reasonable wage levels do not result in unreasonable profit levels — instead of investment in jobs. It must provide security and insurance of various kinds; for example, continued employment even when economic conditions are depressed. It must arrange for health services, old age benefits, and help for the disabled.

It seems to me that trade unions must increasingly turn from their emphasis on wages to their other appropriate functions. Democracy in the work place is still a major challenge for most unions. Helping workers improve their qualifications and their productivity is another. Vocational education of various forms can be encouraged and assisted by unions. Trade unions already have the organisation to provide a major *Harambee* effort. We have seen what relatively unorganised, poorly led self-help group efforts can accomplish. How much more we should expect from trade unions! In addition to training programmes, more attention should be devoted by unions to such activities as consumer co-operatives, saving and credit arrangements for members and housing development.

The trade unions in Africa have not yet learned as much as they should from their African heritage. The sense of family and the sense of community that have existed in Africa for so long can provide a highly relevant guide to our trade unions. This spirit of mutual social responsibility must be adopted by our trade unions or they will become isolated from issues that are the most relevant to Kenya's development. I fear that if they address themselves alone to the immediate problems of their current members, their influence will inevitably wane. They have the organisation and a view of life that could give them a central role in Kenya's total development. I hope this sense of mutual responsibility will grow.

The Government can help unions in their broader efforts and it can also re-examine its own activities to assure that it is not contributing to the welfare of the 'haves' at the expense of 'have-nots'. I fear that, while trade unions may be contributing to the difference between urban and rural standards of living, so is the Government. Everything tends to be better in urban areas — schools, health services, roads, power, water and so on. If policies are to serve national manpower objectives we must make sure that life in rural Kenya is not far less attractive than life in urban Kenya. Above all, it is in rural Kenya that we expect and need our largest gains.

AFRICAN SOCIALISM AND ITS APPLICATION TO PLANNING IN KENYA

Speech in Parliament introducing the motion on Kenya Government Sessional Paper No. 10 of 1963/65, 4th May, 1965

Most countries in the continent have declared themselves to be supporters of African socialism. This has become a very wide umbrella — not that there is anything wrong with this. No one expects communism to be the same thing in Albania as in Yugoslavia. Social democracy in Sweden is not the same as it is in Britain.

The K.A.N.U. Manifesto went some way towards defining Kenya's brand of African Socialism but it was essentially an electioneering document. The Kenya Constitution provides the legal framework within which national aspirations can be implemented. Sessional Paper No. 10 gives both the philosophical basis and detailed proposals for social and economic policies. It is one of the clearest declarations published anywhere of what a nation stands for and where it is going and indeed is one of the three pillars on which Kenya is founded, the other two being the K.A.N.U. Manifesto of 1963 and the Constitution.

For comparison, readers might look at the collected speeches of Mwalimu Julius Nyerere, President of Tanzania, to be read together with his country's Arusha Declaration. The 1968 Mulungushi Declaration of President Kenneth Kaunda of Zambia, although it is not so broad in content, could also be studied.

Sessional Paper No. 10 deals with a subject of vital significance to the development of Kenya, namely 'African Socialism and Its Application to Planning in Kenya'. This issue has been shrouded in confusion, embellished with slogans and pat phrases, and nearly drowned in a sea of contradictory statements and allegations. There are those in the East and the West who have tried to tell us what we mean by African socialism, and there are those at home who twist the phrase to their own petty uses. This state of confusion could be costly to the development of our country. It could slow down the drive towards unity, hamper the inflow of capital and discourage our people from devoting their full share of hard work to the cause of economic growth.

This bickering, unrest and uncertainty have rightly led many of our citizens to request the Government to clarify the situation. Many Members of Parliament have rightly demanded a detailed statement of African socialism and have even tabled motions on this matter before the House. The Planning and Development Advisory Council has also urged the Governments to make its policies on African socialism explicit. The Government has responded to the evident need quickly, as it should and must in a democratic system, and has laboured hard to produce the Paper which now requires the united support of this House to demonstrate to the world and our own people that non-alignment is a positive policy in economic as well as political affairs.

But before I say anything on the paper I want to say a few words about the actual drafting of this paper. I am doing this so as to put an end to malicious gossip by some people who seek to undermine the effect of the paper by suggesting it is not the product of the Kenya Cabinet. As the House well knows, the responsibility for drafting this paper lies with my Ministry. Having drafted this paper, on the instruction of the President and the Cabinet, I submitted it to the Cabinet Development Committee for their consideration. My Assistant Minister (at that time the Hon. Mwai Kibaki, M.P.), spent many, many hours going over several drafts, sentence by sentence, before a version was approved for discussion in the Development Committee of the Cabinet. The Development Committee, with all the Ministers — and I repeat, all the Ministers — taking part, devoted lengthy sessions to the paper, discussing every issue in detail. The version that emerged from this searching scrutiny was then presented to the full Cabinet when it was again thoroughly discussed and after minor modifications unanimously — and I repeat unanimously — agreed in the form in which it is now presented to Parliament. I can assure you that except for the Constitution itself, no paper has been so thoroughly analysed at ministerial level as this one.

It was suggested recently in one of our Sunday newspapers that such a paper as this should be constructed as a consensus of the views of provincial, district and local political and party leaders and Members of Parliament and that we might even sponsor an essay contest to obtain ideas on its substance. Government by essay is in many ways a novel and intriguing idea, but I can assure you that it is not an experiment we can afford in Kenya today. This kind of proposal is based on four false assumptions: firstly, that the Government is out of touch with the people and their representatives; secondly, that the Government has no responsibility to lead but only to follow; thirdly, that we can afford the time involved in soliciting and collecting suggestions, from every conceivable source; and, lastly, that socialism is basically a new idea that has not been thoroughly explored before.

These assumptions are all false. Cabinet Ministers are themselves representatives of the people and they and our President have already earned the reputation of spending more time in personal contact with the people than the Ministers of any other Government in the world today. Kenya's Ministers have an intimate knowledge of the views and needs of the people and if that is not enough we also have our vigilant Members of Parliament who do not hesitate to tell us when we are wrong.

A government that fails to lead, fails entirely. The government is in possession of facts, information and knowledge and has access to expert advice which is not available to people in general. Leading means nothing more than bringing this body of knowledge to bear on the problems of the country in such a way as to make rapid progress toward the achievement of the aspirations of the people. This government will not abdicate its responsibility to lead.

The writings on socialism are extensive and even those on African socialism would run to many, many volumes. Political leaders throughout Africa such as Nyerere, Senghor, Nkrumah and our own President have expressed themselves often and at great length on the subject. More importantly the K.A.N.U. Manifesto (of 1963) and our own Constitution already contain the principles on which any paper on African socialism in Kenya must be based. We have followed those principles religiously in preparing the more detailed paper now before this House. I should like to emphasise here that the mandate given to this Government based on the K.A.N.U. Manifesto, does not end until 1968* when our people will judge us by our record. Meantime, the

---

* The abolition of the Senate and the absorption of its Members into the National Assembly were accomplished by means of a Constitutional Amendment Act in 1967. Under existing arrangements one third of the Senate seats were subject to new

K.A.N.U. Manifesto constitutes the guide for all our decisions and actions, I hope that in the course of this speech I will show how the Manifesto is related to this paper or vice versa.

Socialism has taken several forms in the writings of those political and economic philosophers who have followed Marx. Even wider variations are found when practical socialist systems are examined. This is not suprising because a practical system must modify the universal elements of socialism to fit the needs, conditions and attitudes peculiar to the country and the people concerned.

The elements of socialism that serve to characterise the universal system are well known and include: First, ownership and operation by the State of the fundamental means of production. Secondly, control of those means of production left in private hands. Thirdly, planning the uses of resources to ensure needs are fully recognised in the allocation of resources and, in particular, that the volume of saving and investment is large enough to promote rapid growth and rising standards of living for all. Fourthly, control of the distribution of incomes to avoid excessive concentrations in the hands of a few and to share the benefits of society equitably among all its members. Fifthly, encouragement of the co-operative form of business organisation to establish an identity between those involved in production and distribution and those receiving the fruits of that labour. And, lastly, the guarantee of equal opportunities to all without discrimination or exploitation.

But, as will be seen, these elements of an economic system can be regarded as universal because they are stated in such general terms that they permit interpretation and modification to suit the needs of particular countries and peoples. Each country has its own history, its own culture, its own inheritance of economic institutions and resources, and its own problems. To impose on a people a rigid system that takes no account of their needs, desires, aspirations and customs, is to court disaster and failure. The Government wishes, understandably I hope, to avoid these consequences and therefore has laboured long and hard on this paper to ensure that full account has been taken of our legacies,

---

elections every two years. As a result of the amalgamation some former Senators would not have been able to serve their full term if Parliament had only lasted until 1968. In order to facilitate passage of the Amendment a deal was made whereby the new National Assembly was extended until 1970.

attitudes and problems in formulating those policies that will guide our future development. It has been our concern to define a system and to identify policies that will meet our needs, solve our problems and further our ambitions, and the operative word is 'our' not 'their'. We reject, therefore, those who come to us and say there is no such thing as 'African socialism'. Such people that say this are prisoners of foreign propaganda. Such people betray our traditions and betray our very society. They forget that even in the countries about which they speak so much there are many brands of socialism — Leninist, Marxist, Stalinist, Trotskyite, Maoist, Christian socialist, Democratic socialist, and an endless list of 'ists'.

There is no reason why there should be no African socialism. Our fundamental objectives are very fully defined in the paper. They are points we have not only emphasised many times in the course of our struggle against colonialism but which we have pledged to the country and in the K.A.N.U. Manifesto. They consist of the hopes and aspirations of the humblest man in our community.

To make progress toward these fundamental objectives, we have decided to employ the system of African socialism; we must draw particularly on those African roots that are especially among all tribes in Kenya: political democracy and mutual social responsibility.

In the traditional African society in Kenya only one requirement was imposed on an individual before he could participate fully and equally in political affairs. He had to be a mature, responsible member of that society and nothing else. Indeed, the Constitution already guarantees that 'every person in Kenya is entitled to the fundamental rights and freedoms of the individual whatever his race, tribe, place of origin or residence or other local connexions, political opinion, colour, creed or sex', and the K.A.N.U. Manifesto also states that, and I quote again, 'The K.A.N.U. Government will steadfastly uphold the rule of law and guarantee the position of every citizen according to the Bill of Rights'. Any mature citizen has the right to vote in elections, to join the party and to participate fully in political matters. It is sometimes argued that faster progress could be made if political rights were suspended temporarily. History demonstrates that suspension of this kind has a habit of becoming permanent. During our struggle for Uhuru, we always asserted that only through freedom and human rights could the people co-operate fully with the Government. If I may quote from another African statesman, who has written very much on this subject, Leopold Senghor, he has noted these dangers when he wrote in his *African Road to Socialism*, 'What good is our independence if it is only to imitate European totalitarianism, to replace external colonialism by domestic colonialism?'

It must be clearly understood and recognised that our equality differs considerably from that taken in many countries. In some Western democracies on the one hand, literacy tests are imposed before a citizen can vote and, in many cases, these are administered arbitrarily to prevent many mature citizens from participating in political affairs. It is also the case that in some instances only those who own property are permitted to vote. Such discrimination has been rejected in Kenya and will not be permitted.

In Eastern communist countries on the other hand, stern tests are applied to party membership so that, out of large populations, only a few people qualify for membership of the party. Rule by a party of the 'élite' is regarded there as a temporary phenomenon that will eventually give way to broader political participation, but the facts are that this 'temporary' situation has been going on for generations. Such a sacrifice of full political rights would be in conflict with our Party Manifesto. It is interesting, at this point, to note the contents of the recent report of the Presidential Commission on the Establishment of a Democratic One Party State in Tanzania. The Commission stated — 'We do not see T.A.N.U. as an "élite" but as a mass party through which any citizen can participate in the process of Government'. Mwalimu Nyerere, himself, has said, 'No party which limits its membership to a clique can ever free itself from the fear of overthrow by those it has excluded'.

Thus, in our system of socialism in Kenya every citizen is guaranteed full and equal political rights. Wealth must not be permitted to confer special political concessions on anyone. The disproportionate political influence that has frequently been granted, openly or otherwise, to economic power groups in capitalist societies must not be permitted to gain a foothold in Kenya. Similarly, the fundamental force of religion, which has been denied in many communist countries will be a definite feature of our society in which traditional religion provided a strict moral code. But political rights will not be contingent on religious beliefs.

I should like to turn to the subject of mutual social responsibility. Mutual social responsibility is the extension of the African family spirit to the nation as a whole. The State, in this case, assumes obligations to ensure equal opportunities to all its citizens to eliminate exploitation and discrimination and to provide needed social services such as education, medical care and social security. But the obligations of the State imply reciprocal obligations for the members of society. All citizens must contribute to the degree they are able to the rapid development of the economy and society. As the K.A.N.U. Manifesto clearly states 'We aim to build a country where men and women are motivated by a sense of service and not by a greedy desire for personal gain'. The Manifesto says further that the K.A.N.U. Government and the party are 'confident that the dynamic spirit of hard work and self-reliance which will motivate the Government will inspire the people throughout the land to great and still greater efforts for the betterment of their own communities'. Further, 'Every individual has a duty to play his part in building national unity. Your duties are not limited to the political sphere. You must endeavour to support social advance.' The K.A.N.U. Manifesto also recognises the part of Government as far as mutual social responsibility is concerned. It says, for instance, that 'The traditional respect and care for the aged among our people must continue', and in the field of education 'The first aim of (seven years free education) will be to produce good citizens inspired with a desire to serve their fellow men'. The President himself, in his personal message introducing the K.A.N.U. Manifesto stated, 'The future prosperity upon which our plans, hopes, and aspirations depend, need (everyone's) effort'.

These quotations from the K.A.N.U. Manifesto indicate quite clearly what we mean by mutual social responsibility. We are not alone in recognising this as a key requirement in development. Nkrumah, for instance, has said that 'Ghana must secure for every citizen, at the earliest possible date, an adequate level of education and nutrition and a satisfactory standard of education, clothing, housing and leisure'. This is the duty of the Government. On the part of the people Nkrumah writes that Ghana 'shall expect from each citizen a maximum contribution to the national economy according to his ability and training. It is only in proportion to the contribution which (everyone) makes to the work of the nation that we can expect to share in material gains which . . . development of the economy will make possible'.

With respect to the responsibility of the individual and family I should perhaps here explain that there is no society or country where social services are completely free. So far as the nation as a whole is concerned, every service must be fully paid for. Thus, services can be given free to some members of society only if other members pay for it. If school fees are abolished, teachers' salaries must still be paid. If school fees are reduced, therefore, tax rates must be raised, and higher taxes must be paid. If medical services are to be free then the salaries of doctors and nurses must be paid out of increased taxation. If roads are to be used free of charge, then taxes must be raised to cover maintenance and loan repayments. If land is to be given free to some people, then others must pay for it through higher taxation.

The total amount of goods and services available to the people of Kenya depends on the amount the people of Kenya produce through hard work and efficient use of resources. If the people of Kenya do not grow wheat, maize, cotton, pineapples, coffee and tea to sell, then the Government can collect no taxes to provide roads, education and medical services. If everyone waits around for things to be handed out free, there will be nothing to give because nothing will be produced.

Another related fallacy must also be destroyed. Making things free does not mean that everyone can have all he wants. If school fees were abolished, we still could not teach more children than we have teachers for. And as teachers cost money we might be able to employ fewer teachers than before so that fewer children could go to school.

It is the policy of the Government to move progressively towards the elimination of school and medical fees. But to shout about these things without considering their full implications is merely to play politics and to try to exploit the ignorance of the people. Sometimes some people speak on these issues as though Government was opposed to them while others, knowing it cannot be done overnight are eager for cheap publicity by posing as champions of the poor. Let us all today move away from any propaganda stance and be truthful to our people and especially to our country. As we increase our revenues from taxes so shall we move quickly to creating the foundations for a welfare state which we all desire.

In addition to drawing on African traditions African socialism in Kenya must be adaptable to rapidly changing conditions and circumstances without compromising the basic principles of political equality, social justice and human dignity. Some of our presently pressing problems, such as Africanisation, unemployment, idleness and unitilised land, will be solved or considerably alleviated with persistent efforts in the not too distant future, but others will rise to take their place. The system we adopt must be adaptable to these new problems and circumstances. Indeed, it is the need to be adaptable that distinguishes most practical and viable economic systems from the rigid, doctrinaire, theoretical systems that make good reading but bad practice. Marxian socialism and *laissez-faire* capitalism are both theoretical economic organisations. Both settled on ownership of property as the critical factor in economic organisation and advocated rigid systems based on the state ownership in the one case, and on the other private ownership. But ownership is not an absolute, indivisible right, subject only to complete control or none. Practical systems have demonstrated that the resources of society are best guided into proper uses by a range of sensitive controls each specifically designed for the task to be performed.

Marx's criticism of the society of his time and place was a valid one. Political equality and democracy did not exist in Europe and Great Britain before the middle of the nineteenth century when Marx was writing. The enclosure movement and the Industrial Revolution had created a landless proletariat that was ruthlessly exploited by those with economic power who had much the same absolute rights as those of the feudal lords. Sharp class distinctions had been commonplace for centuries; the close association of political and economic power was traditional; and the general welfare was identified with the welfare of the few. The Industrial Revolution brought out the worst elements of the situation — hours of work were dawn to dusk; few safety precautions existed; there was no job security or protection against injuries, illness and old age; children started work as early as the age of four; and no established avenues of political appeal existed.

Valid as Marx's description was, it bears little similarity to Kenya today. Under colonialism Kenyans did not have political equality or equal opportunities, and their property rights were not always respected. Even so, African traditions have no parallel to the European feudal society, its class distinctions, its unrestricted property rights, and its acceptance of exploitation. The historical setting that inspired Marx has no counterpart in independent Kenya.

As predictive models of what would happen to factory system societies, both Marxian socialism and *laissez-faire* capitalism have been failures. The economic systems in actual use throughout the world today bear little resemblance to either model. The Industrial Revolution quickly led to the social protest of which Marx was a part and this in turn resulted in sweeping political and economic changes as the systems of the world adapted to the new state of technological change. Political democracy was achieved; private property rights were diluted; the State accepted increasing responsibilities for social services, planning, guidance and control; taxes were made progressive to distribute benefits more widely. Capitalism, therefore, did not evolve into Marxian socialism, as Marx predicted, but was indeed modified in directions that Marx may very well have approved.

The adaptability of these systems has a parallel in those countries that have attempted to follow Marx. To become effective, these systems, too, have had to demonstrate an ability to adapt to changing circumstances. These have adopted wage differentials and management incentives, permitted various forms of ownership and utilised interest rates or the equivalent in their planning procedures. All practical economic systems, regardless of their origin, have demonstrated adaptability. The problems of today are not the problems of a century ago. African socialism is designed to be a working system in a modern setting, fully prepared to adapt itself to changing circumstances and new problems.

The system we adopt in Kenya must not depend for its success on a satellite relationship with any country or group of countries. On the other hand, economic non-alignment does not mean economic isolationism. On the contrary, it means a willingness and desire:

(a) to borrow technological knowledge and proved economic methods from any country, without commitment;

(b) to seek and accept technical and financial assistance from any source, without strings; and

(c) to participate fully in world trade, without political domination.

The ability of Africa to borrow advanced technological knowledge, modern methods of industrial organisation and economic techniques of control and guidance from more advanced countries provides the opportunity for us to leap over many of the hurdles that have restrained development in these modern societies in the past. It means also that African socialism as a system can profit from the mistakes made by others. Unlike many countries that have eliminated many successful economic mechanisms on narrow ideological grounds, Kenya is free to pick and choose those methods that have been proved in practice and are adaptable to Kenya conditions regardless of the ideologies that others may attach to them. Kenya, therefore, is free to choose among other things:

(a) a wages and incomes policy that recognises the need for differential incentives as well as an equitable distribution of incomes;

(b) techniques of production that combine efficiencies of scale with diffused ownership;

(c) various forms of ownership — State, co-operative, corporate and individual — that are efficient for different sectors or that compete with each other in the same sector — provided only that the form promotes the objectives of the Government; and

(d) techniques of control that vary with the needs of society and its members.

These then, are the conditions our system must satisfy, to draw on the African traditions of political equality and mutual social responsibility, to be adaptable and flexible in the face of changing circumstances, and to be politically and economically non-aligned and yet free to borrow funds, people and technology from any country more advanced in these material resources than ourselves. African socialism, as we view it in Kenya, will meet these conditions and in addition will ensure that three fundamental characteristics are achieved in practice:

(a) that resources are used, and used properly, for the benefit of society as a whole; this is what we call planning.

(b) that a variety of sensitive controls are utilised each adapted to the need it must serve. This is control and implementation; and

(c) that antagonistic classes do not emerge in Kenya as development progresses. This is the concept of equitable distribution of wealth and income and the separation of economic and political power.

It is a fundamental characteristic of African socialism that society has a duty to plan, guide and control the use of productive resources. This principle, too, has its basis in the K.A.N.U. Manifesto, where it is stated that 'we believe in a wide measure of governmental control of the economy in the national interest (and) there are many ways of participation without acquiring public ownership'. The Manifesto also provides that while encouraging private investment, the Government will ensure that 'the undertaking is being directed according to our national policy and needs . . . while we intend following a liberal policy with regard to foreign capital, investments must be made in accordance with Kenya's interests'. The Manifesto continues 'Special consideration will be given to local investors, but we shall have no time for those who make large profits and then fail to invest them in the country'. And with respect to land, 'the K.A.N.U. Government will not tolerate holding of large underdeveloped tracts of land by anyone'.

This is in keeping with African socialism or traditions in which the concept of ownership and property rights was never the inalienable right it was in Europe. This single unifying African principle has been that no matter who owned or managed land or other productive resources, they were expected to be used, and used for the general welfare. No individual family or clan could treat productive assets as private property unless the uses to which those assets were put were regarded as consonant with the general welfare. Unlike the traditional European approach to ownership, no person could treat a piece of land as his own with the freedom to use it or not to use it as he chose. But it is worth noting that over the past century, the European tradition of absolute ownership has gradually been eroded so that today the right of the State to guide, plan and even order the uses to which property will be put is universally recognised.

These African traditions cannot be carried over indiscriminately to a modern, monetary economy. The need to develop and invest requires credit and a credit economy rests heavily on a system of land titles and their registration. The ownership of land must, therefore, be made more definite and explicit if land consolidation and development are to be fully successful. Many forms of ownership will be permitted because each may serve particularly well different purposes. This approach is in keeping with the Constitution and the K.A.N.U. Manifesto. The Constitution provides that 'no property of any description shall be compulsorily taken possession of, and no interest in or right over property of any description shall be compulsorily acquired', except in strictly defined cases where such action would be necessary 'to promote the public benefit', and in that event 'prompt payment of full compensation' is guaranteed. The Manifesto states, 'Citizens will have the right to follow the profession and trade of their choosing and to own property according to the law'. It goes on, 'We shall welcome both governmental and private investment in Kenya . . . (and) shall encourage investors to participate jointly in projects with our own Government'. Finally, the Manifesto states 'Every farmer must be sure of his land rights'. Thus the Manifesto and the Constitution are clear on these matters. But there is no question of society giving up its rights to determine how resources are to be used.

Under African socialism the duty of the State to plan must be accompanied by the power to guide and control resources used. To imagine, however, that the use of resources can only be controlled through their ownership or that the appropriate ownership will guarantee the proper use of productive assets are errors of great magnitude. Ownership can be abused whether in private or public hands and ways must be found to control resources use in either case. African socialism must rely on planning to determine the appropriate uses of productive resources and on a range of controls to ensure that plans are carried out.

The controls available to us range from the use of taxes, interest rates, duty drawbacks and tariffs as a means of influencing and guiding activities in the private sectors through price, wage, rent and output controls, to outright Government ownership and operation. We feel, however, that excessive control is as inefficient as too little control; there is no sense in using an atomic bomb to kill a tsetse fly when a little spray will do a better job, and no sense in using a bulldozer for the flower garden. Each control must be tailored to its needs, and as economic activities range from barber shops and small *shambas* to tobacco, canning and power complexes and large plantations, the range of controls must be great indeed and each must be carefully selected for the task it must perform.

The use of a range of sensitive controls implies as well varying degrees of private participation and initiative, so that each economic activity can be performed in the way best suited to it. This approach also enables us to attract private as well as public capital and privately employed as well as publicly employed management talent. Variety is an important means of attraction whether it is customers, savings, capital or management that is wanted.

The purpose of a range of controls and of planning is to ensure that productive assets are used for the benefit of society. If an individual, a co-operative, a company or the State owns productive assets, society expects these assets to be used and used well. The holding of land for speculative purposes, the charging of exorbitant or discriminatory prices, the abandonment of land and the production or sale of shoddy merchandise are all examples of violations of the principle of mutual social responsibility.

Finally, African socialism must be designed to prevent the emergence of antagonistic classes among Africans and must eliminate through its Africanisation programme the sharp economic differentials that now exist among the races in our country. The concept of political equality in Africa rules out in principle the use of economic power as a political base. The vigorous implementation of traditional political democracy in the modern setting will eliminate, therefore, one of the critical factors promoting class divisions. The policy of African socialism to control by various means how productive resources are used eliminates the second of the factors supporting a class system. Without its two supporting allies, the concentration of economic power cannot be the threat it once was, but we propose to restrict and guard against this factor as well with regard to both foreign and domestic concentration.

The desirability of attracting private capital from abroad is, I believe accepted and such incentives as the investment allowance, the guarantees against nationalisation without compensation in our Constitution and the recently enacted Foreign Investment Protection Act are sound evidence of the sincerity of the Government in this regard. But the spirit of mutual social responsibility applies to foreign as well as domestic investors. Kenya will not become a playground for unscrupulous monopolists or those who employ unfair market practices whether in dealing with consumers or dealing with workers. Rather, foreign investors will be expected to accept fully the spirit of mutual social responsibility as already defined in the Sessional Paper.

The concentration of economic power in domestic hands carries with it the possible exercise of undue influence in political affairs and must be watched closely. The problem is a complex one because while it is desirable to ensure that the wealth of the country is distributed as widely as possible, it is also necessary for the development of the country to ensure that the steps taken do not: first, inhibit the rapid accumulation of domestic savings; secondly, prohibit methods of large-scale production where they are necessary for efficiency; ot thirdly, discourage the inflow of private capital.

The principal long-term technique for controlling the rate of individual accumulation while at the same time stimulating the rate of national accumulation will be through progressive income, inheritance and capital gains, taxes, and death duties. These will make it progressively more difficult for the wealthy to become more wealthy and to pass on their wealth to members of succeeding generations. At the same time, the collection of taxes will tend to translate private savings into public savings conserving them for development of the nation.

While various methods of ownership will be permitted and indeed encouraged in Kenya, the role of co-operatives in both production and marketing will be given every assistance. Co-operatives have direct roots in African traditions but their extensive use in the monetary sector of the economy will involve greater discipline and training. Those who share in the tasks of the co-operative or who use its services share also in its benefits as the co-operative belongs to them.

This brings me to the end of my review of Part I of the Sessional Paper.

Let us turn from the definitional aspects of African socialism to the important policies presented in Part II of the Paper. It is these that will move our country forward and will enable Kenya to take its proper place in the society of nations.

Let us consider then the application of African socialism to planning and development in Kenya. I want to emphasise at the outset that the desperate need in Kenya today is to get our economy really growing — without, however, ignoring that in our economy there must be political equality, social justice and human dignity. Rapid economic growth, in all countries, is a prerequisite to the extension and intensification of welfare services and to the provision of greater employment opportunities. Therefore, in our policies designed to reorganise and Africanise the economy, provide education and welfare services, control the use of resources, etc., we must keep in mind the overwhelming need for the economy to grow.

In applying African socialism in development planning we have first to recognise that we are in a stage of multiple transition. Some of the important transitions already underway are, firstly, the transition from a subsistence economy to a monetary economy. Secondly, industrialisation. Thirdly, the increase in education and welfare services. (This is in strong contrast to the situation during the colonial era when the development of natural resources was given more emphasis than the development of the African people.) Fourthly, the transformation of our economic and social institutions. Schools are being integrated; co-operatives are being organised in nearly every sector of the economy; new Government-sponsored corporations are springing to life and existing organisations are taking on new functions. Fifthly, urbanisation. This movement to urban areas, typical of developing countries places a significant additional burden on planning and co-ordinating development. The sixth transition is the significant move since independence from a basically unplanned economy to one in which planning plays a central role. We have also today a growing awareness on the part of our people of their needs and requirements in the new and modern Kenya. These transitions are the evidence that we are building a modern economy out of our colonial and African traditional heritage.

Our part as leaders is to ensure that while these changes take place political democracy and social justice are maintained and that the lot of our people is rapidly improved. We have inherited a state of affairs in which non-Africans in this country are richer than Africans. It is non-Africans who own businesses in the main streets and industrial areas of our main towns. This characteristic of our economy must be eliminated. Equally important is the fact that we must avoid creating antagonistic classes among the Africans themselves. All these things, we realise. We all agree that certain changes must take place; it is only in the interpretation of the time factor involved and the most effective way of solving our short-run problems that there might be differences. Some people, for instance, think that we can undertake these changes overnight and that we can cure the existing poverty and under-development of our people by giving things, such as land and Asian shops, free to the Africans. There are no such short-cuts to eliminating poverty and promoting development. Development takes time. Development must not only be concerned with solutions to short-term problems; it must also look much further ahead to avoid crises in the future.

Apart from these transitions, it must also be realised that we face a severe shortage of certain key resources needed for our development: domestic capital required for the level of investment needed for our development; trained, educated and experienced manpower; and of foreign exchange.

The shortage of domestic capital stems from the low rate of domestic saving which, in turn, is due to the low level of *per capita* incomes. What we want is to have people produce more than just what they need for subsistence. With the surplus they can buy bicycles, improve their farms, and so on. It is also necessary that such surplus should not just be a saving buried in the ground in a hut or under mattresses. It must be made available for investment.

In order to increase the level of our saving for the purpose of investment we have to do two things; ensure that our incomes are growing as fast as possible, and have a tax structure which will ensure that these incomes are not just used for personal consumption. The problem here is this: to grow faster we must save more, but to save more we must grow faster. We thus find ourselves in a vicious circle. This circle must be broken. In the absence of local saving we are forced to look for capital from abroad. This brings me to the role of foreign capital in our development.

The incomes of the people of Kenya are very low. If we tried to depend solely on domestic capital and tax surplus, our growth rate might not even keep pace with our rapidly increasing population. Consequently, we have to depend on other countries' co-operation and assistance in order to stimulate our own development. Although our aim is to be able to rely on our own resources eventually and to reduce the role of foreign capital and investments, in the initial period, such as this stage in our development, we need this co-operation. To give up use of foreign capital, as some people have suggested, at this stage is almost tantamount to giving up development itself.

However, it is necessary also to realise that in order to attract and use foreign capital we must be able to finance more of the local costs of development from our own resources. We must also be able to invest on an increasing scale in joint ventures with private capital, and to improve more rapidly our infrastructure. The truth is that the more we can contribute to development, the more aid and foreign capital we can attract. We would also be in a position to bargain for better terms. Therefore, the role of foreign capital in the development of this country must be seen in its proper perspective: that is, as an initial necessity and as a temprary measure. The experience of a number of European countries after World War Two supports this strategy. After the war these countries mounted vigorous campaigns to attract American capital for their reconstruction, and succeeded thereby in accelerating their economic growth. Today, we find that these countries can finance their own development and, in some cases, have introduced measures to curb investments from outside. But it has taken these countries nearly twenty years to reach this stage. It will take us a long time before we can become self-sufficient in the field. This is a hard, blunt fact which we must face, and which it does not help any of us to try to avoid. It would serve no useful purpose, therefore, to continue debating whether or not we need foreign capital. Such debate is sterile and misleading. We must instead decide on policies designed to increase our local savings and strengthen our hands by increasing our inability to meet more of the local costs of development projects. In this regard we should look at the points made about the tax structure and its functions. These functions are defined as follows: firstly, supplying funds for recurrent costs and development; secondly, providing incentives and disincentives to influence the pattern and methods of production and consumption; and, lastly, modifying the distribution of income and wealth.

Other sources of Government revenue must also be more intensively used than in the past. Government assets held abroad should be invested in Kenya to the extent that this is legal; fiduciary issue should be more fully utilised; and more devices should be sought for channelling more domestic savings into Government hands.

Apart from the use of taxation in raising revenue, I should mention briefly the role of taxes in modifying the distribution of income among our citizens. The tax structure must be a major weapon for bringing about a more equitable distribution of income and wealth. We are convinced that every citizen of this country must be guaranteed a certain minimum of living standard, and we are also determined to see that we do not have a society in which there are extremes of wealth and poverty. Therefore, those with high incomes and wealth must accept a greater responsibility to pay the taxes needed for development and provision of social services. To achieve these aims, the following policies will be considered. Firstly, exempting from direct taxes people earning extremely low incomes. In particular, the objective should be to begin at once to eliminate from this group the graduated personal tax, substituting property tax in its place. Secondly, retaining the progressive income tax, lowering allowances, as we, indeed, have already begun to do. Some of these allowances were designed during colonial times to serve expatriate civil servants and settlers who looked overseas for security, vacations and education for their children. They cannot apply today. Thirdly, adopting progressive inheritance taxes: in other words, people should not be born and expect to get something for nothing just because their parents worked harder than somebody else. Fourthly, making any capital gains tax progressive. Fifthly, exempting basic necessities from sales and excise taxes. Lastly, taxing luxury items heavily, for these are usually consumed by those with high incomes.

It is important, however, to ensure that the tax structure will not be made prohibitive or confiscatory. Reasonable levels of profits, property accumulation and standards of living are necessary if we are to achieve and maintain a high rate of growth of our economy. In other words, while we intend to use the tax measures for the purpose of ensuring equitable revenue we do not intend that it should be a weapon to punish or deter those of our people who have initiative and drive. Such people need to be encouraged and assured that they too will enjoy the fruits of their labour. It is also necessary that we ensure that no section of our people will assume that because we intend to use the tax measure there is room for the lazy and idle. Such people must be made to know that our society is only for those who strive for self-improvement.

The second severe shortage is that of local, skilled, trained and experienced manpower. In the process of economic growth we need qualified people to teach in our rapidly expanding secondary school system, teachers' colleges and the university; to consolidate, survey and register land at a more rapid rate; to do agricultural research, provide extension services, train farm managers and operate national farms; to manage private industrial and commercial establishments; to plan and implement forestry development; to engineer and construct roads and irrigation schemes and to administer the affairs of the Government. As with capital, we can grow rapidly now only by supplementing our meagre supply of domestic, trained manpower with skilled people borrowed from abroad.

It takes a very long time to train professional people. This means that shortages of high-level manpower will be with us for several planning periods, and those who are constantly used merely to uttering slogans might care to listen to this. The students now enrolled in Form I (i.e. eighth year in school) will be prepared to take jobs requiring a secondary level education only in 1969. We have 10,000 students in Form I this year and not all the 10,000 students in Form I will go through to university degrees. Maybe 50 per cent will get Cambridge School Certificates. Those who continue with university work will receive degrees in 1975; that is, in ten year's time. Those who go on for advanced work cannot be counted as part of our manpower supply until 1976 or beyond. In the case of doctors, for which the need is so great, none of the students now in Form I this year will be available to us as part of the manpower of this country before 1978 — that is, in thirteen years' time — and the number emerging will still leave us far short of the number we must have.

But our problem is not only to train and educate more people. We must also train and educate them in the right things and in the right numbers. The manpower survey now being completed, and which we hope to publish on the 16th of this month, will show that the position is, and indicates that our additional minimum needs for university graduates by 1970 will nearly be met from our students now studying at foreign universities and here in East Africa, but the clearly balanced aggregate picture is marred by bad composition. Surpluses may exist in some fields, such as non-professional B.A. studies, biology, agriculture, chemistry and mathematics and statistics, while severe shortages in others go unattended. The major shortages indicated will be doctors, mechanical and electrical engineers, surveyors, pharmacists, physical planners and veterinarians. Additionally, the manpower survey shows that we are in great shortage of office workers, i.e. typists, stenographers and book-keepers, and so on. Under these circumstances the Government must now ensure that any funds available are used to assist those who choose the fields that we need most. We must use available skilled personnel to full advantage and urge everyone to contribute to the maximum in the effort of nation building.

So far I have spoken of education as a means of solving our manpower problem. However, the Government recognises that it is primarily through education that we can equalise the opportunities among all our citizens. Moreover, we have already declared our intention to eliminate lack of education among all our people.

The third and last shortage with which I will deal is that of foreign exchange. I think it will be necessary to explain what foreign exchange means. Foreign exchange means other countries' currencies. The importance of foreign exchange arises from the fact that since we do not produce domestically such things as locomotives, tractors and so on, we must buy these things from foreign countries, and to do this we need these countries' currencies. We do not go abroad with our East African pound, we get pounds sterling, dollars, marks, francs, roubles, yen and so on. Some people think that you just carry a lot of East African notes. Somebody even said that if you do not have money then go and print some more. It does not work that way. We can acquire these currencies by selling our goods and services abroad — promoting tourism, borrowing, and reducing our holdings of foreign assets. A foreign exchange problem arises when we cannot pay our bills abroad except by emergency borrowing or reducing our holdings of foreign assets to dangerously low levels. This is dangerous because many of these assets support our currency. Kenya does not now have a foreign exchange problem but great care must be exercised to ensure that the steps we take to promote development, including our foreign policy, do not create this problem. More rapid growth means buying more capital goods to satisfy the growing demands of people with higher incomes. As capital goods do not create immediately enough additional production to pay for themselves, the foreign exchange required to buy them must usually be obtained through borrowing or a surplus of current exports over imports. At the present time, Kenya is succeeding in borrowing from abroad to pay for its excess of imports over exports.

These borrowings are often long-term such as ten, fifteen or even twenty years or more. This creates the danger that we may tend to forget or take lightly our liability and the needs to use such funds efficiently. We must be able to repay the loans when the time comes in the currency stipulated. If we use such funds for the transfer of existing assets or inefficiently in new development efforts, their use will not generate the foreign exchange needed for repayment.

I feel I should now say something about bilateral trade and aid agreements. Too often one hears people say 'Oh well our friends will help us'. Whatever friends ? Bilateral trade and aid agreements can lead to specific trade and aid currency problems. If, for example, we sell goods to a country whose currency is not convertible, that is a country whose money cannot be readily accepted for the currencies of other countries, that foreign currency is valuable to us only if we can find useful goods to buy in that country at reasonable prices. If this is not so then we simply be advancing credit to the more developed country. Furthermore, as the currencies of these countries are not convertible, a serious difficulty arises in financing the local costs associated with the capital equipment these countries can supply in foreign aid.

This is a subject which may not be easily understood by some people in our country. I would like to explain it in simple terms. If we get money from a country as aid, we must be able to use the money to buy the things we need. For example, when recently we received a gift of £1,000,000 from China it was given in dollars through a Swiss bank. This way we are able to use the money to buy goods anywhere in the world. If on the other hand we got the gift in yen we could only use it to buy goods from China or some third country which needs yen, because of the difficulties of conversion. At the same time when we get aid of say tractors or locomotives or assistance to build a factory we must be able to find local costs from our resources or from the donor country or other friends. Local costs include the running of the tractor or locomotive, buying of spare parts and general maintenance or paying for labour and any local materials needed to complete the building of the factory and some of the maintenance cost. Where we cannot use the currency of the donor country for local cost the only alternative is to use the goods of the donor country. In this case such goods would be offered for sale in our country to raise the necessary funds or the goods themselves must be used directly in the project. In such cases we have to watch whether such goods would be competing with our own products and thereby damaging our own industries and affecting employment of our people. There is also the question of prices at which such goods may be offered to us. If they are offered at prices above those for which we could buy similar goods on the world market or elsewhere, it would be a form of exploitation which no country would wish to accept. Moreover, there is the problem when aid is offered but the donor country is unable or unwilling to meet local costs. This means that we may not always be able to accept or utilise such aid unless we can ourselves finance local costs. Finally when aid is in the form of a loan there are repayment problems which must be anticipated. We would have to sell sufficient goods to the donor country to raise enough of the required currency to repay the loan or draw down our limited supply of convertible currencies. This situation has led in some countries to the mortgaging of the output of certain agricultural products for years in advance irrespective of price movements, superior market alternatives abroad or changes in production alternatives at home.

It will be seen from what I have said that as a developing country we must scrutinise all aid offers in relation to our foreign exchange policies.

We now come to perhaps the most important and critical point in our efforts to apply African socialism to planning in Kenya. We already know its definition and I hope we agree on it. We have examined the multiple transitions through which our country is passing. We have now to consider the practical steps and measures that we must take to implement African socialism in Kenya.

The choices that we must make stem from the fact that we want to accomplish a wide range of things while the resources we have at our disposal are limited. We want to grow rapidly; to transform the economy from a subsistence to a market economy; to develop our land and introduce modern agricultural methods; to industrialise; to Africanise the economy; to provide more employment opportunities; to have universal primary education; to expand secondary school enrolments; to build hospitals and health centres; and to relieve the housing shortage. To do all of these things quickly and simultaneously would require many more resources than we have or can quickly acquire. I do sincerely hope that members will study this part of the paper very carefully. It is not enough to dismiss these points casually and to mislead the people as to how fast we can move. Our limited resources dictate that we must choose carefully as to our priorities. It is not enough to mislead the people into thinking that all you need to do is to nationalise the East African Breweries and the Tobacco Company and be able to give every child in this country free education the next morning. That is a very unfortunate and ignorant analysis of the economic situation of this country. It may prove to be a very convenient, political debating point at a particular political meeting, but when hard facts are examined, you may nationalise the breweries, nationalise the tobacco company, nationalise the hotels, but you will still have not got free compulsory primary education for every child in this country the next morning. Instead, what you will really be faced with is to pay compensation to all these companies and to remove from the limited resources we have, the very money we need to begin to get social facilities for our people.

It has been suggested by a few people that if our Constitution stands in the way of massive nationalisation because of citizenship guarantees and by stipulating prompt, fair and full compensation when nationalisation takes place, it should be amended. But is this the real wish of our people? I believe that in fact those who call for nationalisation are thinking primarily of non-Africans who own shops or other means of production. If we amend the Constitution, the amendments would clearly change the rights not only of non-African citizens, but of all citizens, Africans, Asians and Europeans alike.

Many people who speak glibly of nationalisation are really referring to Africanisation. They want the ownership of resources to be transferred from non-Africans to Africans, and find nationalisation a convenient label under which to justify their desires. Should such transfers take place I have a strong feeling that many of these apparent supporters of nationalisation would be calling a completely different tune. Many among them are not asking for nationalisation as a socialist measure, but as a racialist measure. In fact, I have heard the same people protest vigorously against any suggestion of nationalisation of assets owned by fellow Africans or land in the former African reserves. It is obvious therefore that the term is being wrongly used in this case. It must also be noted that our own Party Manifesto specifically excludes any idea of wholesale and indiscriminate nationalisation.

But another reason why we should not tamper with the Constitution is that such action would undermine our standing both in the eyes of our own people and abroad. It would, for instance, affect the attitudes of investors as well as the very valuable aid we get from donors. It would also affect the initiative among local people to save for investment. It would tend to reduce the attraction which may now hold for local as well as foreign investment and this would slow down growth itself.

I feel I must emphasise again that if nationalisation were applied to a given economic activity, such as bus transport, it would affect everyone, African and otherwise, owning productive resources in that industry.

In the Sessional Paper as well as the Party Manifesto we envisage circumstances which would necessitate nationalisation. These include:

(a) when the assets in private hands threaten the security or undermine the integrity of the nation or

(b) when productive resources are being seriously and clearly misused or wasted; or

(c) when the operation of an industry by private concerns has a serious detrimental effect on the public interest; and

(d) when other less costly means of control are not available or not effective.

It must be realised also that a nationalised industry must in most cases be self-supporting. It must be run efficiently and at a profit. It must not become a burden to the taxpayers or just a source of inferior service or goods. Otherwise nothing is gained by nationalisation.

There is, of course, the time when a Government must nationalise a service as part of its responsibility to the nation. In such cases cost would not be the deciding factor. In some countries nationalisation has been resorted to as a weapon against dangerous foreign influence. This kind of decision is political and not economic. It has nothing to do with socialism as such and the need has not arisen in our country at the moment. Nationalisation will be used in Kenya when circumstances require such an action but it would be an error of great magnitude to regard it as a panacea. It would be an error of great magnitude for someone to deceive the public that the answer to their problems of poverty, disease, and lack of education is the indiscriminate massive nationalisation of every means of production. This is ignorance in its highest form.

In the case of the Africanisation of the economy the problem is to reconcile the urgency of the matter with citizenship guarantees and the desire for rapid economic growth.

The Sessional Paper refers to the constitutional guarantees as well as the declarations in our Manifesto regarding the rights of all citizens. This is an important consideration. At the same time we must consider the serious imbalances inherited at the time of Independence. These cannot and will not be permitted to continue. Government's approach to this problem is fully explained in the paper. The bulk of these efforts are directed toward establishing Africans in a firm position in the monetary sector by ensuring that a large share of the planned new expansion is African owned and managed.

Our people also have a legitimate desire for welfare services. Unlike the capitalist countries of the nineteenth century, where the individual was left to fend for himself, our Government recognises that it must provide our people with basic welfare services which are a necessary part of individual dignity and social justice. It is the firm intention of the Government to provide medical and hospital services, old age and disability benefits, free universal primary education, unemployment relief, and financial assistance to all those who need and merit it for university studies. These are our objectives and they are well known, they have been stated time and again, but to provide them fully and freely now is not only in many cases impossible, but would also bankrupt the nation and mortgage economic growth for generations.

However, despite these problems we are making progress. Limited medical and hospital services are being made available to the destitute; primary education is being expanded more rapidly than population and some children from poor homes can be exempt from paying fees; bursaries are available to many in secondary schools and universities; employment opportunities are being created for some of the unemployed: and a National Provident Fund and a National Health Insurance Scheme will be starting soon. These efforts may seem meagre when compared with desires but they are generous when compared with our limited resources. They form the basis for our future expansion of services.

Self-help is an important means for promoting development. Self-help in our country has strong roots in African traditions and has, therefore, important potential for our development. The people have responded vigorously to the call and spirit of *Harambee*, and are putting much money and effort into self-help projects.

But an unplanned, unco-ordinated and uncontrolled self-help drive can lead to major problems. Self-help cannot provide all the resources that are needed to construct a project and keep it running. When a self-help project is constructed, we need complementary resources such as trained manpower and revenues to cover recurrent costs. If these are not forthcoming or have to be obtained at the expense of other planned projects, self-help can slow growth and lead to frustration and demoralisation of the people instead of promoting their welfare and development.

Similar examples could be cited with regard to health centres and other such self-help projects. The conclusion which stands out strongly is that self-help must be planned and controlled. This means that self-help projects must be fitted into the National Development Plan and self-help efforts must be guided into useful channels. If this is not done promptly, the achievement of planned targets is most certainly going to be jeopardised. We need to notice, incidentally, that there are many fields such as co-operative housing schemes in which self-help efforts could be directed with little or no demand for highly trained manpower or significant recurrent cost implications. Such fields must be vigorously exploited, for we have now successfully aroused self-help effort in most parts of the Republic.

The Sessional Paper considers very fully agriculture and land tenure. This is an important field because agriculture is the dominant sector of the economy, and encompasses the whole of the country and provides a living for the majority of Kenya families. Perhaps even more important for the present discussion, our plans in agriculture provide the best example of African socialism at work. Almost every form of organisation will be utilised in this sector including national farms, co-operatives, companies, partnerships and individual farms. It should be clear, however, that national farms and co-operative enterprises are not being encouraged as alternatives to peasant farming. We expect our individual peasant farmers to participate fully in the enlargement of investment in agriculture.

There is the need to have legislation to ensure that no one who owns land fails to use it efficiently. Thus idle and mismanaged farms will not be permitted, whether such land is owned by citizens or non-citizens. This is in accordance with the K.A.N.U. Manifesto which states: 'The K.A.N.U. Government will not tolerate the holding of large under-developed tracts of land by anyone'.

Secondly, the present practice of spending a large portion of the Government budget on the settlement and development of a limited acreage in former European areas must be phased out and future funds directed to the development of the great potential of the former African areas. What our country needs now is development, not merely land transfer.

Thirdly, the urgent need to develop the agricultural sector should not obscure the equally important need for a land tenure policy to ensure that this development is not concentrated in the hands of the few. On the other hand, we need to bear in mind that we cannot limit individual ownership only in agriculture. Any limitation of individual ownership has to cover all sectors, including rights of owners. On the other hand, we need to bear in mind that we cannot restrict these ownerships only by thinking of the acreage of land, it must also be by considering the actual activities, a ranch, egg farm or cereals farm. All these factors have to be considered. It is therefore not something to be done haphazardly, and it is for this reason that the Government has suggested that a working party might be established to consider and recommend on forms of land tenure and possible limitations on property, and to advise on the machinery for making these effective. Again it is important to emphasise that any limitations decided upon must apply to all people and throughout the country. But one thing we can and should do immediately is to eliminate speculation in land; it is for this reason that the Government has decided that no agricultural land should be sold to non-citizens unless approved by the Government.

Recently there have been discussions, accusations and counter-accusations about Government's promise and responsibility to the landless. The Government's position on this question is consistent with the declaration made in the K.A.N.U. Manifesto, and I would like today to take this opportunity to refer to the actual wording in the K.A.N.U. Manifesto in order to remove once and for all the misrepresentation that has been taking place around the country. On page seven of the Manifesto there is a sub-title 'The Landless', and this is what the Manifesto actually says: 'The problem of the unemployed landless will be vigorously settled and resettlement in the Scheduled Areas has a part to play in meeting their desperate needs. At the same time, we are aware that this process cannot continue indefinitely. We cannot afford to fragment economic farms which are making a vital contribution to our national prosperity into units producing little more than subsistence. The main solution will lie in our determination to increase agricultural efficiency in all areas. This will provide a basis for rural and cottage industry and for regular agricultural employment to absorb the landless. Attention will also be paid to the siting of larger projects in rural areas where appropriate. Our plans for urban industrialisation will also help to solve this pressing problem.' Whereas every effort will continue to be made to find land for the landless, this problem cannot be solved by land settlement alone. Even in our traditional society, we had the *Ahoi** and *Jodak** systems. Clearly, the solution lies in the Government's efforts to ensure economic growth and the absorption of the landless into employment both within and outside agriculture. Ultimately, the bulk of our labour force will find employment in non-agricultural activities. It is right that we should be concerned about the landless and those who are suffering. But we must not either try to mislead them, use them for our own political ends or exploit their situation. This is not a problem that can be removed by nationalising or confiscating

* These are Kikuyu and Luo words for tenant.

farms that are being efficiently managed and on which there are thousands of employed Africans. It is to be noticed yet again that those who talk so passionately on this subject have never asked that we take away some of the tribal land that is not under cultivation or that we should all donate land from our own holdings to give the landless in our respective districts. All that some people are talking about is merely the Highlands, the former European areas, and no more.

The Government does not only reject the squatter system but steps are being taken to deal with arbitrary cases of eviction of employees and the misuse of trespass laws. But let us not try to play politics with these sensitive and human problems. Let us instead try to co-operate together to get over them.

I should not leave this discussion of development of agriculture without saying a word or two on co-operatives. Co-operatives have strong roots in our tradition, and they will be a prominent feature and instrument in building a truly democratic, socialist and advanced economy. In the field of agriculture, priority should be given first, to producer co-operatives formed by people such as workers and squatters already employed on land. Such priority could be enforced by having credit facilities made available to such groups, as against individuals wishing to buy land. In fact, this is precisely the line which the Government is pursuing.

The paper goes on to deal with education; public utilities; commerce, industry and tourism; trade unions and consumers. All of these fields are important to our development. I have already discussed critical issues affecting some of these matters. I now move directly to the problems involved in achieving more balanced growth among the provinces.

The K.A.N.U. Manifesto promised vigorous action in developing areas of the country neglected during colonial days. The Government has noted with approval the concern of the Members of Parliament with development of these areas. The problem is not at all easy, given our limited resources and when we consider that these areas do not often have the basic natural resources including water or good land. They cannot compete for development money with other parts of Kenya. In purely economic terms, £1,000,000 invested in one area may raise the net output by £20,000, while its use in another area may yield an increase of £100,000. Investment in the second area is the wise decision, because the country is £80,000 per annum better off by so doing and is, therefore, in a position to aid the first area by making grants or subsidised loans.

However, this problem becomes less difficult to deal with when we remember that the purpose of development is not to develop an area, but to develop and make the people of the area better off. If an area is deficient in resources, the development of the people can best be done by a number of measures: firstly, investing in the education and training of the people; secondly, investing in the health of the people; thirdly, encouraging some of the people to move to areas richer in resources; and, of course, fourthly, developing those limited resources that are economic.

With education and training and some capital, the people of these provinces can make the best of limited resources. If the potential for expansion is small, medical services, education and training will qualify the people to find employment elsewhere. But we must press ahead with plans for these areas. The people there cannot be expected to wait very much longer.

Today, some of the provinces and districts that have genuine economic potential remain under-developed simply because the people will not accept new ways and the necessary discipline of planned and co-ordinated development. In these areas a concerted and prolonged effort to overcome prejudice and suspicion is needed before development can take place. Such efforts must be very carefully organised and planned and implemented through the Government and party machinery.

The policies that have been outlined throughout the Sessional Paper pervade the plans constructed and now being revised for every sector of the economy. These sectoral plans and policies must however be co-ordinated so that they fit into an overall pattern that represents Kenya's strategy for development. The main lines of this strategy have been summarised in the Sessional Paper. The construction of plans for the several sectors have been drawn up with this overall pattern in mind. As time passes of course the order of priorities will change. In particular as the agricultural and infrastructure base grows, increasing emphasis and capital will be directed toward industrial development.

The foregoing discussion shows that we are committed to planning. Indeed, acceptance of effective planning and control of the use of resources are central features of African socialism. In planning and controlling the use of resources we aim at achieving two objectives:

firstly, to find the best ways of using our limited resources — that is, land, skilled manpower, capital and foreign exchange — so that we can attain higher growth rates of our national income and, therefore, achieve higher living standards for all people; and, secondly, we also plan in order to ensure that the resulting pattern of our economy, as growth takes place, conforms to our ideas of democracy, social justice and social values. This latter objective is as important as the former, for higher growth rates of the national income could be attained at the expense of the majority, as happened in the nineteenth century in European countries.

The success of planning depends on its coverage, the determination of the people and the willingness of the people to observe the discipline of planned development. Above all, it is imperative to realise that any activity that uses resources is a proper subject of planning. This is the reason why I said earlier that self-help efforts must also be planned and controlled. Important aspects of planning have all been discussed in the paper. But emphasis must be laid on the need for discipline. Without this there is no hope for success. As the Sessional Paper says, if discipline is rejected, so is planning and with it African socialism.

Sessional Paper No. 10 (1965) on African Socialism and its Application to Planning in Kenya, lists fifty-eight major policy considerations concerning all sectors of the economy. The paper states that the economic, social and political development of Kenya would be guided by and based on African socialism as defined in that paper — two of the most important considerations being that through selective controls on use of resources, determined effort will be made to promote the African tradition of mutual social responsibility in the development of the country, and secondly, the growth of the public and co-operative sectors of the economy would be accelerated to embrace a large enough section of the economy to establish a socialist basis for future development. Other policies enumerated covered criteria and procedure to be followed in the fields of nationalisation and Africanisation of the economy; the development of the welfare services; stimulation of domestic saving; reconstruction of the tax structure; the role of self-help in Kenya's development; agriculture and land tenure; education and training;

development and control of public utilities; industry, commerce and tourism; trade unions and employment; consumer protection; development of the less developed areas of the country; and conservation of natural resources.

The basic aims of these policy measures were to increase citizens' participation in the development of the economy; expansion of the public sector; greater public control of the private sector; and achievement of a number of social objectives such as more progressive taxation and a beginning towards free social services. The paper recognised that these aims could only be achieved within a framework of rapid and diversified development.

Many of these policy recommendations have already been implemented. Here we can only give a few examples. Medical fees for all children and out-patients have been abolished; graduated personal tax for those paying at the lowest rate of tax (i.e. 48 shillings p.a.) has been reduced by 50 per cent. In the field of land ownership, noncitizens cannot now buy agricultural land except in very limited cases which are special, and which must have the approval of the President. The Government is now working on a comprehensive incomes policy, which will cover not only income distribution but also employment, machinery for settling industrial disputes, industrial protection and urban-rural balance, etc.

Legislation has been introduced to help promote the twin policies of Africanisation of personnel and ownership of industry and trade, e.g. the Immigration Amendment Act and Trade Licensing Act; the establishment of a compulsory hospital insurance scheme for incomes above £600 p.a.; free education has been provided at Forms V and VI together with expansion of school fees remission at primary level, expansion of University, Secondary and teacher training education; a National Social Security Scheme has been introduced; new institutions have been established, e.g. the Central Bank, the National Commercial Bank, the Co-operative Bank, the National construction Company, the National Trading Corporation, the Tourist Development Corporation together with strengthening of older institutions such as the Industrial Commercial Development Corporation and the Development Finance Corporation of Kenya; Industrial Estates have been started and in agriculture land settlement and consolidation have continued and in some cases expanded.

Thus Kenya has moved along the path defined in the Sessional Paper. Although most of these policies have been in operation for only two years or so, there is no doubt that they have contributed enormously to the development of the economy. The rate of growth of the economy, i.e. G.D.P. as a whole has only been slightly below the planned rate, and in 1966 it was 10·3 per cent. Rural development has also continued apace and the smallholders, that is African peasant farms, contribute 40 per cent of the total value of gross marketed produce. Africanisation of agriculture has also been pursued vigorously through settlement schemes and assistance to Africans to buy large farms. African farmers, both smallholders and large-scale farmers, are now producing perhaps as much as 60 per cent of the total marketed produce.

KENYA INTELLECTUALS AND THE
K.A.N.U. GOVERNMENT

Speech made on 20th February, 1967 at the opening of National Book Week in Nairobi

Mr. Mboya has taken the initiative on many occasions to stimulate fellow intellectuals to think about the challenges of new nations.

I need not point out to this distinguished gathering that my topic of discussion is a most important and relevant subject at this stage of our economic and social development. I have advocated before that development means change, and rapid change. This change takes place in all areas of our life — in the level of personal incomes, the social structure, attitudes and values, the structure of the economy and in our relationships with other countries. The role of the intellectual in stimulating change and in ensuring that all the change works towards the desired ultimate goal is an extremely important one. I will first explain, very briefly, the aims of the K.A.N.U. Government, and then say something about the intellectual.

I am sure you have all read the K.A.N.U. Manifesto, the Sessional Paper No. 10 on African Socialism and its Application to Planning in Kenya, and the revised Five Year Development Plan. These three documents outline very clearly the short-term objective and aims of the K.A.N.U. Government. When introducing the K.A.N.U. Manifesto, the President said, 'Our achievement of independence, for which we have struggled for so long, will not be an end in itself. It will give us the opportunity to work unfettered for the creation of a democratic African Socialist Kenya'. In the Sessional Paper No. 10, the K.A.N.U. Government elaborated this statement in considerable detail. In paragraph two of the Sessional Paper, it is stated, 'The best of Kenya's African social heritage and colonial economic legacy must be re-organised and mobilised for a concerted, carefully planned attack on poverty, disease and the lack of education in order to achieve social justice, human dignity and economic welfare for all'. This is the K.A.N.U. Government's central objective. It should also form the foundation on which intellectuals base their thinking and observations.

Whenever I have asked any of our young people why they want to go to school or college, the answer comes out quickly and simply: 'I want to be able to help my country and serve my fellowmen'. On speech-days, in every school or college, the visitor or the headmaster tells the young and keen listeners: 'You are the leaders of tomorrow'. They are told that the education they get is to prepare them for leadership — although perhaps the emphasis should be on service rather than leadership. They are reminded of the mass poverty and illiteracy in our country and the responsibility of every educated man to work to remove these conditions. I have recently looked at every letter that I have received from our students abroad and find that each one expresses his urgent wish to come home and join in the task of nation-building. They all talk in glowing terms and with great hopes or expectations of the role they will play when they return.

Resolutions are passed and memoranda are framed in student meetings and conferences telling the world how little has been done to solve world problems and how impatient they as students are to get out of college and put things right.

This is the background against which we must consider the relations between the K.A.N.U. Government and the intellectual, or better still, the role and impact of the intellectual in independent Kenya. We have often said that ours is a country of mass ignorance, superstition, and illiteracy. This means that we recognise the need for more enlightenment, education, and literacy if we are to succeed in our efforts to build the Kenya nation. It goes without saying then, that the K.A.N.U. Government has basic sympathy for and high expectations from the intellectual. What remains is for the intellectual to justify these expectations and to play his part effectively. He has to make himself felt and not sit on the side-lines grumbling and getting frustrated.

The achievement of the ultimate objectives set out in our Manifesto and the other documents I referred to will not be an easy task. It will require extra effort and sacrifice; it will also require hard thinking and effective planning in order to ensure that economic development produces not only more material comforts but also the kind of society which our people desire.

Because of the practices and policies of the colonial administration, the educated people in this country were a very small proportion of the total population at the time of independence.

We have been making remarkable progress in the field of education since independence. The country is now investing a very large share of its output in education. I am making these remarks in order to show that those of us who have had the opportunity to go to schools, colleges, and universities, are extremely fortunate. We are privileged; but let me hasten to add that I know that 'the educated' is not synonymous with 'the intellectual'. However, for convenience and with regard to our situation in Kenya, I will lump the two together. What then we should all realise is that in educating us the country has been investing in its future. Once this is recognised, then our responsibility to the nation becomes clear.

It is fairly easy to forget this responsibility. A student who has struggled hard through his examinations, may come out of the university convinced that his reward for his hard work is a privileged position in the society. He may even go further and expect his salary to be as high as those offered by the international organisations. He calls this his market value — but does not ask which market. If a graduate feels like this, then it means that he does not recognise his responsibility. What may happen if the Government and the society do not intervene is that an élite class, with all the comforts and conveniences of this century, is established, completely isolated from the rest of the population. I need hardly point out that the net result if such a situation is left unchecked, is to introduce intolerable instability in the country.

The danger of an élite class is very real. Because of our shortage of high-level manpower, we must do all we can to increase its supply. But since it takes a long time and a lot of money to increase the supply of highly trained people, it means that not very many people, and certainly not all the people, can have the opportunity or the privilege of going to institutions of higher learning. This, in turn, means that for a number of generations to come, the educated and highly trained people will remain a small proportion of the total population. However, this educated group need not be the kind of élite class I am speaking of provided that steps are taken to prevent such a class from establishing itself. We need to produce high-level manpower which will be emotionally and constantly involved with the problems, difficulties, poverty, and the insecurity of life among the less fortunate people.

Let me elaborate on this by relating it to social intercourse between the élite and the rest of the population. Most of our new élite live in towns where they work. Many of them have relatives living in the same town. They all talk about African socialism. But how many take off the odd evening or the weekend to call on the poorer relations. How many visit the old folks in the 'African reserves'. I do not wish to make this a generalised statement that will cover every educated African, nor do I want to suggest that there are no problems. Many of the educated people share their salaries with swarms of relatives; and one gets to know some of these relatives only when one lands a new well-paid job. But my point is that service through involvement means contact with the people. I also want to emphasise that the intellectual who wants to write about the people or provide answers to their problems and thereby help the country move forward must maintain constant touch with the people.

Another aspect of our requirements which depends on finding dedicated intellectuals is the need in the Government to develop a cadre of professional and technical personnel. So far we have succeeded in filling most of our administrative posts but we still have to find scientists, economists, agronomists, engineers, medical specialists, etc. This is a most exciting and challenging field. It is a challenge which, when met, should give personal satisfaction to the individual as well as the country. But it is a much slower process than, for example, the promotions one gets in the administrative or routine jobs. It requires a lot of initiative and commitment on the part of the individual officers. Too often we have lost prospective candidates because one feels that an economic degree qualifies one to be a specialist. Or sometimes good people just degenerate because they stop reading and studying after joining a Government department. Even more often, we lost a good man because some firm offers him a few hundred pounds more in salary — even though the career is not promising enough. I do not see how we shall be able to build the required number of experts, researchers, and advisers if the educated people are not prepared for the more difficult road towards specialisation. In the older countries, the competition is very severe and it takes years, and a strong will with total commitments for the younger people to succeed. There are many opportunities in our country, but we need clear and firm dedication to realise them. We need genuine specialists and experts and not second-rate persons whose claim may be belated only because of the colour of their skin. They must be able to stand up to the vigorous international standards demanded of similar persons in the same field.

There appears to be a tendency among some of our educated people to think that politics is a field which is below one's dignity. These people therefore refuse to be ordinary party members, and avoid participating in political discussions, especially at the local levels. This feeling seems to come from a conviction that the individuals concerned should devote their attention to lofty ideas, often not well-defined, which should exercise the mind of the nation. The tendency is for discussions, among people of this sort, to be centred mainly on ideological and theoretical arguments. Any conclusion reached is supposed to be the best advice which the policy-makers can only ignore at their peril. There is also a tendency to think that those who really know what should be done are those outside the Government, civil service, and the party. This 'Philosopher-King' approach will not do. Sometimes the party is attacked for presenting 'unqualified' candidates for parliament or local council elections. The educated people seem to think they should be called at such time to become candidates even without ever having done any party work or getting down to know the local branch committee. The educated can never be in a position to lead this country unless they mix with the people more freely, join in day to day local activities and help and assist by providing advice which the farmer, the worker, and peasant so much need.

Here I should point out that there is a growing tendency to underrate the masses' ideas and good judgement. There appears to be an erroneous conviction that all that needs to be done is to inform the masses what is required of them. We in K.A.N.U. do not share this view. K.A.N.U. is a mass party, and we believe that the ordinary people in villages and towns must participate in the policy formulation process. We expect the intellectuals and the educated to play their full part in the party — not only at the national level but also, and perhaps more important, at the local level. Anyone who attends party meetings in the districts would not fail to see how irrelevant theoretical and ideological arguments are. The masses are concerned with their poverty, disease, insecure life and limited opportunities to improve their lot. They want these hardships and difficulties removed. We as educated people should recognise this as a central problem. Compared with countries in other continents, we are very fortunate in that the masses have full faith in their educated sons. They expect their sons, who only until recently were living with them in the villages, to get them out of their difficulties.

This is the responsibility we carry on our shoulders, and unless we deliver the goods, our mothers and fathers will lose faith in us. It is for this reason that emotional involvement in the efforts the people are making and an intimate knowledge of their difficulties and hardship are so necessary. We should recognise the people's problems as our problems, and it would be disastrous if we thought we would relax in comfort while the masses continue to live under the hard and harsh conditions under which they have been living for centuries.

What I have really been trying to do in these remarks is to indicate three important points: First, is the need for the educated and the intellectuals to involve themselves in all the tasks, aspirations and the needs of the masses. They should be the officers in the battlefront in the war against poverty, disease, and insecurity of life which are the lot of the majority of our people. I am not saying, of course, that the intellectuals should abandon their present jobs. What I am saying is that the intellectuals must recognise their role in our efforts to develop and contribute all they have, especially by providing good leadership at all levels. I also expect the intellectuals to devote some of their time thinking about our political and social philosophies. But they should not do this from ivory towers with the aim of gaining some sort of self-satisfaction. Rather, the approach should be practical and constructive with the thinking being based on intimate knowledge of the prevailing conditions and the aim being to guide the various changes towards the declared economic and social objectives. Nothing could be more disastrous than having the intellectuals sit back as professional theorists, finding faults and making forecasts of disaster or upheavals, without saying or doing anything constructive at all.

The second point is that the intellectuals should recognise their responsibility to the nation, and impose upon themselves even more the sacrifice which they expect from the masses. As I have said on several other occasions, rapid and orderly economic and social development requires certain sacrifices. In our own particular case, we have already stated that in accordance with our philosophy of African socialism, the privileged must be prepared to sacrifice proportionately even more, so that the gap between the rich and the poor can be narrowed down as fast as possible. We cannot tolerate a state of affairs where those who have go on having more while those who have little or nothing remain in the same position. Here I should point out as far as the educated are concerned, it is through sheer luck that we are in a better material position.

All the educated Africans will, I am sure, agree with me on this — if only because we all have ex-school mates who were not lucky enough to go to higher institutions of learning and who to-day have to do all they can to get a subsistence income in the rural areas. This is basically because it has happened so suddenly. But this instability can be turned into strength if the educated and the intellectuals work hand-in-hand with their less fortunate brothers for a more prosperous Kenya characterised by equitable distribution of income, human dignity, and social justice.

The third point which I want to indicate concerns the discipline which the educated and the intellectuals must impose on themselves. Rapid economic and social development and national dignity could not be achieved without discipline. Through effective enforcement of various Government measures, discipline is, in fact, being imposed on the masses. But discipline must be imposed, and more effectively and ruthlessly, among the educated too. The kind of discipline I have in mind is more than going to the office at the right time and paying one's taxes promptly; it covers the total behaviour of the individual. No intellectual or educated person who is determined to discharge his full responsibility to the nation will spend most of his free time in bars getting drunk, leaving his students in classrooms while he wanders off to some vague duty elsewhere, use his privileged position to acquire more personal wealth through corruption, indulge in empty theorising on ideologies thereby confusing the people who expect guidance from their educated sons, or neglect his duty and concentrate on complaining that he is not being given a chance or promoted. Worse still is that man who thinks he can be an honest intellectual and a tribalist at the same time. We often say that education should help us achieve unity. The masses expect leadership and will often respond positively. But how can we help them when we are the first to be tribally minded? There have been complaints of tribalism in giving jobs or promotions or even in helping those in need. Here is an area that requires absolute discipline. There will, of course, be those people who will not observe this discipline and the Government should not hesitate to introduce and enforce the necessary corrective and preventive methods. I do not have to remind you that the popularly elected K.A.N.U. Government derives its strength from the masses, and they expect to see the Government provide firm leadership in the effort to establish social justice while developing Kenya into a prosperous African Socialist State.

From this, then, you will see that the K.A.N.U. Government, and indeed the entire society, expects a lot from the educated and the intellectuals. We are still at the early stages in the task of nation building. A lot still needs to be done in our development planning techniques, in carrying out already planned programmes and projects, and in setting up administrative and legal structures necessary for our increasingly complex economy and society. Kenya is, therefore, a fertile field in which the intellectual can play his part fully. We expect our educated people and the intellectuals to work closely with the Government and the party in this very challenging task of nation building.

At this point, I would like to pay tribute to those of our intellectuals who have been responsible for the promotion of art — Paa-ya-Paa and other individual exhibitions, the various writers and authors who have introduced us to new African books; the East African Institute with its monthly journal, Publishing House, Seminars and Radio broadcasts; the East African Academy and some of the groups of lecturers at our University College, for all their efforts to introduce real intellectual activity based on our country's problems. Among our civil servants too there have been occasions of real intellectual inspiration and creativity. But we have just begun and there is a lot of room still to be filled. I recall one particularly inspiring incident some years ago that held great promise for genuine incentive and stimulation of intellectual activity, but which was never repeated. I refer to the 'Kenya We Want Seminar' of 1962. We need more such activities where our own people from all walks of life can come together and discuss the country's problems. Here, too, I should compliment our women's groups for their seminars and group activities in recent years.

Before independence was achieved, the colonial regime, tried all they could to impose their culture on the African people, essentially by destroying our traditions. Africa is now trying to decolonise itself in this respect, and we shall need all the ability of our intellectuals. As I see it, it would be a totally negative approach to look backwards and try to re-establish all our old traditions. The constructive approach is to combine our valuable traditions with what we have learnt from foreigners' achievements in the same way that the colonialists underrated them. We do not have to exaggerate. Africa has a lot to show, and indeed teach the world.

WOMEN'S ROLE IN NATIONAL DEVELOPMENT

Address at the Conference organised by the East African Institute of Social and Cultural Affairs and the National Council of Women of Kenya, 24th April, 1967

Mr. Mboya's concern for and interest in women's role and place in independent Kenya has earned him a high place in women's organisations throughout Kenya. He is a regular speaker at important Women's Conferences and is often involved in assisting women leaders with their activities. The following speech on Women's Role in National Development is one of many important speeches he has made in recent years at Conferences convened by women's groups.

As mothers and housewives, women are in the vanguard of the new struggle for economic reconstruction and social progress. The future of all those ideals and objectives that we have defined for ourselves rests heavily on their shoulders. As mothers and farmers — let me repeat farmers — they hold the key to the success of the programmes of development that we have designed for our rural areas. Because of their position in the family and clan and tribe and the homes across our land they have a continuing influence in the shaping of the society that we must establish in Kenya. It will, therefore, be seen from what I have said that there can be no concept of national development which does not seriously take into account the role of women. Any attempt to plan or even to implement our plans without seeking the full co-operation of women is doomed to failure and cannot be regarded as a serious attempt to move forward, and you are the people best placed to ensure this co-operation. There are also other voluntary organisations — the Child Welfare Society, the Red Cross, the various children's homes and homes for young people in which many members and affiliates of the National Council of Kenya Women are doing a most praiseworthy job for our people. Women have also made great contributions in community development projects, in the prison service, in the medical service and in the teaching profession. Increasingly they are taking their place in Government departments and in the monetary sector of the economy. For all this we must thank and encourage the women leaders whose energetic work and persistent efforts are beginning to pay off. I would like to refer to one of the most impressive but silent revolutions that is taking place in our country today. I refer, of course, to self-help programmes. During my tours around the districts of Kenya I have come to realise how these efforts depend so much on women. Linked with this is the spreading of the nursery school system in most of the rural areas. I believe that in the next decade every child going to school will have passed through some form of nursery school. This will represent a major step forward in our educational efforts. It will bring younger and better prepared children into all our primary schools.

Whatever I am going to say to you is said with all these points very much in mind. We can discuss the role of women in national development from a sense of achievement and based on the challenges that still lie ahead. We need not start from a zero point but we must be concerned with the need to facilitate greater participation and involvement of our women in the total struggle of nation building.

I would like us to look first at three rather obvious features of our country. We are primarily an agricultural country, and our future economic development must be based on the development of this sector. Second and related to the previous point is that most of our people live in the rural areas. In fact only 7·8 per cent of our total population of nearly ten million live in urban areas. More significant for African population is concerned, the proportion is even smaller — it is about 5 per cent who live in the urban areas. More significant for our discussion is the fact that as far as women are concerned, there are very few of them living in the urban areas — although their proportion is increasing rapidly. And finally, it is worth noting that there are more women in Kenya than men — and if only because of this factor women must play a very big part in our development efforts.

These three features are important in our development strategy. Those who have read our Development Plan will know that the strategy we are following is based on rural transformation, i.e. the development of natural and human resources in provinces and districts. By developing the human and natural resources available in the provinces and districts, we hope to remedy one of the great injustices and weaknesses of the colonial era.

But let me mention at once that the effort being made by the Government in this direction is not confined to agricultural development. I should perhaps point out that those experts who tell us that all that is needed to secure rural transformation is to improve agricultural practices tend to over-simplify the problem. Rural transformation must be tackled on a much wider front with attempts to cover every important aspect of rural life and economic activity — development in adult education, health, agricultural practices, housing, water supply, marketing facilities — all these must be part of the plan. It would in fact be desirable to have a programme which tackles all these problems simultaneously. Unfortunately, such a programme would be very costly — both in terms of finance and the high-level manpower which would be required. It is, however, essential that a beginning be made in each aspect of rural life and economic activity, and our Development Plan contains projects and programmes which, when implemented should add up to a definite step forward in rural transformation.

I have made these few remarks on our strategy for development because they help in indicating the role of women in our economic and social development. The emphasis must coincide with that we have set in the plan. The changes which are necessary in securing rural development cannot take place unless the women play their full part. Indeed, these changes can only take place if the women themselves change their attitudes and practices and accept new ideas whose implementation will lead to greater material benefits and better living conditions. This is because in the African society women play a very big part in every activity — in farming, looking after the house, and the family and so on. Furthermore, in some parts of Kenya it is often the women who play the biggest part in agriculture. Consequently if modernisation of agricultural practices is to be achieved, agricultural extension advice must also reach women. The same thing is true in promoting health and better hygiene in the rural areas. The Kenya Government has recognised the role of women in introducing the necessary and desirable changes. This is one of the reasons, for example, why in Farmers' Training Centres, husbands are encouraged to bring their wives. It is also the reason why we encourage women to become

Agricultural Instructors and Home Economics Extension Workers. We recognise that in the modernisation of our agricultural sector women must play a big part. However, my point is that in the general effort to transform the rural sector, the role of women must be recognised. It is not only in fields like nutrition, childcare and hygiene at home in which women are going to play a big part. By the very nature of the characteristics of rural life, women must be seen as producers in all economic activities. This, in fact, is only recognising what is actually true.

Perhaps you will permit me to mention that too often there is discussion only about the modern or monetary sector of the economy when we think of the role of women. This sector is of course important and it is natural to think of jobs and posts within this sector. But let us not lose sight of the fact of our total population of ten million only about six hundred thousand are wage-earners. And even then over half of this number work for wages in the rural areas. The role of women like that of men must be considered in the light of these facts. National development as I have pointed out is not merely a process of urbanisation and industrialisation — it must have its roots in the rural areas. Nor is it merely a question of raising agricultural output — it must include social change. New attitudes are needed to overcome traditions which may stand in the way of development. Efforts to instil a new sense of values among our youth is needed to guard against the possible vacuum that may be created when old customs face the challenge of education. There is the danger that people begin to consider rural life as of less attraction than urban life. We also face the danger that our few educated people including women may tend to be attracted to the urban areas and deplete the leadership required in the rural areas where the majority of our people still live. Lastly we must guard against the danger of being preoccupied too much with the problems of the urban population at the expense of our people in the rural areas. This can happen very easily when the articulate leaders and the well organised groups spend all their time on the urban problems to the exclusion of the rural problem. I hope you women leaders and organisations will always keep these points in mind in deciding your work programme and the role you must play. In our efforts to improve rural life and so reduce the apparent attraction of urban life we intend to expand on social services, education and health facilities, water development and communications. But such efforts depend not only on Government plans but also on the people. I have already referred to the good work which women's groups are doing in Kenya. It is for you to help them intensify their efforts to create the necessary attitudes among our people that will promote our programme of rural transformation. The leadership which you can give in this area is very important and I hope you will accept this challenge. Government will do what it can to help with leadership training among women and is sponsoring training schemes including co-operatives and social work. Some women have been sent overseas to come back and play a greater role in these fields. But it is important that such women appreciate and accept the need to continue to work in the rural areas.

Let me now turn to the non-agricultural sector of our economy. The women's role is at present small in this sector. This is especially true when one compares our country with the industrial nations where women are to be found in practically all occupations. But we cannot jump from our present stage of development to the level of economic development achieved in the industrial nations in one or two years. The process will take time. But as the country develops, the pattern of our economy will also change. The changing pattern of our economic activities will not only diversify the economy generally but will also lead to new opportunities and jobs being created. Women can therefore expect to play an increasing part in the economy as a whole. The main subject of this conference is therefore a good one — for ours is a changing economy and society — and the role of women should be seen from two angles. First, women must contribute in initiating the necessary and desirable changes. Second, in the changed (but still changing) economy, women must play their full part in all activities of the nation. I suggest that this would be a useful approach in discussing this important subject during the five days ahead of you. I have already briefly indicated the role of women in initiating change in the rural sector of our economy. I will now say something about their role in the monetary sector.

As I have already observed, women's contribution in this sector is at present small. However, already a beginning towards increasing their contribution in this sector of the economy has been made. The number of women in employment increased from about 55,000 in 1963 to over 82,000 in 1965. As far as African women are concerned, the increase was from 44,300 to 72,000 over the same period. Female employment between 1963 and 1965 in the main sectors and by race is indicated by the following figures:

SECTOR	YEAR	NUMBER OF EMPLOYEES			
		African	*Asian*	*European*	*Total*
Public Service	*1963*	7,278	1,425	1,935	10,638
	1965	12,931	1,332	1,304	15,567
Private Industry	*1963*	5,019	2,836	3,964	11,819
and Commerce	*1965*	8,921	3,946	3,656	16,523
Agriculture and	*1963*	32,035	6	110	32,151
Forestry	*1965*	50,072	8	91	50,171
TOTAL	*1963*	44,332	4,267	6,009	54,608
	1965	71,924	5,286	5,051	82,261

From these figures it will be noticed that the number of African women employed in the three main sectors has increased rapidly. However, the number of African women employed in commerce and industry is still very small, and one expects that in future the number of African women employed in this sector will increase more rapidly than it has done in the last three years.

Women's contribution in every sector of the monetary economy will depend, of course, on a number of factors — especially education and training. One of the reasons why employment of African women in some sectors is insignificant compared with the number of men employed is that education and training of women was not given the emphasis it required in pre-independence days. Since independence, however, education of women has been fully recognised. Of the total enrolment in primary schools of 1,050,000 about 40 per cent are girls. In secondary schools, enrolment of girls has risen from 8,970 in 1963 to 16,391 in 1966. In other words the number of girls in secondary schools has doubled since independence.

The preparation of women to play an increasing role in the economy is not confined to academic education: many more girls are now being trained as nurses, home visitors, social workers, community development assistants and officers, secretaries, teachers, etc. than was the case in pre-independence days. These are actually some of the fields in which we have serious middle-level manpower shortages. For instance the Manpower Survey published by my Ministry in 1965 indicates that we shall have a short fall of 3,164 primary school teachers and over 400 staff and general duty nurses in our requirements in 1970. These shortages are and could actually be more serious in future because the Government is making a much greater effort to provide certain essential services, e.g. health and education. For example, a manpower survey undertaken now could indicate a much greater shortage of nurses because the Government has introduced free medical attention for all children and outpatients. Furthermore, the manpower projections of demand and supply contained in the Manpower Survey I referred to are aggregates which do not show the requirements of African high-level and middle-level manpower. In fact the shortage of African high-level and middle-level manpower is already proving a bottleneck in the Africanisation of some sectors of our economy.

All that this amounts to is that women must recognise that there is ample scope for them in many activities of the economy. What they should also realise is that many of the jobs in which they will be working — such as being secretaries, nurses and community development officers — must be tackled with confidence. Women must realise that in doing these new jobs properly and with confidence they will not only be serving the country directly but also indirectly in the sense that those who are prejudiced against women in certain jobs or in positions of authority will see that such prejudice is irrational. It is unfortunate, but true, that women will be expected to prove that they can handle new responsibilities effectively.

Women leaders have, I think, recognised the point I am making. In the last few years there has been a tremendous increase in activities organised by our educated women. These women have accepted and must continue to accept, a very heavy responsibility. In fact they have initiated the kind of revolution in the rural areas to which I have already referred.

Another important contribution of our educated women has been that they have managed to attract the older and illiterate women in some of their activities. I have already referred to the *Maendeleo ya Wanawake* movement and its local groups which have become important centres of activities. Here the only suggestion I would like to make is that the activities of this and other groups should be related to the activities of other organisations and especially to work with chiefs and key government departments operating in the rural areas — particularly the Department of Community Development. Women's activities, and those of other voluntary organisations, should be complementary with the effort being made by the Government. Moreover, the Government has many more resources at its disposal which should be used to assist voluntary effort. But before such assistance is increased, voluntary effort must be planned and related to Government schemes.

I am not suggesting that voluntary organisation should relate their schemes and projects to the effort being made by the Government in similar areas or fields only because of financial reasons: indeed these organisations can help enormously in ensuring that opportunities to achieve certain social and economic objectives are seized as they arise. As far as women's organisations are concerned, the Government will be ready to assist in schemes aimed at educating the older and illiterate women. It is, in fact, the illiterate who constitute the bulk of our population.

Another suggestion I would like to make concerning our educated women is that they must avoid being exclusive at all costs. It is very easy for organisations to become exclusive clubs, even if the initial objectives for forming the organisations were excellent, unless a conscious effort is made to tackle the practical problems facing the country. The challenge before our educated women is a very clear one: it is the general education of the older and illiterate women.

The last suggestion that I want to make is the need for your organisations to wage a campaign for a public consciousness of women's activities and efforts. It is my impression that most of our elected representatives even including Ministers, Members of Parliament and Municipal and County Councillors do not fully appreciate your efforts. Do not sit back and wait to be seen and recognised. Go out and sell your projects and where possible involve the local Member of Parliament, County Councillor or even Party Chairman. Rope them all in and see that they work more with you to encourage the public to come to your aid. Demand to speak on your work at Chief's *Barazas** and

---

* *Baraza* is the name for the traditional form of meeting in Kenya. It has been democratic to the extent that anyone can attend, but in fact such meetings have usually been dominated by men, if not exclusively male.

some of the Constituency Meetings. You have a message for the people which deserves a prominent place in the affairs of our nation. Do not allow yourselves to be drawn into discussing some of the casual problems such as national dress, cosmetics and so on. Think big and speak on national issues so that your organisations can be consulted on matters of policy and specially on social and economic policy.

I have discussed the role of women in the economic development of Kenya. To end with, I will say something on the women in politics and public life. As I said earlier women constitute the largest block of voters in Kenya. As is now generally appreciated women played an extremely important role in the struggle for independence. But today the part being played by women in politics is distressingly small. This is something which must be somehow corrected. As far as the constitution is concerned, women have equal rights. What is now needed is for the women to be active. The older and illiterate women are still interested in politics. They turn out in thousands to hear party leaders, their local Members of Parliament and Government Civil Servants. These women I feel certain would like to see the younger educated women participate in politics so that we can have women Members of Parliament at an early date. Those educated women who stand aside are only delaying the day when women can join Parliament. It would be a great error for the educated women to stand aloof expecting that one day they will be invited to stand for Parliament. Apart from the fact that participation in local party matters and politics is a good experience, people expect to see anyone interested in standing for Parliament participate fully in local matters and political activities. Furthermore, not everyone of us can go to Parliament at the same time, consequently, women, just as men, must be prepared to contribute in the political development of the country at all levels.

I would like to refer to just one more aspect of our development which requires the support of our women. Being much closer to the traditions of our people, the women will understand better what we mean by African socialism. I know that there have been attempts to misrepresent this philosophy or to use it to cover up for the weaknesses of some of our people. For example some people who like idle life demand support from relatives by invoking African socialism. The truth is that under our traditions there was no room for idlers. Each one was expected to contribute according to his ability before he could expect support from the relatives or clan. The women can help us eliminate this menace. Yet another commitment we have made is to watch against the development of antagonistic classes among our people. The danger of the few educated people living in isolation cannot be ignored. In traditional society the women play a very important part in preserving the complex family structure. Our educated women must not ignore this role. We must beware of the consequences arising from the cost of high living — a condition which unless watched can lead to serious complications among the new élite in our country. There is also the danger of tribalism to be watched. Women have a definite interest in all these matters.

Finally, I would like to summarise my remarks by saying that in the changing society, the traditional division of labour between men and women is slowly losing meaning. Indeed, it should, for in some cases its continuation would impede development. Our women must expect to play an important role in every kind of economic activity — from agriculture, health, education, Government service to politics.

Part Two

PAN-AFRICANISM

During the revolutionary decade of the 1950s, the old pan-African movement led by Dr. W. E. B. DuBois and his American and West Indian supporters, was transformed from a foreign-based movement, preoccupied with the problems of racism, into an African-based movement whose major objective is African Unity. The former move- ment organised six congresses in foreign lands: London (1900), Paris (1919), London (1921), London and Lisbon (1923), New York (1927) and the sixth in Manchester (1945). The major challenge facing the leaders of the Pan-African Congresses was the colour problem. As Dr. DuBois proclaimed at the 1900 Congress: 'the problem of the twentieth century is the colour line — the relation of the darker to the lighter races of man in Asia and Africa, in America and the islands of the sea.'*

The new movement, now based in Africa, was inspired by different objectives. Mr. George Padmore, a West Indian theoretician who from 1939 increasingly became an influential pan-Africanist, has summed up the challenge of pan-Africanism in these words:

'In our struggle for national freedom, human dignity and social redemption, pan-Africanism offers an ideological alternative to com- munism on the one side and tribalism on the other. It rejects both white racialism and black chauvinism. It stands for racial co-existence on the basis of absolute equality and respect for human personality. Pan-Africanism looks above the narrow confines of class, race, tribe and religion. In other words, it wants equal opportunity for all. Talent to be rewarded on the basis of merit. Its vision stretches beyond the limited frontiers of the nation-state. Its perspective embraces the federation of regional self-governing countries and their ultimate amalgamation into a *United States of Africa*. In such a Com- monwealth, all men, regardless of tribe, race, colour or creed, shall be equal and free. And all the national units comprising the regional federations shall be autonomous in all matters of common interest to the African Union. This is our vision of the Africa of Tomorrow — the goal of pan-Africanism.'†

Dr. Kwame Nkrumah gradually emerged as the leader of the new

---

* W. E. B. DuBois, *The Souls of Black Folk*, 1903. New York.
† G. Padmore, *Pan-Africanism or Communism?*, Dobson, 1956, London.

movement. He regarded himself, not only as the successor of Dr. DuBois but also as the natural President of the proposed *United States of Africa*. His claim to presidency was further enhanced in 1957 when Ghana became the first black African colony to win its independence.

Mr. Tom Mboya was involved in this new movement right from its inception. As a result of a meeting between Dr. Julius Nyerere and Mboya in the latter's house in Nairobi in 1958, a decision was made to found the Pan-African Freedom Movement of East and Central Africa (P.A.F.M.E.C.A.), which was formally launched on 17th September, 1958 at Mwanza, Tanganyika, by representatives of nationalist movements in Tanganyika, Zanzibar, Nyasaland, Kenya and Uganda.* Up to 1960, PAFMECA was essentially an East African Organisation. But in February 1962, it held a large meeting in Addis Ababa at which Ethiopia and Somalia were included for the first time. It was also decided to expand the organisation to include Southern Africa, its name being changed to the Pan-African Freedom Movement of East, Central and Southern Africa (P.A.F.M.E.C.S.A.).

Throughout this period, Mr. Mboya played an active role in the work of this organisation whose existence had raised a question that was to grow in importance: the relation of regional unity movements to a pan-African movement. The issue culminated in the famous debate at the Cairo meeting of the Heads of States and Governments of the O.A.U., July 17–21, 1964, between Drs. Nkrumah and Nyerere. Nkrumah contended that 'To say that a Union Government of Africa is premature is to sacrifice Africa on the altar of neo-colonialism.' To which President Nyerere retorted that 'To rule out step-by-step progress in a march to unity is to rule out unity itself.'

In December 5–13, 1958, Dr. Nkrumah called the first All-African Peoples' Conference (A.A.P.C.), which was generally regarded as the successor to the Pan-African Congresses. 500 Trade Union and political party delegates from twenty-eight African countries, most of them still colonies, attended, together with observers from many non-African organisations. The purpose of the Conference was, as Nkrumah said at the opening session, to plan 'for a final assault upon imperialism and colonialism'.

* See Mboya's article in the *East African Standard*, 26th September, 1962.

Mr. Mboya, then only twenty-eight years old, was elected Chairman partly to pay tribute to his active role in the fight for Kenya's independence, and partly to sound a warning to the European settlers and businessmen in East and Central Africa. The A.A.P.C. brought many African nationalist leaders from colonial Africa into contact for the first time with others from independent Africa. Among other things, the issue of pan-African Trade Unionism was decided upon in principle.

Summarising at the end of the Conference, Mr. Mboya said:

'Some have said Africans are not yet ready to be free. Others have said we are not yet civilised enough. To this we give a simple answer:

'Civilised or not civilised, ignorant or illiterate, rich or poor, we, the African states, deserve a government of our own choice. Let us make our own mistakes, but let us take comfort in the knowledge that they are our own mistakes.'

He concluded,

'Whereas seventy-two years ago the scramble for Africa started, from Accra we announce that these same powers must be told in a clear, firm and definite voice: "Scram from Africa".'

The second meeting of A.A.P.C. was held in Tunis in January 1960. The main issue discussed at this conference was that of pan-African trade unionism, and the bone of contention was the famous question of 'disaffiliation' (from international trade union structures). The East African Contingent, led by Tom Mboya, who was personally absent from Tunis, opposed disaffiliation. Consequently, no decision was taken at Tunis. Disagreement over the disaffiliation issue was partly responsible for alienating Mboya from Nkrumah.

The third and last meeting of the A.A.P.C. was held at Cairo from 25th to 31st March, 1961. Speaking at the Conference Mr. Mboya urged that 'Africa's ultimate redemption will only come from Africa'.

Another pan-African organisation in which Mboya has been involved a great deal is the United Nations Economic Commission for

Africa. At the twelfth General Assembly of the United Nations on 26th November, 1957, it was resolved that the E.C.A. should be established as a U.N. regional instrument for promoting economic and social development, as well as economic co-operation among African countries. It was established in 1958, and it held its inaugural meeting at Addis Ababa from 29th December, 1958 to 6th January, 1959, at which Mboya represented the I.C.F.T.U. In 1965, he became Chairman of the Seventh Session of E.C.A. In 1967 he made his final speech as Chairman of the E.C.A. at its Eighth Session held at Lagos Nigeria (see pp. 182–208).

Mr. Mboya's concern for pan-Africanism and African unity was also manifest in the role he played in the Pan-African Freedom Movement of East and Central Africa. He was also a member of various working parties and committees whose work led to the creation of the East African Community. More recently he was a member of the six-man negotiating team — two ministers from Kenya, Uganda and Tanzania, charged with negotiating the terms of association with countries who have applied for admission to the East African Community.

Another aspect of his work of international publicity for the African nationalist cause was his writing. Among his publications during the 1950s were:

The Kenya Question: An African Answer published by the Fabian Colonial Bureau, 1956, with a Foreword by Dame Margery Perham, then of Nuffield College, Oxford.

Kenya Faces the Future published by the American Committee on Africa, 1959.

He also contributed widely to publications, especially those dealing with African affairs. In 1964 his first full-length book, *Freedom and After*, was published by André Deutsch.

AFRICAN FREEDOM

Address delivered on the First African Freedom Day, 15th April, 1959,
Carnegie Hall, New York

I am glad to be in New York to launch today the world-wide celebration of African Freedom Day, April 15th was decided upon as African Freedom Day at the first Conference of the Independent African States held at Accra in April 1958 and was later endorsed by the first All-African Peoples' Conference also held at Accra. These conferences marked the discovery of Africa by Africans. This is in complete contrast to the discovery of Africa by Europeans in the nineteenth century.

What is this Africa and what do we mean by the word Freedom? This is what many of us are thinking and talking about today throughout the world. Africa is still associated in the minds of many people in the United States and some European countries with the nineteenth century. They think of the Dark Continent, the jungles, the wild beasts, the Africa as presented to them by Hollywood — the fierce, ignorant or merrily- and furiously-dancing tribesmen. Little is it realised that Africa too shares in what we call the twentieth century: modern cities, schools, roads, airfields, houses, cars and so on. As we celebrate this day, therefore, we might usefully stop and ponder these questions.

Africa desires to be understood and to be recognised from the viewpoint and perspective of her own people. Africa is no longer willing to be referred to as British, French, Belgian or Portuguese Africa. Africa must create and assert her own personality and speak for herself. She cannot be a projection of Europe nor any longer permit herself to be interpreted or spoken for by self-appointed interpreters. It was this conviction that moved African statesmen and political and trade-union leaders to hold the two conferences at Accra in 1958.

The Conference of Independent African States marked the birth of the African personality. The representatives of the African states at Accra unanimously agreed on the need for Africa to rise and be heard at all the councils of world affairs; and to achieve this objective they created the Organisation of African States, which now consults on all questions affecting Africa before the U.N. and which represents the united will of all Africans on such issues. Equally important was their decision that Africa's total liberation was the task for all Africans.

To implement the latter decision, non-governmental representatives of African people from the entire continent met at the All-African Peoples' Conference in Ghana in December. That Conference gave birth to the African community. By a unanimous vote all five hundred delegates from political parties, nationalist organisations, trade unions and similar groups from every part of Africa agreed to work together in full co-operation for the total liberation of all Africa.

Thus both conferences were characterised by a spirit of unity based upon the same, predominant concepts and ideals — above all, those expressed in the common purpose: independence for all Africa. There was agreement that the independence of one territory is incomplete and meaningless unless it is accompanied by total independence for all territories. This, indeed, was but the practical application of the moral principle expressed earlier and more elegantly that 'no man is an island', and less elegantly but in language every American recognises that 'we must all hang together lest we hang separately'.

The year 1958 also saw the inauguration of the United Nations Economic Commission for Africa at Addis Ababa in Ethiopia. This marked, in fact, the U.N.'s functional recognition of Africa's legitimate place and role in the world's economic and social community and was another useful addition to the twentieth-century discovery of Africa. It provided a long-delayed vehicle for pan-African economic planning and co-ordination.

There are those who complain that the discovery of Africa and the African personality and community by Africans is taking place at too fast a pace. Such people should be reminded that Africa is many years behind the rest of the world and that in these circumstances we cannot afford the luxury of wasting time. They might well remember the old but true adage that 'he who is behind must run faster than he who is in front'. In the case of Africa we do not have only to run faster but we have, at the same time, to try to avoid the mistakes and pitfalls of those who 'run before us', a considerable addition to our task. Lest any believe we are really running too fast, let me recall to them that colonialism has existed in Africa for over four centuries.

Most people seem to agree that colonialism is on its way out. It is, therefore, doubly difficult to understand why nations which are signatories to the United Nations Charter and which have committed themselves to the Declaration of Human Rights have not found it possible to give effective support to the African's struggle for freedom. Most of them have been noted for their compromising attitude and their desire to please the colonial powers or each other at the expense of democracy and human rights. How can anyone honestly believe that a compromise is possible where human rights, democracy and Christian ideals are concerned and still expect the African to have confidence and faith in him?

Of 220,000,000 Africans only 70,000,000 live in independent states free of white minority domination.* The rest have yet to be liberated from colonialism and European domination. Surveying the situation of the 150,000,000 people still not free one will immediately see what the African talks about when he condemns colonialism and European settler domination.

Africans are convinced that economic and social conditions cannot be considered apart from their political setting. Self-government and independence open great possibilities for economic and social development. Self-government permits people not only to embark on development programmes serving purposefully the needs of their own country which they know best, but also enables them to establish relations with other countries on the basis of equality and to co-ordinate progressively the economy of their country with that of others. Full economic and social emancipation is not possible without political emancipation. Above all, it is through becoming masters of their own fate that the energies of the people are fully released for the arduous task of economic and social development.

The subjection of a people in any form, including forced labour, apartheid, or colonialism under the guise of assimilation, is wholly inimical to economic and social development. This is one answer to those who argue that we must wait until we have a viable economy and have acquired enough experience before we have the right to demand our freedom.

---

* At the end of 1968 some 30 million Africans out of an estimated 300 million were still under colonial or white minority rule.

This argument for delay, which smells of a passive betrayal of democracy, ignores the fact that, so far, experience has shown that it is only after independence that most of our countries have embarked on large-scale economic and educational projects and that in all cases it is only after independence that the world has begun to be conscious of our economic and social problems. In fact, the foundations for stable government have been laid only after independence, which makes nonsense of the plea of colonial governments that they are training us for self-government. In every case, colonial powers have left their African territories only when the organised pressure of our people has made it impossible for them to govern without serious consequences.

In addition to crying caution and go slow, opponents of African freedom have raised other objections. While most of the opposition arises from those who fear that independence will cost them status, economic advantage, or other special privilege, I would like briefly to consider the questions that are posed to me time and again by non-Africans.

For example, I have repeatedly been asked about the use of violence to achieve freedom. To this I can only answer that we are totally committed to non-violent positive action. Nevertheless, I must call attention to the wise words of the great English reformer, John Bright, who in 1866 declared:

'I have never said a word in favour of force. All I have said has been against it — but I am at liberty to warn those in authority that justice long delayed, or long continued injustice always provokes the employment of force to obtain redress. It is the ordering of nature and therefore of the Supreme that this is so, and all preaching to the contrary is of no avail. If men build houses on the slopes of a Vesuvius, I may tell them of their folly and insecurity, but I am not in any way provoking or responsible for, the eruption which sweeps them all away. I may say too that force, to prevent freedom and to deny rights, is not more moral than force to gain freedom and secure rights.'

Secondly, there are those, perhaps affected by the guilty conscience which the general record of western colonialism must unfortunately lead to, who fear that we Africans may yield to the not unsurprising temptation to victimise minorities — particularly the formerly dominant whites — when we gain independence. To them I can only repeat what we resolved at Accra in December: citizens' rights in Africa will be recognised and guaranteed, regardless of race or colour. Our quarrel is only with colonialism and European domination. With these we shall never compromise.

Lastly, there are some who are only too ready to try to make capital out of some of our teething problems. They expect perfection from us and lie in wait to ridicule our demand for freedom every time they see — or fancy that they see — any error or misjudgment by an African. I am flattered by these people because whereas they have not yet attained perfection themselves, they believe we are better fitted to achieve it before them. We have nothing to apologise for; but while we will always welcome constructive criticism, we do not and cannot allow interference with the sovereignty of our independent status. Any problems we meet during our early stages of independence reflect on the utter failure of colonialism as a training ground. We have no reason to believe that if the colonial governments had another hundred years the situation would be better.

But is it really necessary for us to justify our demand for freedom or even to answer as to our readiness to shoulder the responsibility of self-government? If so, to whom are we accountable and by what and whose standards are we to be judged? What right has any other person to set himself up as our tutor and judge?

I submit that we have a right to self-determination. It is a birthright which we need not either justify or explain. We know and understand our desires and responsibilities to our people, our countries and world peace. The other nations would do well to co-operate with us in our efforts instead of setting themselves up as our judges.

Too often we have heard of those who insist that African freedom involves a risk of communism. To them, all I want to say is that if they spent all their efforts in practicing the democracy that they preach they would have nothing to fear from communism.

Let us, therefore, join together and match the internationalism of communism, item by item, with the internationalism of democracy. Let us co-operate in the effort to eliminate disease, poverty and ignorance from the face of the earth and we shall have dealt a death-blow to the root causes of most of the 'isms' that currently bedevil the world.

To those who count upon military bases, established in colonial areas without the consent of — or even notice to — the local inhabitants, for security against the false prophets of the world, I commend a thorough study of recent events. Military agreements negotiated with colonial powers will necessarily be, as they are today in Morocco, subject to the will and the needs of the African people when they gain their independence. I humbly submit that only Africans, whatever their colour, background or race, may rightfully decide matters which vitally affect the future of Africa. We African people seek the same peace, stability, security and well-being that all decent people seek the world over, and we are unwilling to be used willy-nilly as pawns in a great power struggle. For this reason we adamantly oppose the use of any African territory, even the most desolate wastes of the Sahara, as a testing ground by non-Africans of their new and ever more devilish instruments of destruction.

What specifically, therefore, is the task of Africans who seek to achieve that standard of well-being which is now recognised to be the decent and proper right of all peoples? It was clearly summarised by Dr. Kwame Nkrumah, Prime Minister of Ghana, when he called upon the African peoples to aim at four stages of advance: the attainment of freedom and independence; the consolidation of that freedom and independence; the creation of unity and community among the Free African States; and the economic and social reconstruction of Africa.

To this great fourfold task we shall devote our full energies until a new, proud, free Africa is able to contribute constructively and equally to the great adventures before mankind.

RELATIONS BETWEEN PRESS AND GOVERNMENTS IN AFRICA

Address to the International Press Institute, Paris, 17th May, 1962

Although this address was delivered before Kenya's independence, it is still surprisingly valid today. It is unfortunately true even today that much reporting about Africa by the outside world is ill-informed and ill-disposed, reflecting more of the prejudices of the writer than the reality of the situation.

Some improvements have been achieved by the opening of bureaux in Africa by international news agencies and by other leading news media. The creation of national news agencies in many African countries has also helped to ensure the flow of more accurate news both within the continent and to the outside world.

There have been considerable advances in the Africanisation of staffs of newspapers published in Africa. In this regard it is fair to point to the work carried out by the International Press Institute Journalist Training School in Nairobi. A significant indication of the growing importance of the flow of news both about and in Africa, was the holding of the I.P.I. Annual Conference in Nairobi in 1968. Since independence, the press and news media have remained remarkably free in Africa. This is particularly noteworthy if one considers the crises through which the continent has passed. This freedom has generally even extended to hostile reporters from foreign news media.

What attitudes or relations are created between the Press and the new governments of Africa will depend to a large extent on the background and reactions in the period of the nationalist struggle.

The most important factors which must weigh heavily in deciding these future relations will include such questions as — was the Press hostile or sympathetic to the nationalist cause; was it reactionary or progressive; was it identified with the imperialist forces and money interests in the former colonial countries; and how far is it still regarded as a tool of foreign penetration and an agent for neo-colonialism.

The local Press in Africa may in this regard also suffer from the reactions of the African countries to the attitudes of a hostile foreign Press.

In trying to analyse these factors a number of questions arise. The most important to you, I am sure, relates to the freedom of the Press.

Most Africans are bound to ask; what is this freedom of the Press? Does it include licence to do and say what they please, even if it means directly or indirectly wrecking all our efforts at consolidating our dearly won independence and our efforts for economic reconstruction?

Does this Press in Africa recognise that in our special circumstances it has a duty to Africa and that in fact we expect it to make its own constructive contribution towards our general efforts?

Can the Press in Africa afford to behave and write as though it were operating in London, Paris or New York, where the problems and anxieties are entirely different from those current in Africa?

These and many other questions keep coming up in the minds of many Africans as they try to decide what freedom of the Press should mean in the African context. It is, therefore, important that the Press should concern itself with finding out what goes on in the mind of the African.

In the majority of cases the world Press is served by foreign journalists who pay short visits to the various parts of Africa and on whom the world's verdict over Africa may rest. The news agencies are often relying on such journalists or reporters, who may not themselves know enough or physically be able to cover the area assigned to them to be able to interpret the African scene.

The result is that news coming out of Africa is often, if not always, related to the already biased and prejudiced mind that keeps asking such questions as — is this pro-East or pro-West? Very few, if any, of the world's Press ask such logical and simple questions as — is this pro-African?

Let us look back now for a moment and see some of the reasoning that will influence relations between the Press and the African Governments in the emerging nations of Africa.

'Government of the people, by the people, for the people' is one of the most respectable objectives in the philosophy of the democratic world. It is one of the best-known, and probably one of the simplest definitions of ordinary democracy.

In all the so-called 'free nations' of the world the human eye can hardly follow the speed with which politicians on platforms, and editors on leader pages, rush to the defence of this sacred principle, and congratulate themselves on living within its shadow.

Some of the mass-circulation dailies, the ones that have tears in their eyes, would give away the Statue of Liberty, or bound copies of the British Constitution, with every issue if this were mechanically possible — and if, of course, it would justify an increase in advertising rates.

'Liberty, Equality, Fraternity' is one of the most cherished, and certainly the most direct definition of the ordinary brotherhood of man. It has drawn widespread emotional response, in terms of loyalty and readiness to struggle and even in terms of spiritual peace, for a very long time.

It is a clean philosophy, a noble idea, easy to understand. It has been perpetuated in the minds of men by successive waves of politicians and statesmen, who could find nothing better to say, and by those generations of leader-writers and feature-page tricksters who found their task made easy by having such resounding words to represent.

The Press, in other words, has triumphantly upheld for many generations — with burning sincerity in periods when such values were threatened — the principle of self-determination, freedom in all its guises, and the dignity of men.

This has not necessarily prevented variations in what are called Press standards — standards of reporting, or of comment, or of taste. It has not prevented differences in presentation of the flavour of democracy or in ideas about how it should be maintained. It has not prevented fortunes being made.

But this defence of simple notions about the right way to dignity and to administer a human society has long endured.

My task today, against all this background, must seem on the face of it — unusual. I have to explain and comment on the remarkable fact that the nationalist struggle in Africa (for self-determination, freedom in all its forms, the elementary rights of man) has been carried on so frequently amid a general chorus of protests from the Press.

I have to deal with the strange but simple fact that in many countries, especially in East and Central Africa, independence has been attained, or brought within early reach, despite — this is the point — a general Press hostility.

By 'the Press' in this context, of course, I mean the national news-papers and reviews of Africa, edited and published by experienced overseas technicians, taken for granted by those of European up-bringing, increasingly available to and consulted by the African people with the recent growth in literacy, and assumed internationally to represent the mature voice of an otherwise unsophisticated country.

These are the pillars of influence, the builders of an image, increasingly supplemented — in the editorial and business sense — by subsidiaries printed in some major vernacular. I also include the Western Press and especially some of the influential papers published in the metropolises of the Colonial Powers.

The perspective of time is also important here. I am not talking about the tone or the opinion of a newspaper that you may have picked up today, or last week, or on any odd occasion in any particular year.

I am talking about the whole tendency of the Press to disparage, belittle and oppose, to be fearful or sceptical or simply patronising, during the whole period of emergence of the African personality and African political power. I do not in this include the nationalist Press or the African-owned Press.

This attitude of the established Press in Africa — rooted as it has been in overseas traditions and capital and professional ideas — has generally expressed itself in three principal ways.

Firstly, there has been a fundamental dislike or distrust by proprietors and editors of change. You will all remember when Mr. Harold Macmillan, speaking of Africa, produced a phrase that has been made tedious by repetition, although Ministers in the House of Commons still include the phrase in their speeches as though they had just invented it — 'the wind of change'.

On the whole, in the Press of Africa, the Prime Minister's words and their implication had a very grim reception. Change was disliked by all those who sought and found comfort in ancient institutions in the solidity of sameness, and who shied away — as part of their code — from new ideas.

Change was distrusted by those to whom Africa was, and must always be, the arena of a carefully stratified society, the right clubs, home leave every two years or so, and the natives permanently in their place.

Change was alarming, as a concept, to those whose business interests were attuned to a *status quo*, and who could not or would not move with the times of new forces, new needs, new markets, new competition, new balance-sheets, new editorial themes.

Secondly, there has been a professed sense of outrage in nearly all newspapers and reviews at the jargon in which all along there has had to be openly expressed the beliefs and the ambitions, and even the demands of African nationalism.

It came as a shock — or was presented as a shock — that we who have represented the African people in their struggle should make demands for such outrageous things as self-determination, freedom in all its forms, human dignity and human rights.

It aroused something like astonished resentment when we spoke of a move away from privilege and towards equality, away from restrictions and towards liberty, away from racial injustice and towards fraternity.

It led to something like fear when the frustrations of our people or the frustrations of their leaders in the emotional atmosphere of meetings and rallies generated passionate strides along the road to inevitable truth.

It drew carefully designed bewilderment when we met palliatives with impatience, strategy with better strategy, intrigue with rebuff. This, as some of them suggested, was not cricket.

How right they were. The freedom of our people, the creation of outlets for their latent talents and ambitions, the substitution of self-respect for wretchedness, the achievement throughout Africa of such things as health and learning and economic security . . . these things are not a game.

Thirdly, there has been a campaign, rooted in some complex of superiority, and conducted with maddening paternalism, designed to show that the people of Africa were unready for self-determination, incapable of controlling and enjoying freedom, inherently unaware of (or indifferent to) the dignity of man.

It had been argued in the Press for years — referring again in particular, to the newspapers and reviews of East and Central Africa — that the grant (as they called it) of liberty would extinguish freedom.

In tones varying from despair to ridicule, the Press has submitted that democracy would lead to the collapse of administration, the extinction of industrial enterprise, the running-down of agriculture and marketing structures and communications and social services and the whole fabric of an ordered society.

It is difficult to work out, in all this, just what the Press was hoping to accomplish. If their campaign had succeeded, it logically follows that a sense of inferiority might have crippled the energy and zest of our people.

There is little doubt that constant gloomy prediction about the fate of major industries and services — and the people undertaking them or employed by them — has contributed greatly to the uncertainties or ordinary families, to lack of confidence and flight of capital, factors that have magnified difficulties out of all proportion to conceivable hazard. The Press has not provided understanding.

It has never strengthened us with faith. It has discounted — in the fields of economic planning and executive skill — African potential, calibre, or concern.

In nostalgia for the past — and in fear of the present, it has hesitated on the threshold of the future, never committing itself to belief — or even hope — that stability and material progress, and acceptable social justice, would assuredly follow the unleashing Africa of the spirit of man.

The African leaders are not saints; few of them have pretensions to genius; not one would minimise the challenge and problems that must — especially in the early days — mark a change of regime. But all of them have been in pursuit of that most noble theme of British justice: 'Let right be done'.

All of them drew strength from the knowledge that the discipline and judgment and dedication — and the economic potential in all spheres — of our people, are virtually untapped.

Despite the most careful or casual misrepresentations in the Press, these assets are there; with them we can win the struggle to build a new Africa. Without them we could never have begun.

We have arrived, as a result of all this, at a stage of peculiar relationship between new or emerging independent governments and the established Press. It is a stage distinguished by some heart-searching on both sides.

The Press, therefore, reaches the conclusion that it has to get on terms with new sets of values, with a whole new realisation, and with us. This is a state of mind which we have to watch and which — whenever it seems discreet to try — we like to encourage.

The African leaders realise full well the advantages of having a free and professionally competent Press, carrying out an informative function, a critical function, often an educational function, and with some of its columns of features providing outlet for eccentricity or inventiveness or grief.

But what we look for in all this, as a not unreasonable ambition, is a national Press that is in every sense rooted in the country of its publication, instead of being an organ or an echo of interests overseas.

Basic capital establishment of a modern Press has generally depended, like other industrial enterprises, on investment from overseas. It would be helpful if, without damaging any primary interests, more participation in the Press by local talent could be achieved through the process we call Africanisation.

Public companies independent of the government of the day — could approach their task more effectively if their whole lives and prospects and rewards were welded into the country, and they themselves had to live with the outcome of their proposal or their condemnation.

Of course, apart from finance, this is a problem of personnel. Newspapers and reviews have too often been staffed with recruits from overseas carrying the National Union of Journalists card, and in that sense competent, but some of them having no real interest in or knowledge of Africa — not even knowing the language of the people; some of them thinking a two or three-year contract in Kenya (or wherever it might be) would be amusing; some of them glad to get the job after Fleet Street had waved them good-bye.

The standard of objective reporting — on which comment could properly be based — has therefore been generally low. At times it has even been slanted; splashing a sentence out of context; seizing on a word ill-timed; preferring a story about failure or fear to a story of achievement or endeavour; stressing every day the clash-of-personality angle rather than common purpose and dogged advance.

This is not easy to resolve. We have not — as yet — produced our own flow of experienced journalists that professional editors would be eager to engage . . . but this must come.

Meanwhile, the African leaders might sometimes be forgiven for saying they would prefer some interim inefficiency to what has often been apparent lack of scruple.

Africanisation would be helpful in this sphere, as well, bringing to newspaper production the boon of familiarity — not the familiarity that breeds contempt, but that which makes a watchdog valuable and gets by with only honest mistakes.

Looking to the future in Africa, there is only one constructive line to take. The established newspapers and reviews in East Africa can be confident that they need not be suppressed or be absorbed into some Government propaganda machine. But they will have to find their feet.

What they are facing now is not really a political challenge but a business dilemma. They must have scruples (just as justice must be seen to be done) which must be seen to be maintained. Their coverage of news must be accurate and comprehensive. Their comment must be relevant and fairly based.

They must cater for a new public in Africa, one that has never existed before, a whole new personality on the world stage. And if, as business enterprises, or as editors responsible for conducting such enterprises, they do not meet these basic needs, they will simply be put out of business by people who can and who will.

Lastly, I should really make some mention of the treatment of Africa by the whole of the international Press. I could complain about some occasional treatment; publication of stories about riots that never occurred; about mobs that were never formed in streets that simply don't exist; stories of gloom and despondency, quoting people who carry no weight, or misquoting people who do; comments of correspondents who, after twenty minutes in Africa, write pungent stuff which seeks to turn back the clock of history at a time when the production of our history needs sympathy, sagacity, cold reason, to help it to reality and make it all worth-while.

One point I will make. You, the world Press, must understand that Africa today is something new. Our policies and approaches and determinations — and failings — are not governed by those considerations, or emotional reactions, that are familiar throughout so many countries of the world.

Our lives are not coloured by daily obsessions with East versus West. At a time when the world is old, and the thoughts of the great developed nations have broken through the bounds of space, which could well lead to universal destruction, we in Africa are creating something new.

We are building a society that is pledged not to distort the cherished values of dignity and freedom, is committed to justice and effort and effective independence.

It is a society that has a new discipline to offer, forceful enough in the world councils to repel the manœuvres of two great armed camps, and bring the world back to understanding that the dialectic of both these sides is no substitute for duty to the physical well-being and spiritual contentment of man.

This should be a story of construction and compassion, a story that has never yet appeared in print.

If at any time you think this rates a column, and you'd like to come and cover it, we should place no restriction on where you'd be able to travel, or on whom you'd like to see.

It would give us no measurable pleasure to say that we achieved all this despite the world Press. We'd rather have your shrewd appraisal, and be jolted — at times — by constructive ideas.

In this speech I have tried to show the trend of thought in Africa as it may affect the Press in future. In being frank I have tried to draw attention to the urgency of the situation.

The Press needs to recognise that it has a duty in our society as well as its normal and popular functions and service. It must respond to the challenge before us constructively.

It must recruit and train local people rapidly and it must identify itself with the African aspirations, understand and share our anxieties and join us in the task of nation-building.

It must learn to treat Africa in her own context on the basis of her people's emotions and not in the East-West context or on the basis of foreign interests.

These things it must do, or face the charge of traitor. This is the hard fact that is Africa today and which will, of necessity, shape the relations of tomorrow.

CONFLICT AND NATIONHOOD
The Essentials of Freedom in Africa

Anniversary Address delivered to the Annual General Meeting of the Africa Bureau in London, 30th September, 1963

It is probably still not widely enough appreciated how much is owed to a few organisations and individuals in Britain in building the good relations between the former power and the former colonies. The help given by organisations such as the Africa Bureau to nationalist leaders did much to temper the racial and international animosities which colonialism and settler contacts might have left in their wake. In this speech Mr. Mboya discusses this unique contribution.

I am honoured and privileged to be asked to be the guest of the Africa Bureau. This invitation comes at the most appropriate time for me. As you all know we are in London to attend the final Constitutional Conference before Kenya's Independence. This is therefore a suitable opportunity for me, on my own behalf and on behalf of my country and even other parts of Africa, to thank the Africa Bureau and those of its dedicated workers like the Rev. Michael Scott and Jane Symonds, for the assistance and help they have given to us during our struggle for independence.

In fighting the British colonial regime and the white supremacists, we have been encouraged, strengthened and inspired by the spiritual, moral and human courage, understanding and standards adopted by some of the British people and Members of Parliament such as are represented by the Africa Bureau. It is organisations like the Africa Bureau that have helped us on both sides to emerge out of conflict in friendship ready to forge new relationships based on respect, fairplay and equality. I believe therefore that Africa and our independence struggle as a whole owe something to bodies like the Africa Bureau for their contribution towards our victory for independence.

I further believe that both Africa and Britain owe to such bodies a lot in that their efforts have helped to remove racial hatred and bitterness against the British people. Through their efforts we have come to realise that in fact there are many good white people and that not all British people support colonialism. We have thus been able to confine our struggle only against British colonialism and racial injustice and not against the British as a people or against white people as a whole. As we emerge into independence we come with love for fellow human beings, ready and willing to establish friendship and co-operation with our former colonial masters. We recognise that our countries cannot survive on isolationist policies and that we need the co-operation of other countries and peoples if we are to fulfil our objectives.

This then is one of the lessons of our struggle and the contribution made by those who supported the Africa Bureau and such like other bodies. I say these things because at times during these past years I have heard people who have charged African leaders with all sorts of wild allegations. It has been said by some people that we would victimise and even persecute the white people after independence. This argument has been used to defend tyranny in South Africa and to defend the policies in Southern Rhodesia. To support these charges the case of one irresponsible white journalist or businessman deported by an African state has been blown up and sensationalised as proof by those who did not in any case ever support African freedom at any time. But look at the other side of the picture. New African states have given Europeans full citizenship, right of ownership of land and property, personal protection, equality before the law and in employment and salaries. This is despite the bitter experiences we have gone through and despite the fact that millions of our people still suffer at the hands of European supremacists, in South Africa, Southern Rhodesia and the Portuguese territories — not to speak of the persecution of Negroes at the hands of white racial extremists in America and some of the indignities suffered by coloured people in Britain.

I am happy that we have been able to defeat colonialism and at the same time to crush possible racial bitterness within ourselves. Some African leaders have said that our struggle for freedom is twice blessed. That is that in winning freedom we release ourselves from hate and from an inferiority complex. The second blessing is that we release our colonial masters from the sin of suppressing fellow human beings and give them the freedom and moral capacity to contribute once again to the general effort to secure human rights throughout the world.

I have already referred to the continued oppression of Africans in Southern Rhodesia, South Africa and Portuguese territories. Some of you will congratulate yourselves for the fact that the Central African Federation breaks up formally in December this year. Nyasaland becomes independent in July next year while Northern Rhodesia is well set on the way towards a one-man one-vote democratic government next year too. Of the three territories, Southern Rhodesia remains in a precarious position; Winston Field now thinks he too must have a date for independence soon.

The difference which must be pointed out to Winston Field is that whereas Dr. Banda and Mr. Kaunda speak for the people of Malawi and Zambia respectively, he (Field) does not speak for Zimbabwe. The question is, for whom does Winston Field speak? If indeed he feels confident he represents the genuine wishes of the majority of the people in Southern Rhodesia then we would all of us support him in his claim for independence if he will agree that his leadership is put to the test through a one-man one-vote election. This is the procedure that has been used by the British Government in every other African territory. It was used to ascertain Nyerere's support in Tanganyika, Obote's in Uganda, Kenyatta's in Kenya and Banda's in Nyasaland. It will be used in January to ascertain Kaunda's standing in Northern Rhodesia before he can get a date for independence. Why should the same procedure not be used in the case of Winston Field?

Only the British Parliament can pass the necessary Act giving Southern Rhodesia its independence and therefore we find it ironical for any one in Her Majesty's Government to plead that they have no effective authority over Southern Rhodesia. To refuse to take appropriate action to ensure that independence for Southern Rhodesia would have meaning for all its people would not only be to abdicate a clear responsibility on the part of the British Government, but it would also definitely affect the relations between the British Government and the African States who are now members of the Commonwealth. In the face of any betrayal by the British in Southern Rhodesia the African States would find it difficult to stay in the Commonwealth without being accused in Africa of condoning the betrayal of their own brothers.

There are those who regard the giving of independence to African territories in Central and East Africa as a policy of abandonment of kith and kin. Such persons are clearly ignorant of the new forces in the world and also ignorant of the true interests of those white people who have decided to make Africa their home. Any policy which encourages racialists will not safeguard white interests in Africa. Instead it will destroy the basis upon which new relations need to be established to ensure safeguards for all people in the new nations. Nothing can be a stronger safeguard for the white community in Africa than a genuine and willing acceptance of white citizens by Africans as equals in the new nation.

As far as South Africa and the Portuguese territories are concerned, I am led to the conclusion that the world is too preoccupied with polite diplomacy to do very much to help. These two countries are impervious to world opinion, Christian or moral teaching, to be bothered. In fact, they have come to regard resolutions at the United Nations and threats of economic sanctions as a regular but harmless game in which some people and nations indulge without any intention to act. It appears that only one alternative is left and that is — force and violence.

The brutality and finality of the road taken by the South African Government is one which can only lead to destruction. They have gone well beyond the point of 'no return'. Only the world can save them from themselves. The African states will not succeed merely by closing their airports or seaports to South African airlines or ships. Nor is a trade boycott by African states unsupported by effective economic sanctions by other nations going to bring South Africa to her knees.

These measures are important and they show that we are willing to sacrifice even our own economic interests in aid of the struggle for freedom in South Africa. But to avoid violence the other nations must be prepared to act. American banks and businessmen, British business-men and industrialists and even some Eastern and Western European countries must be prepared to act and not just talk. Trade with South Africa is in fact support for apartheid. It keeps the Nationalist Party in power and helps to secure the suppression of Africans. No explanation can be advanced to justify these business activities except in terms of the selfish interests of those involved.

What does it matter, if some of our own people in South Africa or Portuguese territories suffer a little or 'die a little' as a price for complete freedom? As it is, they are already suffering and even dying while the world powers continue their casual and carefree attitude. Britain can play a very real part in this campaign against South Africa and

Portugal. It is not the question of 'centuries of friendship' with Portugal that is involved. It is the question of human rights and Britain's future relations with the new nations that must be considered. To continue to sell or send arms to South Africa or Portugal in any form or under any excuse must provoke African nations and expose Britain's hypocrisy on the South African and Portuguese issue. There may be those who will accuse me of preaching violence in this speech, I must remind them of the words by John Bright in 1866 and merely reiterate that any long delayed or long continued injustice, provokes the employment of force to obtain redress.

Every African state today accepts as a duty to help and assist other territories to gain their freedom. This is why for us the South African or Portuguese territories must remain the concern of the whole of Africa. We reject completely the plea that the treatment and conditions of people in South Africa based on race segregation can ever be a domestic affair of the Republic. It is not possible for Africans to feel completely free or to enjoy respect all over the world while any part of Africa remains under colonial rule or European domination. With complete freedom of Africa will come the respect and dignity of coloured people elsewhere in the world. This accounts for our interest in the treatment of Negroes in America and coloureds in Britain and elsewhere.

Freedom, or independence, is not an end in itself. It cannot mean merely political sovereignty with a national flag. Independence is for us the means by which to ensure self-expression in social, cultural as well as economic fields. As I have already stated elsewhere, independence must be followed by efforts in economic reconstruction and political development. The African nations do not need to be reminded of the great responsibility that must come with independence. It is not only right that the responsibility for development should pass on to the shoulders of the African nations, but it is true that the only way to ensure that development has meaning to the man in the street is for the government and other agencies to be those of the people, responsible to the people.

Sometimes this point is lost sight of by critics of African independence who would have us believe that economic development would be best achieved under continued, 'stable' colonial government. It must be recognised that no colonial government can be stable in this twentieth century. Long years of experience under colonial rule have convinced us that economic development under such a system cannot reflect the genuine interests of the people, nor can it secure the response and active support of the people.

For Africa to develop rapidly it is necessary to capture the imagination of the people themselves and to have their full co-operation in the various programmes. The new nations must re-examine and review as a matter of urgency the entire economic theories and institutions developed during colonial days. At that time for example the emphasis in many cases was based on extractive economic activities. In some countries mineral extraction became the only interest of the colonial powers or investors to the complete neglect of agriculture and other industrial possibilities. In other countries interest centred around agricultural cash crops to the neglect of other forms of production or industrial possibilities. In every case social services, i.e. Education and Health, lagged behind and were always a matter of secondary interest. In every case the potential of the African as a consumer, producer and skilled craftsman was ignored, played down or left without incentive.

A new government in Africa must revise these attitudes and in many cases replace them with dynamic and positive policies. Some of our friends become very upset and critical when we try to give new emphasis to our economic programmes. They try to put a label on what we do and ask why we do not in every case just continue from where the colonial power left off. There are those who seem to think that because we seek to change some of the economic theories and institutions we do not recognise or welcome the need for investments from abroad. On the contrary, there is complete recognition of the need for investment from abroad and in every African state no effort has been spared to induce more investment even with greater protection than was possible during the colonial days.

There are two points that do not seem to have been brought out in previous discussions of this subject. The first one is the resistance one meets in the attitude of permanent officials and civil servants left behind at the time of independence. These people have traditional ideas about things which need rehabilitation before they can fit into the new mood and pace adopted by the new governments. This is met through the different civil service training programmes and Africanisation schemes that we adopt. Although the civil service should be independent, it would be highly dangerous if it did not respond to the new policies and moods of independence. Sometimes, the efforts of the new governments to secure this rehabilitation are mistaken by Africa's critics for attempts to involve civil servants in politics. The second area where rehabilitation is necessary is that on the part of the international agencies which we must deal with in the future. These agencies, e.g. World Bank, Commonwealth Development Corporation, United States Assistance for International Development, etc., are sometimes too committed to old ideas and theories about Africa's economy. This commitment often results in ill-conceived report and analysis or even disagreement on the merits of the projects proposed by the new African governments.

To summarise these new attitudes and to assert the new trend of thinking on the future of Africa's economy, many African states have now adopted as their goal the creation of an economy based on African Socialism. It is a term which has led to many debates and enquiries and which remains to be defined precisely in writing. In brief, it reflects and implies the development of a society based on our own ideas and concepts, with our own relations between man and man, between labour and profit and the attitude to work or production and its results.

Some of the ideological views in Europe are foreign to us and in any case they are part of European history. They have changed and developed or assumed new dimensions according to changes or attitudes in Europe. In Africa these ideologies are sometimes irrelevant and in conflict with our traditional and cultural relations. The adoption of the policy of African Socialism is not merely an attempt to be different from everyone. It is not based on any inward-looking policies but on sound, meaningful and positive attitudes that can best promote the spirit and atmosphere within which the urgent task of economic reconstruction can take place.

Africa is well aware that this next phase in our struggle is by far the most important and laborious. It will need patience and restraint and it may even mean failures at times. But this remains the test of our resolve to build a nation. No people have succeeded in building a nation except with their own effort and sweat, with discipline and resolution. This is what we too must do. There is no short cut and we cannot hand over this responsibility to anyone outside Africa.

Despite these very urgent responsibilities Africa is unable to ignore her international responsibilities. Immediately on independence, we take a seat in the United Nations, we have to compete for the markets of the world and in the event of a war we would not be excused the repercussions that accompany such conflicts. Although many people profess to us their sympathy for the under-developed countries we have come to learn that we cannot depend on such sympathy. In fact, neither at the United Nations nor in the world markets is anyone prepared to give Africa a probationary period. An African country is expected to master the intricate international financial, trading and diplomatic system and language, from the very moment a country becomes independent at midnight on the night preceding the date of independence. . . . In fact if you do not, then you are used as an example of the reason why Africa should not be free. No one seems to understand or even suggest that these are circumstances which call for understanding on the part of the older nations!

I do not say these things in an attempt to plead for sympathy. I am pointing out that we have to know the world and accept our part fully without looking back.

I am saying also that when any state becomes independent she assumes obligations and responsibilities similar to those expected of the older nations and cannot agree to be treated as a junior partner in world affairs. I am saying that we cannot agree that world peace is a monopoly of the big powers and finally I am saying that the new nations in order to make an impact must aim at economic independence, and refuse to exchange one form of colonialism for a new form. In the days of Secretary of State Dulles it was a sin to adopt the policy of positive non-aligment or neutrality. Today this policy is in fact accepted and sometimes actively promoted by the big powers. If Africa is to influence world opinion and effectively to safeguard her interests and independence then it is right that we should stand by this policy in the future.

In concluding my speech, I should refer briefly to Kenya and East Africa. As our conference is still going on I cannot refer to our discussions on the constitution except to say that we are concerned as a government that the constitution should fulfil two main aims. It should be workable and flexible to stand the strains of independence. It should be an instrument that assures unity and removes contention, based on faith and confidence in the future of the Kenya nation. The atmosphere under which we met in London at last year's Lancaster House Conference was false — full of deliberately generated fears and leadership claims. There was panic and exaggeration of possible tribal conflicts. We ended up with a constitution based on a massive compromise and arbitration by the Secretary of State. Since the elections in May this year, Kenya has a stable and popular government. Tribal and racial fears are fast disappearing and we are confident that economic recovery is well on the way. The people of Kenya of all races and tribes look at the future with hope, confidence and great expectations. We are resolved not to disappoint them in this. Many Europeans have decided to stay and will take on Kenya citizenship in December, this year. This applies to many of the Asians too. We have managed to create a new atmosphere in the country and our Prime Minister, Mzee Kenyatta, has proved to the cynics that despite previous propaganda, he is giving effective leadership to Kenya.

Kenya is committed to all the resolutions passed at the recent Conference of African States held at Addis Ababa. At home and together with our neighbours we are working hard for the establishment of an East African Federation.* We are convinced that this is a necessary step both for economic and political reasons. We are confident that it will be possible to establish the Federation very soon after the Independence of Kenya and Zanzibar.

* Although political federation has not been realised, economic co-operation has been maintained and strengthened by the establishment of the East African Community.

AFRICAN UNITY AND THE O.A.U.

Article in the East Africa Journal, *October, 1964*

I was fortunate to be included in the Kenya delegation to the O.A.U. Conference held at Cairo from 17th to 23rd July, 1964. For individual participants like myself it was a rare privilege to be able to meet and hear practically all of Africa's great leaders. It reminded me of another equally important occasion when African leaders met in Accra, Ghana in 1958 for the first two conferences of African leaders to take place on the African soil. In April 1958 leaders of nine African states met to plan African unity and exchange views on the role of independent African states in the struggle for Africa's liberation. They also discussed the steps to be taken towards harmonization of policy — especially on foreign affairs and at the United Nations. From this conference emerged resolutions that have since helped to accelerate the liberation of dependent territories and bring about practical steps towards pan-African Unity. It was agreed to form the African group at the United Nations.

The April Conference was followed by another historical conference the same year. At Accra in December 1958 inspired by the earlier conference, African leaders of political parties, trade unions and other organisations met for the first time. This was a nationalist convention and as its chairman I was privileged to observe at close quarters the dedication of the leaders to the struggle for liberation. From this conference every leader went home assured that he was no longer alone in the struggle and that there could be no doubt in the ultimate victory that lay ahead. Every leader went away committed to pan-Africanism and pledged to work for the unity of the African continent. The conference established the All-African Peoples' Conference as a permanent body with a secretariat in Accra. It was decided to meet regularly each year and a steering committee was set up. The A.A.P.C. was a non-governmental organisation and included ruling parties as well as opposition parties, it also included some parties in exile who seemed to want to use it as a platform against some of the independent African states. The period after 1958 and until 1963 was one of intense activity in many ways. But from the point of view of the 1958 conferences and pan-African unity four things stand out.

1. The liberation movement gathered momentum and in 1960 more than ten African territories gained their independence! Leaders like Lumumba became household names in Africa and the world conceded the birth of a new Africa. This new Africa was impatient with imperialism and European domination and there was increasing determination to gain independence at home and to convert the whole world to support the struggle for freedom.

2. The A.A.P.C. conference continued but its permanent body was quickly overtaken by events. Independent Africa quickly required some responsible voice through its new governments. The use of A.A.P.C. by dissident groups working against other African governments, made the A.A.P.C. suspect in the eyes of such governments. Instead of receiving the full support of the African states the A.A.P.C. was suspected and regarded as an agent of one or two African states. Some speeches made from its platform and some of the methods used in organising its conferences tended to justify these allegations. However, it was to be expected that as more territories became free there would be a need for an organisation of African Governments and statesmen to replace the group of nationalists and opposition leaders. Governments had to ensure that resolutions passed would reflect well on their image taking into account their responsibilities to their own people at home, their responsibility at the U.N. and their relations with foreign countries. The A.A.P.C. was clearly not the body to perform this function and as a result its influence began to diminish. In fact even today, the A.A.P.C. has not been formally dissolved but everyone assumes that it has served its purpose. We have seen the end of pan-African conferences of the A.A.P.C. type and from now on will see more of the governmental type.

3. At the April 1958 conference in Accra the heads of state did not decide on any formal machinery for consultation or the actual basis upon which to build pan-African Unity. The 1958 All African Peoples' Conference on the other hand discussed the outline of the structure for pan-African Unity. It resolved that in view of various problems,

i.e. geography, communications, different economic structures and the big job of consolidating independence in the immediate post-independence period and the task of economic reconstruction, the movement towards an eventual pan-African government should be by way of regional organisations. Five regions were proposed, viz: Northern, Eastern, Western, Central and Southern Africa. This decision was made in the realisation of the problems of unity but also in the belief that issues on which there was unity far outweighed those on which there were differences. In other words unity as a goal was accepted right from the outset. The only matter for consideration was the methods of achieving unity. In the period immediately after these 1958 conferences there were various steps taken towards the unity of the different African states. There was the proclamation of the Guinea/Ghana Union. This was followed later by the proclamation of the Guinea/Ghana/Mali Union. There were the various attempts which produced different groupings such as the Casablanca Group, the Monrovia Group, the Brazzaville/Malagasy Group and even the Magreb Group. These last few years might be regarded as Africa's period in the search for unity. It reveals Africa's complete commitment to pan-African unity. It reveals dedication and resolution in the effort towards unity. Of course it has also revealed that not so many of our foreign 'friends' are really for African unity. The African states demonstrated without exception that they did not regard their own independence as enough in facing the world. They believed that Africa's influence could only be felt in unity. They saw this as the only way of being able to act effectively in dealing with problems of economic reconstruction at home.

4. At the December, 1958 conference an important meeting took place but was not sufficiently reported at the time. This was the meeting of trade union leaders. It was agreed to convene a conference of trade union leaders later on to discuss the future of African workers. Their role in the independence struggle and their role thereafter. In the period since 1948 several conferences were convened. Groups developed and affiliation to international trade union centres was brought forward as the main issue in the unity of the trade union movement. The fact is that this too was part of this general search for unity. Trade unions are sensitive to attitudes and policies of their individual governments

and countries and before some pan-African machinery for the organisation of the relation between the states emerges complete trade union unity is impossible.

I have mentioned these four points because they have a bearing on subsequent events and on any discussion of the Organisation of African Unity. It is important to note that these activities and the determination of the African states to find unity led to the historic conference of all the heads of African states and government at Addis Ababa, Ethiopia, in May 1963. At this conference the O.A.U. was formed. It was decided to abandon the various groups and to use the O.A.U. instead as the vehicle for promoting African unity.

The first Ordinary session of the Heads of State and Government of the Organisation of African Unity was held in Cairo on 17th July to 23rd July, 1964. Apart from the Heads of State of Ivory Coast, Upper Volta and the Congo (Leopoldville) all the others attended in person, the King of Libya being represented by the Crown Prince. This itself shows the seriousness with which the organisation is regarded by every African state. The different groups were dissolved and O.A.U. began to play an active part almost immediately after the Addis Ababa Conference. During the first year of its existence, O.A.U. did not have a budget or permanent secretariat. But the Emperor Haile Selassie made a significant contribution by providing a temporary secretariat and donating funds to cover the first year's expenditure. This great son of Africa has proved one of the greatest statesmen and a consistent worker for unity in Africa.

The work of this session must be considered in the context of the activities that took place in a year since the Addis Ababa conference. Although a permanent secretariat had not been established, important structural decisions were taken. In addition to establishing the Council of Ministers, that is ministers of foreign affairs and the committee of nine charged with the task of giving asistance to freedom movements with a view to accelerating the liberation of areas still under colonial rule, it was decided to set up a number of specialised commissions. These would deal with the special subjects of areas of interest. In the course of the year the number of commissions established included the one of jurists; labour and social affairs; defence and military affairs; scientific research; sanitation and health, etc. It is the intention that through these commissions African states under O.A.U. will come together to share experiences, exchange views, agree to harmonize policies and to pool resources and plan joint action. At the Cairo Conference much urgency was given to the need to take immediate steps to improve communications between African states. At the end a special commission for communications and transport was set up.

Clearly this approach and the decisions taken indicate a businesslike approach to the question of unity. The charter of the O.A.U. emphasises the sovereignty of all member states and the fact that no state may interfere in the internal affairs of another member state. By the setting up of the commissions this provision of the charter is preserved while at the same time facilitating greater scope for consultation. Although the O.A.U. is not itself a government of Africa the commissions could lead to a state where on practically every issue there could be an O.A.U. decision to guide or even commit all member states. The manner in which this is being done does not permit for the cheap propaganda which accompanied some of the previous decisions taken in Africa in the pre-O.A.U. days.

One of the issues which occupies the minds of O.A.U. and which is the subject of discussion in the council of Ministers concerns Africa's position *vis-à-vis* the Cold War. Many member states have no military power and defence from external threats would be possible only if an African military high command were established. Such a command could also help to establish an African policing force that could be used to help a member state in difficulty at home, e.g. the present Congo (Leopoldville) situation. Such a decision requires careful consideration. It has many political repercussions and it was obvious that many countries while accepting the objective, felt the details needed careful consideration. This was another proof of the businesslike approach of the O.A.U. to African unity. It did not take time, however, for the member states to agree on a general resolution calling for the denuclearisation of Africa. This means we have adopted a self-denying ordinance not only to refuse others to use Africa to test or produce nuclear weapons but not to begin to manufacture such weapons ourselves even with the aid of friends from outside Africa. But the member states pointed out that this did not mean a denial by Africa from sharing in the benefits of peaceful uses of atomic energy. In fact, Africa would welcome this to help conquer her deserts and forests, improve her soil, increase her water supply, etc.

Perhaps the most significant achievement of the year for the O.A.U. was the positive part played by African statesmen in resolving the explosive border fighting between Morocco and Algeria and between Somalia and Ethiopia. The significance of this event lies in the fact that in the absence of the O.A.U. these incidents would surely have been referred to the United Nations Security Council. In that event they would have ceased to be African problems. They would even have ceased to be simple border disputes. They would have become world problems and that immediately draws in the Cold War. For once African problems were resolved away from Europe and away from Cold War influences, encouraged by this achievement, the Heads of State and Government resolved unanimously to set up permanent machinery. They approved a protocol of conciliation and arbitration. To this new machinery all future disputes would be referred instead of being referred to the United Nations. This is a most decisive step on the road towards African unity. Of course the conference recognised the potential menace of border disputes. A resolution was accordingly passed pledging all member states to accept and recognise the borders bequeathed to us by the departing colonial powers and to desist from expansionist tendencies.

The work of the Committee of Nine was examined and this led to the exchanges between President Nkrumah of Ghana and President Mwalimu Nyerere of the United Republic of Tanganyika and Zanzibar. There is no doubt that this exchange brought out some very important developments in the search for unity. For one thing it revealed that a stage had been reached when African states will not be dictated by mere emotionalism or slogans. It further revealed the sincerity of African leaders in their commitment to unity. There is agreement that unity will not come about if people try to run away from reality and appeal merely to emotion. Whereas the ultimate objective is on all-African government, this must be approached carefully and deliberately and the conference decided, in fact, that this process did not have any special or new machinery. It would come out of the discussions already taking place in the different commissions and at regular meetings of the Heads of State and Government. There was even agreement that one of the ways it could come about is through regional unity. Although the foreign press tried to make something out of it, this incident helped to bring out the point of maturity reached in the search for unity. It no longer was a delicate plant to be protected from the winds of argument and debate. It is strong enough to stand scrutiny.

One weakness of the Committee of Nine was that according to the original decision member states could only contribute to the Freedom Fund if they so wished. It was decided to remedy this and to make it mandatory for each state to contribute according to a formula laid down.

One question of importance that was never discussed formally was that of the developments in the Congo. The Congo is a member of O.A.U. and she could not be debarred from attending the conference. According to the charter, O.A.U. must respect the right of the Congo people to decide on their leaders and on who should represent them at O.A.U. conferences. Despite this it was clear that Tshombe's decision to attend would, as the saying goes, have put the cat among the pigeons. Fortunately for everyone he did not come. But one or two countries took the opportunity to restate these facts from the conference rostrum and the hope was expressed that in this case time may help to heal the wounds. But there was clear concern about the future of the Congo. Would Tshombe really succeed ? What about Gizenga ? These questions were often asked in private discussions between delegates. But there was no clear answer. Today we know one or two answers but the situation remains the same and Africa's anxiety continues.

Looking at the future, the next year will see even more activity. Resolutions were passed which require continuing attention by the African group at the United Nations. Some committees were set up to look into different questions. And the Labour Commission was asked to study and report on the question of trade union development in Africa. In the colonial scene Angola, Mozambique, Southern Rhodesia and the Protectorates will receive greater assistance. Measures are to be taken to discuss the future of the Protectorates after they achieve independence. They will need protection against any threat from South Africa. A special department is to be set up at the Secretariat to help intensify the campaign for sanctions against South Africa.

The Permanent Secretariat is to be set up at Addis Ababa with Diallo Telli of Guinea as Secretary General and four assistants one each from Kenya, Nigeria, Algeria and Dahomey. The next conference will be held in Accra next year and meantime the Council of

Ministers will carry on its task of consolidating O.A.U. gains in the search for unity and exploring new steps that could be taken to increase the areas of unity. Here is a body that the world cannot afford to ignore. Africa is at last coming into her own.

When this article was written the O.A.U. was little more than a year old. Since that time it has done much to fulfil the hopes that were expected of it. The Organisation has fostered the unity of its name. Certainly there are differences of outlook and policy among the independent states of Africa but the O.A.U. has prevented the entrenchment of ideological blocs in Africa which could have provided an entrée for Cold War and other Big Power interference.

With the support of sister African states through the O.A.U. the Congo (Kinshasa) has entered a more stable period. The O.A.U. was active in getting rid of the white mercenaries who had been such a scourge. One field which has not been much publicised is that of refugees. A great deal of humanitarian work has been carried out with the Organisation's support in dealing with this problem.

Mediation by the O.A.U., especially through the good offices of President Kaunda of Zambia, ended the dispute between Kenya and the Somali Republic. The O.A.U. has helped to relieve similar tensions between Ethiopia and Somalia.

The practical success of the O.A.U. is all the more noteworthy in that, unlike most regional groupings it is not dominated by one or two great powers able to impose their will.

THE ROLE OF THE CIVIL SERVICE
IN DEVELOPING COUNTRIES

Address to the East African Staff College,* Nairobi, 25th November, 1965

At the very outset I would like to declare my support for the establishment of the East African Staff College on a permanent basis. I think you agree with me that we in East Africa have produced political leaders of international repute. But we have yet to produce administrators of international standing. The main reason for this obvious gap is that we have had limited facilities and experience in the art of producing administrators. The record of our African administrators who have been promoted to positions of great responsibility since Independence has proved without a doubt that they are just as capable as any other administrators. I am convinced that given adequate facilities and opportunity we could produce top-ranking administrators before long. This is the main reason why I support the East African Staff College idea whole-heartedly.

The importance of the civil service as a whole cannot be over-emphasised. In our own lifetime, indeed in post-war European history we have seen countries suffering from a perpetual change of governments. Curiously enough in some of those countries the administration has remained stable and effective. The credit for this stability is rightly attributable to the civil service. Quietly and conscientiously the civil service has governed while the politicians squabbled and even exchanged physical blows in parliament.

---

* The East African Staff College was established under the East African Common Services Organisation (now the East African Community). It brings together local people in managerial, administrative and executive positions and in public life to courses designed to help them in their jobs with a better understanding of East Africa.

In Kenya there is also the Kenya Institute of Administration which often organises similar courses. The K.I.A. has been used to bring together civil servants, Members of Parliament and leaders of public opinion to get to know one another, discuss policy problems and create a development conscious leadership in the country. These two institutions are complementary.

I have chosen to address this seminar on the role of the civil service in developing countries for two main reasons. First, I would like to clarify some points which, in my opinion, have brought about unnecessary conflict between the civil service and politicians. Second, I believe the civil service has a significant role to play in developing countries like ours.

My observations will be directed mainly towards the civil service in Kenya. I have no doubt, however, that most of my observations are equally applicable to other countries represented at this seminar.

At this juncture I should point out that most of our civil servants have assumed responsibility at a considerable disadvantage. It is an open secret that during the colonial regime politicians like myself and civil servants were at loggerheads. Provincial and district administrators regarded politicians as intruders who had come into the scene to 'educate' the masses to revolt against authority and to remove civil servants from their jobs. Thus they thought that their task was to oppose politicians. The politicians, in turn, regarded the colonial administrators as antagonistic perpetrators of colonialism and domination of the governed. As one would expect there was a great deal of conflict between the two groups. Over the period both sides regarded each other with suspicion and distrust.

Unfortunately the conflict between the civil service and politicians is one of the colonial relics which we seem to have inherited. By and large the senior civil servant is regarded as a bigoted and privileged individual who is not really interested in the welfare of his country as such. Not so long ago a Member of Parliament in Kenya urged that civil servants should take their orders from politicians irrespective of their rank and position. This was obviously intended to cut the civil servant down to size. Others have advocated a substantial cut in the salaries of civil servants whom they regard as extravagantly paid. I could quote a number of other instances to demonstrate the conflict between civil servants and politicians. Some civil servants on the other hand, continue to look upon an elected representative as an intruder, with whom he cannot co-operate or share confidence.

I submit that such a conflict is most unhealthy and detrimental to the development effort. For neither the politician nor the civil servant can give of his best independently of the other. The politician should count on the civil servant to implement the Government's programmes in the district. On the other hand, the civil servant should count on the politician to support and help him in educating the people to carry out such programmes and protect him from undue public criticism. I believe that it is only in such an atmosphere of mutual trust and confidence that the politician and the civil servant can render their best service to the country.

It appears to me that the main source of conflict between politicians and civil servants is lack of a clear definition of roles. Both have an important part to play in their society. I regard their roles as complementary rather than competitive. Unless their roles are clearly defined, however, conflict is bound to arise.

As the elected representative the politician is the mouthpiece of his constituency as well as a legislator. Although ideally he should not promote sectional interests at the expense of the national interests it is an open secret that the desire for being re-elected at the following election might interfere with his objective judgment considerably. Indeed there might be times when the politicians might disagree with and even oppose Government policy openly.

The civil servant, on the other hand, is supposed to be a loyal and disciplined servant. The civil servant is expected to promote and implement Government policy at all times. This position must not be influenced by the nature of the party in power or his own feelings. Should the civil servant feel strongly against a certain policy then he has only one course open to him, namely to resign. He should never attempt to meddle in politics for in so doing he steps on the toes of the politician and conflict is inevitable. Thus the civil servant is expected to remain objective at all times and to promote Government policy energetically.

The senior civil servant, however, should not be a passive sponge, a routine implementor of Government policy. By and large the civil servant is better educated than many of the politicians in his area. He should be able to contribute in evolving the social, economic and political machinery best suited to his country. He must be dynamic and an innovator full of new ideas. It is his duty to persuade the politician who, in turn, would propagate new ideas and, if successful, in convincing his colleagues, translate them into Government policy.

In Kenya, the Government has decided to preserve the distinction between the civil service and politics. Our civil service might be described as 'neutral' by which we mean that civil servants are not permitted to participate actively in politics. But what is the civil service neutral from? Neutrality is a negative force which implies non-participation in a given course of action. I must point out that the civil servant is expected to further objectives of Government, to become fully committed to Government policies and personally involved in the promotion of the aims and aspirations of his society. He is, to that extent, not neutral at all.

What the tradition of political neutrality seeks to establish is the professionalism of the civil service. The civil servant is expected to make an objective appraisal of a given project or programme, to consider its feasibility, the cost/benefit ratio, the choice of the best means of achieving the objective and many other variables which go into the making of the project programme. These are the aspects of policy formulation on which the civil servant must concentrate. After making his appraisal the civil servant is expected to advise the politician who, in turn, subjects the advice to such considerations as the preference of the people between projects and the determination of priorities. These are essentially political considerations.

Thus, the civil servant is not neutral in the sense of taking no interest in the political activity of his country. As the advisor to the politician on the technical aspects of the country's programme he himself must not only be well informed but also personally involved in the hopes and aspirations of his country. It is worth noting that during the colonial regime the civil servant spared no efforts in the promotion of the British Empire. Indeed many civil servants earned such titles as Member of the Order of the British Empire for their distinguished service in the promotion of the Empire. It is my sincere hope that the names of our civil servants will figure prominently in the history of our countries on account of their outstanding service to the nations.

The civil service has been frequently accused of the 'island mentality', an attitude of detachment from the rest of the society. This affinity to clubs has tended to create a class that strikes the observer as distinct. I must make it clear that in Kenya the civil service is an integral part, and an important one at that, of the society at large. As such it must of necessity have the same objectives as the rest of the society. In the case of Kenya, it is important for the senior civil servants to understand and to be able to interpret to other people the objectives as defined in the K.A.N.U. Manifesto, the Sessional Paper on African

Socialism, the constitution of the Republic and important policy statements by the President and the Government.

I must confess that I have been horrified by the manifestations of colonial relics in our society. In some places including Government offices and institutions, I have seen expatriates and well-dressed, educated Africans given preference over the less fortunate, uneducated men and women who have, at times, been waiting for hours. This is clearly contrary to the objectives of our society.

As our President said recently, 'We may be underdeveloped and our people may walk barefoot but we are a proud people — proud of our heritage, our traditions and ancestry'. We must always remember this. Indeed it is impossible to promote political equality, social justice and human dignity in a society in which preferential treatment is given to an individual on account of his colour, possessions or education or some other quality. We must always remember that whether a man is an important dignitary or an uneducated peasant, he has his rightful pride as a free citizen of Kenya. He must be treated with respect. I submit that it is only when we observe this cardinal principle that we can claim to respect ourselves fully. Others will respect us automatically. The civil servant has an unlimited scope for setting an example in his daily dealings with the public.

As I pointed out earlier one of the objectives of our society is to provide high and growing *per capita* incomes. I am convinced that in a developing country this desirable goal can only be achieved in a planned economy which seeks to derive maximum advantage from the available resources, both domestic and foreign. Implementation of development plans calls for a sound and efficient civil service. Our society has no room for the civil servant who is idle or unable to carry out his duties efficiently on account of drunkenness. Nor do we have room for the civil servant who misuses public property or embezzles public funds. We must rid our civil service of such misfits. Indeed we are determined to have civil servants who are fully committed to the attainment of our declared objectives and the promotion of our national hopes and objectives.

As I tour the various districts of Kenya, I become increasingly aware of the decisive role the civil servants can play in a developing country such as ours. Many times local people are full of enthusiasm and energy. They are ready to work and want to share in building the nation. Here the civil servant can be an 'ideal man'. He must help find something useful in the area to which to channel these before the enthusiasm dies. Then there are cases where people are engaged in a project — they need encouragement and to feel that Government notices their work. The civil servant must convince them of the importance attached to their work. Too often people think of development in terms of a large project costing so much money: sometimes they think it is a question of new industries and many times they ask how much money has been voted for development in their areas. But development could mean introducing a new maize seed and fertilisers in an area or shifting from potato to beans production, introducing modern methods of planting the same seeds or organising the tractor units on hire basis. These measures create higher productivity and attract more development. In the final analysis the initiative on the part of the civil servant rather than the local politician can decide whether or not an area will develop. Each civil servant has to accept this challenge. I have often asked our civil servants in the districts as to how many of them already have nicknames. By this way our people express approval or diapproval of a person. It also helps to identify the preoccupation of that Government officer in their eyes.

My address would be incomplete if I failed to mention that the civil service is expected to play an important role in the promotion of national unity. Tribalism which developed by leaps and bounds during the colonial era is still a separatist force in our society. Indeed in some cases pride of the tribe has superceded pride of the nation. This is obviously incompatible with our idea of a nation. We are all duty bound to promote national unity. The civil servant has had much greater opportunity for mixing with people from other tribes and understanding them. He should set an example in condemning tribalism and the petty thinking from which it is derived.

THE IMPACT OF MODERN INSTITUTIONS ON THE EAST AFRICAN

Address to the East African Academy Fourth Symposium, at Makerere University College, Kampala, 19th September, 1966

The reaction of people to rapid, social and economic change has long been a concern of a subject for study by anthropologist, sociologist, psychologist and, perhaps to a lesser extent, economist and historian. The literature on this subject is, I am sure, very large indeed. Certainly the Industrial Revolution in England itself prompted scores of such studies and other studies have followed that Revolution as it has spread throughout the world. Now we are concerned both as scientists and men of practical affairs, with the impact of its modern counterpart on people throughout the developing nations. I have been asked to speak to-day, as a man involved in creating change, on an even smaller portion of this problem, namely, 'The Impact of Modern Institutions on the East African'.

The larger, indeed world-wide, problem of which this is a part is the creation of effective change. Effective change is in my view the resolution of two often opposing forces — an initial innovation and the reaction of people and society to that innovation. The nature of the change which emerges will depend on the characteristics of the initial innovation, the type of social reaction which takes place, and the way in which the two are permitted to interact.

The world of today has become adept at creating initial innovations. Indeed, technical research which lies at the root of so many of these innovations has itself been institutionalised. The production of technological innovation is today a massive industry, much of it conducted by government organisations because of the large injections of capital required and the uncertain nature of the outcome. None can doubt, however, that the large-scale organisation of technical research has produced the basis for enormous and world-wide social and economic change. We are only on the verge of the new technological revolution and it is not yet possible even to visualise its extent and implications. The splitting of the atom, computer technology, automation, space travel, communications satellites, transistors and laser beams are only the visible portions of the potential changes that are nearly upon us.

As these technological innovations are introduced, the nature of economic and social life must change. It is indeed unfortunate that the massive expenditures on technological research are not being matched in even a small way by expenditures on social research. The painful dislocations and adaptations associated with rapid change might then be reduced, the path of change smoothed, and the rate of genuine progress, which is not always synonymous with change, accelerated.

The adjustment to change is therefore a world problem and the present manifestations of it are only an indication of the scale the problem is likely to assume in the future. If innovations are introduced too rapidly and without an appreciation of the problem of social adaptation this resistance may solidify, the innovations may be rejected and effective change may be nil. This social resistance to change can be documented throughout the world. The difficulties the British are having in increasing productivity, the resistance of many trade unions in the United States to automation, and the problems encountered in introducing collective farming in the U.S.S.R. are well-known examples.

Social research on a large-scale is necessary if means are to be found to overcome social inertia and make effective change both acceptable and desirable. The alternative of forcing change on people is not an acceptable solution. Such a procedure displays no regard for human dignity and social justice and in the extreme can lead to social and moral bankruptcy. Certainly the social upheaval accompanying the Industrial Revolution had undesirable characteristics that might have been avoided with better social research and preparation. But this is a hypothesis that will, I think, be tested again and again, and in country after country throughout the world, over the next several decades. Suffice it to say that we in East Africa are aware of the problem and are determined that effective change and economic progress here will not entail the avoidable social costs and human suffering that have marked the history of so many of the countries of the world. How successful we in government will be in our efforts will depend in no small measure on the advice and research of those of you who are social scientists.

The modern institutions — by institutions I mean the methods, both formal and informal, by which social behaviour is organised — that are being created in East Africa are partly borrowed, partly indigenous, and partly original innovations. Those that are planned — and certainly not all of them are — are modern in the sense that they are based on the most recent thinking, advice and experience, and are designed to further social progress and economic development. The institutional change is necessary in East Africa in order to achieve these ends is scarcely a matter for debate. Neither the traditional institutional arrangement indigenous to East Africa, the institutions inherited from colonialism, nor the strange amalgamation of the two that has occasionally emerged offers a sound institutional basis for future progress. That indigenous arrangements are too steeped in sufficiency and subsistence living to be constructive without modication in a modern, specialised economy and the colonial institutions were too often designed with the narrow view of maintaining law and order, or creating an economy supplementary or complementary to metropolitan needs, a necessary but certainly not a sufficient condition for progress. It has been, and indeed continues to be, necessary to modify existing institutions and to design and introduce new ones. Such a process is a continuous one in any country but the urgency of the matter for East African countries upon independence has been equalled only in other newly independent nations.

The nature of the institutional changes needed is determined largely by our goals and aspirations and the type of society we are seeking. Sessional Paper No. 10 of 1965 entitled, 'African Socialism and Its Application to Planning in Kenya' deals at length with these matters as they apply to Kenya while the Development Plans of the three countries contain concrete evidence of the institutional arrangement which will be employed in East Africa to attain the very similar objectives of the three governments.

Institutional arrangements govern the entire range of group behaviour and can be religious, family, social, political or economic in nature. Religion of various forms and kinds has had a strong influence on the people of East Africa and will undoubtedly continue to be a major social force in the future as well. In the main, religion is expected to make a positive contribution to development by promoting the high moral standards and integrity so fundamental to the effective division of labour, specialisation in production and development of an exchange economy. While separation of Church and State is practised in East Africa, freedom of religion is guaranteed by the State and positive support to religious institutions is encouraged by the State. It is also true that unlike some countries religion has not so far been a decisive force in East Africa and tribal or even racial identity is still stronger than the religious identity. Religion has of course had its impact on the East Africa. In particular we find that some traditional attitudes and customs have changed as a result of new religious — for example, new attitudes regarding polygamy, witchcraft and even the status of women and children.

The emergence of new political institutions has been a more complicated matter. The indigenous political arrangements in East Africa largely were systems of tribal organisation and government. While these clearly differed, sometimes substantially, from one tribe to another, the systems typical of most tribes in Kenya assured every mature member of the tribe a voice or at least an influence in tribal decisions, such influence or voice depending more on age grouping rather than wealth.

The appearance of colonialism in East Africa meant that another set of political institutions was superimposed on the traditional arrangements. While the new set was in many ways distinct from the old in the sense that Africans even in the later years had only very limited participation in the political system, the new institutional arrangement did affect the traditional system. In the first place constraints were imposed which reduced the political power and freedom of the tribe. Secondly, the political organisation of the tribe was often utilised to administer and enforce decisions which were in fact made by colonial authorities. Finally, and as a result of the first two points, the African felt less and less a participant in the political process and naturally resented the imposition of outside authority.

The struggle for independence brought with it the birth of the nationalist movement. This movement represented the first attempt to introduce a national as against a tribal or racial outlook. The existence of a common enemy, namely the colonial powers, and agitation for freedom helped to promote the movement. Every effort was made to play down or even eliminate tribal differences and identities. The nationalist movement represented a new force with potential for future unity even after independence. The impact could be felt and seen.

Party slogans and leaders emphasised the oneness of the people and the peasants and workers accepted this new relationship.

But it would be naïve to imagine that this process has been entirely successful. As soon as independence was won tribal loyalties began to emerge, manifesting themselves in different forms — sometimes as demand in the name of a tribe; sometimes as a case of alleged discrimination or favouritism in relation to this or that tribe. In some cases strong doubt has been expressed about the impartiality of leaders or even Government servants when they are dealing with people who do not come from the same tribe. And then there is the yet unresolved question of race relations. Thus we in East Africa have sovereign states with democratic constitutions guaranteeing equality for all citizens but we have still to achieve complete nationhood. Such nationhood requires commitment, a sense of identification and the submerging of tribal as well as racial loyalties to national loyalty. It is for this reason that we must seek to ensure that our political and Government institutions create the desired response among our people and persuade and assure them that their interests, security and welfare lie within the nation state instead of the tribe or race. Somehow this point has not quite been reached. While our parliamentary institutions including elections may have had an impact in terms of the people's right to choose their Government, our local authority system and the general administrative machinery have yet to produce the necessary results. I have a feeling that we shall have to experiment a little before we find the right formula. Here we are concerned not merely with the impact that physical institutions may have, but also the ideas and concepts implied as well as the goals and targets that we have set for ourselves. We are especially concerned with the impact of these institutions on our primary objective as governments in a developing region, i.e. the development and progress that takes place within our new nations.

Our indigenous social institution that has received the greatest attention in East Africa is the extended family. As pointed out in the Kenya Government's Sessional Paper No. 10 of 1965, the extended family system has both advantages and disadvantages with regard to successful economic development. Many of the newer social and economic institutions tend to threaten the extended family system. This therefore is an area in which resistance has occurred and the Governments of East Africa are concerned to maintain the best elements of that system while at the same time modifying those elements that are not conducive to development. We, in Kenya, are attempting to convey the spirit of the extended family to the State and the Nation through the principle of mutual social responsibility. This concept was fully explained in Sessional Paper No. 10 as follows:

'Mutual social responsibility is an extension of the African family spirit which can be extended to even larger areas. It implies a mutual responsibility by society and its members to do their very best for each other with the full knowledge and understanding that if the society prospers its members will share in that prosperity and that society cannot prosper without the full co-operation of its members. The State has an obligation to ensure equal opportunities to all its citizens, eliminate exploitation and discrimination, and provided needed social services such as education, medical care and social security.

'Drawing on this background African Socialism expects the members of the modern State to contribute willingly and without stint to the development of the nation. Society in turn will reward these efforts and at the same time will take measures against those who refuse to participate in the nation's efforts to grow. Sending needed capital abroad, allowing land to lie idle and undeveloped, misusing the nation's limited resources, and conspicuous consumption when the nation needs savings are examples of anti-social behaviour that African Socialism will not be countenance.

'While the modern economy is more complex than traditional society, the principle remains that to be successful society and its members must each acknowledge fully and willingly its responsibility to the other. But the movement towards a modern, monetary economy changes the nature of these responsibilities and the mechanisms by which a member contributes to society shares benefits among its members. The people must be continually and carefully informed of what society expects of them and how these efforts will promote the welfare of all.'

While the many positive features of the extended family system are recognised and efforts are being made to develop appropriate institutions for retaining them, it is also clear the system has operated in the past and, indeed, in many cases continues to operate today in a fashion detrimental to progress, change and development. The difficulty lies largely in the system of social security implied by the extended family and in its effect on individual motivation. The extended family customarily encompasses many distant relatives who may in some cases number into the hundreds. Within this group many activities are conducted on essentially a communal basis. Among these are the joint ownership and operation of land for subsistence purposes and a system of social security appropriate to a subsistence society according to which the income of one is shared with others when the need arises. While appropriate in a subsistence economy these aspects of the system can be detrimental in the context of the modern, monetary exchange economy we are now attempting to create. Growth depends on initiative, and initiative can be badly stifled if the individual who makes the effort is required to share the reward with many others whose claims can only be justified on moral grounds.

In every part of East Africa, one can witness the undesirable situation in which a member of a family whose income increases is suddenly and constantly besieged by demands for support from a large number of distant relatives. This continues to be part of our lives. It holds true of the small shopkeeper and the European-trained professional man. In social terms, such a man contributes to society in accordance with the pattern of an economy based on individual initiative essential to success in any mixed economy is scarcely encouraged by the necessity to meet obligations which are made the more imperative because they arise out of the deepest ties that an individual can experience. This is, at any time a deterrent to productive effort and is especially costly at this time when East Africa needs its own indigenous entrepreneurial ingenuity. In short, the system is a drag on initiative because it provided everyone with automatic but unreliable insurance against want, thereby diminishing mobility, thrift and entrepeneurial drive.

As the State gradually assumes increasing responsibility for social security and health and medical care the individual will be relieved of many of his present extended family obligations. Indeed, we regard essential social services as a fundamental human right that should not be subject to the uncertain ability and generosity of distant cousins. Already the activities of governments in the welfare field and other institutional arrangements have had a noticeable impact on the extended family. More and more people are looking to government for their social needs and security permitting the employed person to retain more of his income for his immediate dependants.

Another aspect of the traditional society that has been undergoing rapid change is the role of women and children. As the monetary exchange economy and education grow in importance and size, women will be less willing to undertake chores that have been typical in traditional society. Women and men now work side by side in office and jobs of all kinds are open to both sexes. The horizon of women is extended to include national and world affairs as opposed to a narrow, preoccupation with household matters. More modern methods of farm production, increasing urbanisation and the strong and growing desire of parents have tended to free children from many of their traditional duties and replaced these duties in most cases with formal primary education. Parents increasingly are taking a longer view and are planning the affairs of the family well into the future.

I have already noted the profound effects of religion on traditional attitudes such as those discussed above. Education has also been influential in this regard and is expected to play an even greater role as the number enrolled increases. Indeed, formal and informal methods of education and training form a principal means for modifying attitudes and promoting an undertaking of our changing economies. By providing a standard means of of communication, education is also promoting understanding among tribes and acquainting those in one part of East Africa with the problems and aspirations of others.

In creating new economic institutions in East Africa we have tried to draw as much as possible on existing modes of behaviour but with all the care we can exercise, it must be granted that changes in our economic institutions will often be, and indeed already have been, quite pronounced leading to significant problems in the social process and absorbing them. The principal economic institutions being introduced are:

(a) economic planning
(b) specialisation in production
(c) money as a medium of exchange and a store of value
(d) the co-operative form of organisation
(e) the discipline of an increasingly industrial society
(f) modern concepts of property and land tenure
(g) the use of financial incentives for promoting development

(h) the assumption by the state of the responsibility for social security and welfare measures.

I have described the last institution in connection with the extended family problem but would ask your forebearance while I speak briefly on each of the others and the impact they have had so far on our people.

To date planning in all three countries has been largely a central exercise which has yet to be appreciated by the man in the rural area. To make planning an effective institution we must bring it to the people through local district party machinery. It is my personal experience that the people in East Africa are anxious to have this exercise carried forward. They look sympathetically on planning and indeed expect more of their governments in this regard than we have so far been able to produce. We are all searching for appropriate means to utilise existing administrative arrangements and also to supplement these by bringing in local governments and party leaders. I believe that the people of East Africa readily accept planning but I am also sure that many problems will arise which we have not yet anticipated.

Among the economic changes that planning must assist to bring about in the conversion of the subsistence sectors of our economies into market economies. This cannot be done without providing for specialisation and also markets in which exchanges can take place. There is, however, some natural aversion on the part of Africans in the subsistence sector to undertake specialisation in a whole-hearted fashion.

The advantage to them of a subsistence economy is that they themselves are responsible for all aspects of their daily needs. Specialisation by definition means the dependence upon others for many needs and the opportunity to exchange one's own produce for the produce of others. This requires, therefore, not only trust in others but also a trust in the economic system itself. Governments have the responsibility here to ensure that the needs of the people who specialise are met in the event that some type of emergency or catastrophe should nullify their efforts to produce for the market economy.

The resistance to specialisation as a result of risks involved requires that Government introduces educational measures as well as new organisational arrangements. In sectors which promise large incomes such as growing of coffee, tea and so on this incentive has already proved a major force and many of our people are already involved in specialised market production.

The use of money as a medium of exchange is closely related to our desire to develop a market economy. Both statistics on currency in circulation and personal observation in innumerable rural areas disclose that money has become the accepted medium of exchange in every rural area in East Africa and is having a very apparent effect on the rural way of life. Markets are expanding and the variety of goods being offered is increasing. As methods of transport improve markets are serving wider areas and production for the market is increasing. Credit facilities are being used more extensively and every African knows about borrowing and repaying money even if he is not in a position to do so himself. Finally growing numbers of rural workers are demanding to be paid in money rather than in kind. Money is clearly an established institution which will make easier our task of introducing other economic institutions.

Money and other financial claims must also serve to a greater extent as a store of value. This is a problem to which, in my opinion, too little attention has so far been paid. The use of money and financial claims for savings purposes depends upon the existence of appropriate claims and a knowledge and understanding on the part of Africans that such claims are both safe and useful. I think a great deal more can be done by our Governments and the commercial banks in East Africa to provide a wider variety of saving instruments designed to meet the need of our people.

Unfortunately some of our experience in the past with some insurance companies and building societies have led many of our people to distrust financial institutions as a medium in which to store their savings. Such unsatisfactory experience tends to discourage financial savings on the part of many of our people. Nevertheless, the Post Office Savings Bank is servicing a rapidly growing number of small accounts and more and more Africans are becoming aware of the value of insurance and provident funds. Private security arranged in these ways will make government security programmes more effective and further reduce the burden of the extended family.

Many of the new production efforts being undertaken in East Africa are being organised through co-operatives. This institutional arrangement we regard as being deeply-rooted in African traditions and have found that this form of organisation is readily accepted particularly in the agricultural field. Nevertheless, our modern co-operatives differ in many respects from economic activities, involving a formal and permanent organisation, being more complex and frequently large in scale, and having a considerable impact on East Africans. The co-operative is first of all a means of ensuring a wider distribution of income. Secondly participation in co-operatives provides training and experience in a wide range of operating and managerial skills. Finally the co-operative is a means for turning the traditional communal spirit of the extended family into modern productive efforts. Here as in the creation of other new economic institutions we must guard against failure, because failure tends to generate distrust among our people.

The modern industrial society and indeed modern agricultural methods of production require a disciplined work force. The idea of work for wages is now part of the life of our people. This is one of the greatest impacts of modern institutions in East Africa. Obviously the role of organised labour is a most significant one in this respect. Our unions started off as protest organisations with only one objective of bettering the wages of their members. Today, however, the trade unions are beginning to initiate positive steps which should have a useful impact on our economies as well as their members. These include training for members both in the skills of their work and in the importance of their contribution to their country's development, the encouragement of thrift and savings among their members, the initiation of housing co-operatives and the assumption of responsibility for improving the discipline of workers.

Nevertheless our people have not yet accepted fully the need for discipline in the labour force, and have been slow to learn the intimate relationship between productivity and standards of living. There is still a hangover from the past and worn-out, rusty slogans are still used in a totally different situation. There is also the problem of importing ideas from older countries which are not relevant to our own situation. In many cases, I fear, it will take a new generation of leaders and the considerable expansion of our educational facilities before our objectives in this regard are realised.

Discipline is not only needed to make our labour force fully effective in modern industry and agriculture but also in relations with Government. The State cannot be regarded as a perpetual source of benefits unless the individual fully accepts his responsibility to pay taxes. This, too, is a function of education as well as a matter of discipline. There is still resistance in East Africa to the payment of taxes. This resistance can be traced to use of taxation as a punitive measure in the Colonial days when Africans had to be forced to supply labour for the early settlers and administrators at nominal wages.

The growth of the monetary economy has brought with it a rapid expansion of our urban centres. These have been growing for many years at an annual rate in excess of 6 per cent while the East African population has been increasing by less than 3 per cent per annum. The growth of urban centres has meant that more and more Africans have divorced themselves from the land and extended family groups to take up permanent positions and residence in cities. There has also been a substantial increase in the transient population in urban areas, many being unemployed or seeking only temporary work. This development has created many of our urban problems. Our urban centres are, however, an important means for bringing together people of different tribes thus promoting understanding of each other. The separation from traditional ties with land and family stimulates self-reliance and the varied aspects of urban life are constant sources of enlightenment to large numbers of East Africans. Undoubtedly the shift from rural to urban living requires substantial social adjustment but much of this is necessary if we are to progress toward a modern economy.

The traditional view of property and land tenure is simply unsuited to a modern economy. The identification and registration of land titles and the consolidation of land are mandatory if farm production is to be economic and financial credits for improvement are to be secured. The reorganisation of property rights and the system of land tenure is enormously complicated in East Africa by the variety of existing systems of land tenure. These range from the titled European holdings through communal family and tribal land to fragmented unregistered individual holdings. The techniques being used to modify existing systems of land tenure include settlement schemes, villagisation projects, land consolidation and registration of titles.

I think I can safely say that our new institutional arrangements with regard to land tenure have been enthusiastically accepted by most of our people, but have aroused natural resistance from some who are adversely affected by efforts to introduce new economic social institutions. Changes in land tenure policy are already having a profound effect in many parts of East Africa although the programmes are far from complete. It must be recognised that the shift from the communal holding of land to a system in which the individual holds an exclusive title to land is a radical one. It has meant, however, that individuals can now borrow readily through mortgages and can use these funds from development of the land without fear that the benefits will accrue to others. As a result productivity is increasing and standards of living are improving in those areas where the new system is established. Other evidence that the new system is being accepted is to be found in the rapidly expanding markets in land. This itself represents a major change in the outlook of our people. In order to make these incentives fully effective we must not only succeed in modifying the extended family system but must also educate, train, finance and give experience to a substantial number of Africans who will become the leading innovators and entrepreneurs of our society both in government and private commerce and industry. This is an enormous task for which we have created parastatal bodies, institutions and agencies. I should also mention here the practical and necessarily innovative experience so many Africans are now receiving in the service of their governments and the East African Common Services Organisation.

Our efforts to institutionalise entrepreneurial activities have been well received. Indeed the desire of our people to own and operate commercial, industrial and agricultural enterprises is both manifest and growing. But many of our people do not yet fully appreciate that success in business depends on more than the possession of property. Knowledge, experience, credit-worthiness, integrity in business affairs, hard work and ingenuity all have their roles to play. This talk is another example of the critical place that our formal and informal means for education and training must undertake in developing.

I would like to raise three points by way of conclusion and as a basis for debate. We in East Africa do not live in isolation nor, if this were possible, would we want to. This means that the institutions which affect our East African citizens are not limited to those which we create or develop within our boundaries. We are also deeply affected and often concerned by the institutional arrangements common in other countries and international bodies. In business matters there must be a mutual adjustment between ourselves and those with whom we do business; our interests in cultural affairs are influenced by our travels abroad and by those who visit us; many of our people are educated abroad and are affected by the institutions native to the country visited; and much of the technology employed in East Africa has had its origin elsewhere. Most of our varied relationships with other countries and industrial organisations, including organisations like the U.N. and O.A.U., have had a very healthy impact on our citizens. In particular, our people are becoming internationally minded and responsive to world affairs. We are also developing in East Africa a cosmopolitan outlook that derives in part from the various countries to which we travel and in which we gain experience and education. This outlook is however always tempered by our own backgrounds, traditions and aspirations. Our domestic institutions benefit from this varied knowledge and our judgment in world affairs is not therefore based on narrow domestic considerations.

I have attempted to assess the impact on the East African of various domestic and international institutions. This cannot obviously be a definitive assessment because we are still in a state of transition and indeed always will be. Our institutions themselves are changing and those we have are affecting our populations unevenly and in diverse ways. In such circumstances any attempt to generalise the social impact of our institutions must always to some extent be a distortion of facts. The rapidity with which change is occurring in East Africa is of course a principal reason why East Africa is an especially fruitful area in which to investigate social change. We in government have need of your efforts if we are to be successful in minimizing social maladjustment while maximizing economic growth. But whatever studies we undertake, it must be realised that East Africa is part of a changing world and further that the East African is a child of and participant in the events of the twentieth century. If we do not bear this in mind we might arrive at false conclusions in the mistaken belief that our present day East Africa belongs to the Africa of the nineteenth century. In fact some of what we call modern institutions have been conceived right here in East Africa and are neither foreign nor alien to our people. The impact of such institutions would differ from those imported from abroad.

A DEVELOPMENT STRATEGY FOR AFRICA: PROBLEMS AND PROPOSALS

Address at the opening of the Eighth Session of the United Nations Economic Commission for Africa, Lagos, Nigeria, 13th February, 1967

As Chairman of the Economic Commission for Africa — 1965/1966 — Mr. Mboya spent much time thinking and discussing development problems facing the African nations. In his speech at the Eighth General Session of the Commission he gave a detailed analysis of the problems and proposals for an action programme. This speech has been referred to as a proposal for a Marshall plan for Africa but it is more than that. It is interesting to read Mr. Robert McNamara's statement to the World Bank Conference 1968 promising to treble aid to Africa within five years. Also to be noted is the O.A.U. meeting of African Ministers of Agriculture held at Arusha, Tanzania, August, 1968, to discuss problems of surplus production in food crops.

My aim in this opening address of the Eighth General Session of the Economic Commission for Africa is to examine in some detail the problems we, the African countries, face in our efforts to secure rapid economic and social development for the benefit of 310 million people of the continent. During the two years in which I have had the honour to be the Chairman of E.C.A., I have been impressed by the difficulties we face, the efforts the African countries are making and the innumerable opportunities which are yet to be recognised and exploited. I do not have to point out to this distinguished gathering the fact that ultimately the job of developing this continent is entirely ours, and that through co-operation the job will be easier in the sense that the objective of a sustained and a higher rate of development in Africa will be achieved earlier. But truly rapid development will also require the advanced countries to increase their assistance to Africa and to carry out some obviously necessary reforms in their aid programme.

During the course of my speech I will propose for your consideration a programme of action covering the following especially critical areas:

construction of a continental infra-structure; expansion of food production, storage and marketing; development of human resources; and
collection, analysis and dissemination of economic information.

I have chosen this occasion and this platform to make this statement
because here all those intimately concerned with the task of development in Africa are gathered together to consider and identify possible
areas of co-operation and collaboration. At the same time the E.C.A.,
being a regional organisation of the United Nations, provides the
practical agency through which to speak to most, if not all, interested
nations and international organisations.

My statement will inevitably be long. However, it is not intended
to be conclusive or exhaustive, but rather a basis for discussion which
will hopefully lead to an agreed plan of action. If we genuinely desire
action, then it is fitting that the initiative should come from Africa.

The first six years of the U.N. Development Decade have passed. It
had been a period of disappointment bordering on failure, whether
measured in terms of U.N. targets, expectations in developing
countries, or possibilities as indicated by the wealth of the advanced
countries. Over that period the average person in the wealthy countries
improved his income by approximately $220 to $1,800 per annum
while *per capita* income in the very poor nations advanced by perhaps
$7 to $90 per annum. Admittedly the $7 could have been less, and it is
therefore a measure of both slight accomplishment and major defeat.
If progress continues at this rate we will be able in retrospect to rename
the Development Decade the Dollar-A-Year Decade.

Where is the flow of official capital that was to approach one per cent
of the gross national product of the advanced countries? Where are
the softer loans and the longer maturities? Where are the reduced
trade barriers, the effective commodity agreements and the improved
terms of trade? Where is the assault on ignorance and the development
of natural resources? These objectives remain visions of intellectuals
and promises of politicians. The harsh reality is that too little has been
done. Indeed, if we base our future outlook on the present state of
affairs our pessimism is fully warranted. We are in danger that the
bright promise of the Development Decade, already tarnished, may
yet dissolve completely in the dull reality of abject and prolonged
poverty.

The Stagnation of Aid

The net flow of long-term capital from the rich world to the poor is not increasing. O.E.C.D. has estimated that in 1961 the net flow (including the cost of technical assistance) of official and private capital was $9·2 billion, that it dropped to $8·3 billion in 1963, but rose in 1965 to $10 billion. The flow of official capital, which reflects better the policies of governments, has scarcely changed over this period moving only from $6·1 billion to $6·4 billion, and commitments in 1965 were actually $1·6 billion less than in 1964. None of these figures has been adjusted for price changes. It is probable that the 1965 flow would not in fact buy more investment goods than the 1961 flow. During this same period the terms of trade have deteriorated, populations have grown and the terms of loans have hardened, all of which has reduced the value to developing countries of the 1965 flow as compared with the 1961 flow. The flows are disappointing also in terms of the target of one per cent of gross national product in the advanced countries. In this respect the net official flow has fallen from 0·60 per cent in 1961 to 0·49 per cent in 1965.

But the full picture is even worse than this. The figures reported by O.E.C.D. are not of repayments of principal and the repatriation of capital, but no account has been taken of other reverse flows of capital, such as investments in industrial countries by residents of developing countries, and interest and dividend payments.

The outlook, when these factors are taken into account has been stated very clearly by Mr. Woods of the World Bank:

'These (reverse) payments are continuing to rise at an accelerating rate, and in a little more than fifteen years, on present form, would offset the inflow completely. In short, to go on doing what the capital-exporting countries are now doing will, in the not too long run, amount to doing nothing at all.'

Let's face it — the developing countries are in the greatest danger of not developing at all. Hampered by bare subsistence-level incomes, domestic capital can scarcely be accumulated, even with the strictest of taxation measures, at a rate sufficient to maintain *per capita* incomes in the face of growing populations.

The prospect that foreign capital may dry up occurs at a time when the wealthy nations are achieving unprecedented rates of growth.

Indeed it is not unlikely that *per capita* income for the whole of the rich world may double over the next thirty years from $1,800 to $3,600 per annum. Even astounding success in the very poor countries could not narrow this gap. Increasing incomes by ten times from $90 to $900 would still mean that thirty years hence, the gap would be $2,700 as compared with $1,710 today. But to be threatened with no growth at all is intolerable.

The shrinkage of foreign capital is already having a number of undesirable side effects. First, spheres of influence, from which all newly independent nations want to escape, are instead continuing and indeed in many cases becoming clearly defined. Declining aid means that bilateral sources are becoming more and more selective in determining which countries should be privileged to receive it. After all, a 'friends first' policy is not illogical so long as the bulk of aid is bilateral in nature. The obvious pressure on the developing nations to choose or suffer is regrettable but real. Second, the developing nations themselves finding their joint efforts to increase total aid unavailing — are being reduced to scrambling, competitively and ignominiously, for the limited funds that are available. When Country A gets a soft loan from the International Development Association, everyone knows that there is less for the rest. Finally, declining funds means that all aid negotiations and preliminary red tape are prolonged — perhaps simply to keep corps of experts busy; possibly to make the shortage of funds less apparent.

The growing complexity of aid negotiations, some of which are beyond the means of developing countries to cope with, is also contributing to an apparent ambivalence toward foreign capital among developing countries. The stark reality of the need for foreign capital is opposed by the irritation of bargaining for it, the frustration of growing numbers of refusals, and the increasing external supervision which at times borders on interference in domestic affairs. The ambivalence is therefore, and to an increasing extent, the mere reflection of the scarcity of foreign capital and the onerous terms on which it can be obtained.

This dire outlook is only hardened when one notes the growing hostility to foreign aid in the advanced countries. When aid is not received with the 'appropriate' degree of humility and gratitude, that fact is noted in political forums everywhere. The priority accorded aid is reduced and it frequently is given the status of a sacrificial lamb — something to be given up whenever other problems arise. Thus, aid, much of which must be a long-term commitment to be effective, is curtailed as a means of alleviating short-term balance of payments problems even though these problems are largely the result of dealings among the developed nations themselves. Aid may be cut if recessions threaten, wars escalate, or political parties change power. Thus aid becomes unstable and an impossible basis for planning; its effectiveness is considerably reduced. The growing hostility towards aid also reinforces the attitude that aid should be tied — to direct imports even though at higher than world market prices, to quality standards even though they make no sense in a poor country, to glamour projects even though these are of marginal value to development, and to political support even though the support is not genuine.

The Future of Aid

The present status of aid today holds no promise for the future. Optimistically it means gently rising *per capita* incomes to achieve for the very poor countries perhaps $200 per annum by the end of the century; it means rising debts and perennial balance of payments problems; it means continuously falling terms of trade and continued barriers to the sale of industrial products; it means no escape from the abyss of primary production.

This future cannot be regarded with complacency anywhere in the world today. It is a future that is unacceptable, unstable and unrealistic. But that future will not be changed unless the urgency of change today is recognised and the wheels of motion unlocked. It is no longer enough to exaggerate our meagre accomplishments and to disregard the enormous problems that remain unsolved. We have a choice which is really not a choice at all — we can wait for the débâcle, we can sit idly by while our hopes and aspirations turn into despair; or we can recognise the signs and initiate a constructive and co-operative programme for the development of the poor countries of the world to the mutual benefit of both the rich and the poor. The generation ahead will be decisive — we either solve this problem or set the stage for world-wide turmoil and catastrophe.

In one sense we seek a world-wide revolution in values and priorities;

in a financial sense, however, we need only a minor change. To achieve either, the problem of uneven development throughout the world must be seen as a world problem and not as a case of charity to the poor. Both the urgency and the enormity of the problem must be appreciated and the spending priorities in developed nations readjusted accordingly. Today the world is spending well over $150 billion per annum on the actual or potential destruction of lives and property as compared with the capital transfer from rich to poor countries of about $10 billion per year.

The distortion in world values can be found in the budgets of nearly all advanced countries. The recently announced U.S. budget is an example. Of a total budget of $169 billion over $73 billion is earmarked for defence of which nearly $22 billion is allocated to Vietnam. By comparison, only $3·1 billion is set aside for a foreign aid and of this figure over one-half billion is for military aid. The cold war and ideological differences account for the bulk of the world's defence spending. These are issues which therefore reduce development capital and at the same time put pressure on developing countries to take sides.

We in the developing nations are not interested in a blind commitment to one side or the other. The problem of development transcends such issues. The developing nations in Africa have made their approach clear — a mixed economy with room for both public and private investment but with government policy a deciding factor in promoting growth and ensuring an equitable distribution of income. The ideological debate is essentially irrelevant. In any event, a concern with it should not disguise the fact that the growing breach today is the gap between the rich and the poor nations. Solve that problem and we can all play intellectual games together.

The distortion of values that leads the developed world to spend over $150 billion per annum on defence is to be deplored, but it is not likely to be quickly or drastically changed. What a dream world to imagine that sum being transferred annually as development capital to the developing nations. It is true that the poor nations need a massive infusion to them — a pittance to the advanced countries. Another $10 billion per annum is a massive increase in capital which would double the present net flow. Yet that increase is only 6 per cent of the world's defence expenditure and a bare 0·8 per cent of the gross national product of the wealthy nations.

If the urgent needs of the developing nations are to be met, the advanced countries must themselves accept a different image of foreign aid and see capital flows to developing countries in true perspective. 'Aid' has the unfortunate connotation of a gift whose donor receives nothing in return except perhaps the biblical satisfaction of being a 'good Samaritan'. A good share of aid is not a gift, however, and much of that which is labelled by O.E.C.D., 'Grants and Grant-like Contributions' is not for development purposes but rather is intended for military aid. The term covers also subscription capital furnished to multilateral organisations, sales for recipients' currencies and loans repayable in recipients' currencies.

To a considerable extent, therefore, aid is falsely advertised and information is not available to correct the illusions involved. On the $6·3 billion of net official aid in 1965 at least $1·0 billion and perhaps as much as $1·7 billion was for military aid. About $0·8 billion was sales for recipients' currencies, mostly for famine relief, and over $1·0 billion was for technical assistance. Assuming the balance was intended for development capital, approximately $3·0 billion of the $6·3 was for that purpose. Of this amount $2·0 billion was in the form of loans net of repayments, and $0·5 billion was grants and subscriptions to multilateral organisations, most of which, incidentally, reaches developing countries in the form of loans.

All of these forms of aid are important to the developing countries but we must distinguish between them in order to judge their impact on development and the extent to which development capital itself is financed by grants as opposed to loans. Granted that there is some scope for substitution among the various uses of foreign capital, it is nevertheless useful and necessary to identify major categories of aid both by countries of origin and by recipient countries. The major categories are those I have mentioned — development capital, technical assistance, military aid and food supplies payable in recipients' currency.

Official development capital is transferred mainly through the mechanism of loans. There is an element of aid in these loans because many of them are tendered on softer terms than the developing countries could obtain otherwise. Nevertheless, if 'aid' is given the connotation of 'gift' or 'grant', the inclusion of the principal amounts as aid is another example of false advertising. The amounts involved could equally well be obtained for the same repayment, partly as grants and partly as loans at commercial rates. In 1964, for example, official bilateral loans were extended at an average interest rate of 3 per cent for an average maturity period of 28·4 years. If we assume that the developing countries could have borrowed on the capital markets in concert or through a joint development bank at 6 per cent, approximately 29 per cent of the amounts advanced could be regarded as a grant, the balance being commercial loans. The importance of this approach in measuring aid as opposed to capital flow is made very clear when a similar computation is made for 1965 when official bilateral loans were advanced on the average for twenty-two years at 3·6 per cent. Only 20 per cent of the amounts loaned in 1965 would qualify as grant as compared with 29 per cent a year earlier, indicating the very substantial hardening of terms that has occurred.

The effectiveness of technical assistance and development capital must be viewed in a larger context than has been usual in the past. The primary aim is to raise *per capita* incomes which must be done by striving to increase the ratios of capital and high-level manpower to less skilled labour in the context of modern technology. All developing countries are characterised by a shortage of capital relative to less skilled labour and most also are short of high-level manpower. The ratio of capital to labour in the poor countries can be improved in four ways — through an inflow of capital, domestic saving and investment, an outflow of labour, i.e. emigration and family planning.

The developing nations do, however, have a major responsibility to slow the rate of growth of their populations through appropriate family-planning programmes. An important reason for the more rapid rates of growth of *per capita* incomes in the advanced countries is the slower rates of growth of their populations — for example, in Europe, 0·9 per cent per annum and in North America 1·7 per cent. In contrast populations in developing areas, in which two-thirds of the world's population already live, are growing much more rapidly — for example, 2·3 per cent in Africa and Asia and 2·8 per cent in Central and South America.

Increased emigration of less skilled labour would also ease development problems, but immigration barriers in advanced countries are too firmly rooted and entrenched. The developing nations cannot hope to solve their problems by sending abroad the illiterate, unskilled and unemployed thus enabling essentially the same output to be shared among fewer people. Indeed immigration barriers can today be hurdled only by the relatively well trained and educated. Thus the developing nations with their limited resources are subsidising the advanced nations whenever highly trained people educated at the expense of developing countries emigrate to richer countries.

The fact that people cannot move readily from poor to rich nations magnifies the burden that must be placed on the flow of capital from the rich to the poor, if the capital-labour ratio is to be noticeably improved in the developing nations. Moreover, the difficulty of moving capital to the poor nations is compounded by trade barriers imposed by the richer countries against the products of the poorer countries. The removal of these barriers would make many investments in developing countries both profitable and attractive by providing access to markets that are not now available. Advanced countries cannot impose restrictions on trade and the movement of labour and then argue that capital should freely seek its most profitable opportunities. Capital, in turn, must be regulated, cajoled, induced and subsidised to flow to the developing nations if any headway is to be made against the other injustices.

Finally, technical assistance and development capital, even if financed by grants, are not devoid of benefits to the richer countries which supply them. The bulk of development capital is immediately used to buy investment goods produced by the richer nations and thus create incomes and employment in those countries. And much of the income created in the developing nations increases the demand for consumer goods imported from abroad. Indeed, much of the potential growth of the richer nations is conditional on a rapidly growing external demand. That condition can be created at very little cost in the developing areas of the world in which over two-thirds of the world's population now lives. A small investment today will pay handsome returns in the future. It is now, however, an essential ingredient of any formula to expand the flow of development capital that the richer countries perceive correctly their own stake in doing so. Expanding the flow of development capital is clearly a matter of mutual interest and benefit. Indeed, so long as resources are underutilised in any part of the world, we cannot be satisfied with the level of material welfare anywhere.

A Strategy for Africa

The next step logically would be to outline the specific problems of each of the major developing areas of the world, to propose positive programmes for alleviating them, and to suggest procedures for mobilising the required manpower and capital. It would be presumptuous for me to undertake this kind of assignment for Asia or Latin America, and indeed I hesitate to do so for Africa with whose problems I feel some affinity and familiarity. I will, however, attempt some tentative soundings and offer some preliminary sketches of these matters as they relate to the African developing area.

We need, as my friend Mr. Traore of Chad has suggested, a Marshall Plan for Africa — a massive infusion of manpower and capital. Admittedly, the situation of Africa today differs in many respects, as I will point out, from that of Europe after World War Two, but the imaginative concept and vigorous approach are readily adaptable. The Marshall Plan involved a capital movement twenty years ago of nearly $14 billion from only one country over a three-year period, 80 per cent of it being outright grants. Since then, gross national product in the rich nations has doubled and all of the countries in that category are eligible to assist Africa, perhaps none more than the European countries which benefited so directly and greatly from the original Marshall Plan, and which also were the colonisers of Africa. It is for us in Africa to identify our problems, to prepare a comprehensive, co-ordinated and integrated programme suited to the specific needs of Africa, and to interest the advanced nation in the implementation of that programme.

There are today in Africa thirty-nine independent countries as compared to four prior to 1950 — South Africa, the United Arab Republic, Liberia and Ethiopia — and ten prior to 1960. In the Development Decade itself, therefore, twenty-nine African nations have emerged from colonial rule to political independence, and the struggle to eliminate colonial and fascist domination of our people is not yet over.

The belated achievement of independence status by so many African states is the major reason why a massive development programme in Africa is so essential today. It also explains why development needs in Africa differ in so many ways from requirements in other developing parts of the world. These differences mean that a development programme in Africa must be especially designed to solve our

problems. Indeed many of the global policies and institutional arrangements that now govern the distribution of development capital were
created before Africa threw off the yoke of colonialism, and in many
ways are better fitted to the needs of the older developing nations.
New policies and institutions may be needed to achieve more rapid
development in Africa.

Developing areas in Africa shared with Asia the rather doubtful
distinction that at the beginning of the Development Decade approximately 90 per cent of the population lived on areas where *per capita*
incomes were less than $100 per annum, while only 4 per cent of the
Latin American population lived in countries this poor. Between 1960
and 1964, however, according to O.E.C.D. estimates, production in
less developed Africa has grown at only 4 per cent per annum while
Latin America achieved 4·4 per cent, Asia 4·9 per cent and the Middle
East, 6·7 per cent. Africa is therefore not only among the poorest of
developing areas but is also making the slowest progress. It will take
the massive and co-ordinated effort of which I speak to achieve at more
presentable record. The achievement of independence by twenty
African nations since 1959 is the first major step in that direction.

The problems of achieving independence and building national
unity and political stability have occupied some of our best minds so
that it is only now that we can concentrate on our economic problems.
We have had to reorganise and in some cases to create government and
tax structures suitable to independence, to find equitable means for
accommodating minority groups, to overcome the fears and pessimism
of domestic and foreign investors and to prevent flights of our precious
capital. I would not suggest that all of these problems are finally solved,
but I do feel that the time has come when we must co-ordinate our
efforts in a major pursuit of economic development. Africa contains
20 per cent of the world's land area and 9 per cent of the world's population but it has been estimated that 80 per cent of our natural resources
potential and 90 per cent of our potential of human resources have yet
to be realised. Our people, fresh with independence, are eager to
advance. We must use that eagerness for development if it is not to
degenerate into disappointment and despair.

I propose, therefore, that we in Africa should take the lead in
planning and co-ordinating a programme for the economic development
of our continent. This programme will require a massive inflow of

technical assistance personnel over ten to fifteen years. It will also require — and this is not a simple task — the close co-operation and full support of all independent developing African nations. Such a programme should include the following four critical aspects:

(a) the construction of a continental infrastructure;
(b) the collection and analysis of economic information;
(c) the expansion of food production, storage and marketing;
(d) the development of human resources.

I have not mentioned industrialisation explicity in this list, but you will find as I go on that several of these aspects are directly related to more rapid industrialisation. I have in fact discussed two of these aspects as they relate to industrial development in a recent address delivered in Addis Ababa at the E.C.A. sponsored meeting of Industrialists and Financiers. I shall take the liberty, however, of going over some old ground for the sake of completeness.

The Continental Infrastructure Programme

As the colonial powers withdrew from the continent of Africa, they left behind a substantial infrastructure built up with extensive investments in those facilities needed to make the colonial system effective and profitable. As African countries have gained independence, further large investments have been made in extending and modernising that infrastructure.

Today throughout Africa one finds modern harbour facilities capable of handling and servicing the largest of ships; railways with efficient rolling-stock running inland from these ports; a rapidly growing mileage of modern, often hard-surfaced roads serving both railway and harbours; efficient posts and telecommunications; large, modern airports accommodating the world's largest aircraft; extensive and rapidly growing power facilities; and well-staffed systems of governmental administration.

But the infrastructure inherited from the colonial powers was designed mainly to facilitate trade between the colony and the metropolitan country. The main aim was to maintain 'spheres of influence' and to link their 'possessions' as effectively as possible with the home economies. The railways constructed ran from the interior to the coast; roads were built to serve the railways; posts and telecommunications also served primarily the need for communication between colony and homeland. The infrastructure effectively tied Africa to Europe but the African territories could scarcely communicate or trade with each other. There were practically no transverse roads and railways linking the African countries with each other. Even today it is virtually impossible to travel from Addis Ababa to Nairobi except by sea and air; goods cannot be transported by railway across the continent; and telephone calls between many African countries must still be routed through London and Paris.

This kind of infrastructure development was and is today reflected in the pattern of Africa's trade. It is almost entirely with countries outside Africa. Indeed, one-quarter of African production is sold abroad and one-third is imported. Even the exports and imports of the United Kingdom, a country often said to be exceedingly dependent on foreign trade, constitute only 18 and 22 per cent respectively of her national output.

Obviously the development of any continent must depend in part on trade with other continents, but the full potential for development in Africa cannot possibly be realised without a rapidly growing internal trade among neighbouring countries. The advantages of external trade are well known, but without an extensive and efficient pattern of internal trade, Africa may be unable to generate the degree of specialisation necessary to compete effectively in the sale of industrial products in international markets. Certainly the rapid growth of the United States has coincided with a rate of growth in internal trade much more than in external trade, and a principal impetus to the European Economic Community was the realisation that barriers to internal trade would only retard development. Until we in Africa can generate more trade among ourselves we must continue to rely for industrialisation on import of our industrial and processed primary products.

But import substitution itself is limited in Africa by the physical and technical barriers to intra-African trade. The extent of import substitution depends critically on the size of the market that can be served. When it is recalled that many African nations are smaller in population — twenty-five have less than five million people — than the larger cities in the United States, Europe and even India, the urgent need to promote intra-African trade as a means of accelerating development becomes apparent. Indeed, until these physical obstacles to trade have been overcome, it is difficult to imagine import substitution playing the important role in development that it has already played in Latin America and Asia.

An effective continental infrastructure is also a necessary means for promoting the export of industrial, mineral and agricultural products. Many areas of the continent still do not have economical methods of transport to the coast or the electric power to develop natural resources. A wealth of opportunities therefore awaits the development of infrastructure. Indeed, that development is a principal method by which private foreign capital can be attracted to Africa in large amounts as an important and ever growing supplement to official development capital. It must be noted, however, that the elimination of trade barriers abroad must be successfully pursued if the full potential of Africa is to be realised.

The importance of national infrastructure to development has always been recognised but the need in Africa for an extensive and effective continental infrastructure is even more critical. The problem does not exist in quite such an urgent form on any other continent and this may account in part for its being neglected in Africa, there having been no significant prior experience on which to draw. Building the needed infrastrusture will require massive capital invested in roads, railways, waterways, harbours and ports, and power and communications facilities. This is a momentous task requiring co-ordinated economic planning, political co-operation and of course both foreign and domestic capital. Economic advice on the kinds of infrastructure needed, the appropriate order of priorities, the pace of implementations and possible sources of finance is an obvious function for E.C.A. to perform. It should also take the lead in organising the co-operative effort that will be essential for success.

The Information Programme

The development plans prepared by African countries are a demonstration of how much can be done in a positive way on the basis of very limited data. But every development plan emphasises the urgent need for more information if better and more effective plans are to be formulated and if the implementation of plans is to proceed on schedule.

Sources of assistance frequently seek information which is not readily available; potential investors inquire about opportunities about which we ourselves know very little; and data for evaluating our progress are sketchy and often become available too late to be fully useful. Substantially better basic information is not only needed for national planning but also for the planning of our continental infrastructure.

The known resources potential of Africa is huge and greatly under-utilised. It is also true that much of our resources wealth is unknown or inaccurately assessed. We need to mount, therefore, an intensive and thorough survey of our natural resources. Indeed, such a study must proceed concurrently with the planning of our continental infrastructure because the most economical location of transport and power facilities can only be determined in conjunction with our production and marketing potential. There are many obvious and immediate needs for infrastructure so that the programme can proceed directly, but the ultimate shape of the African infrastructure will be affected by our knowledge of resources potential. I am not speaking solely of mineral resources. We must also learn more about our watersheds and the best ways of sharing our water supplies among countries and for irrigation, power, transport and conservation purposes. Our knowledge of soils and rainfall is also limited. Our efforts to learn more about our physical resources must be accompanied by extensive land-use surveys as a basis for improving our advice to farmers and our decisions on other users of land.

We also know amazingly little about our human resources. Even our estimates of numbers are in many areas little better than guesses. Our statistics on births and deaths are abominable and we know very little more about migration trends and the attitudes of people. Yet the purpose of development is to further the welfare of these very people about whom we know so little.

Progress on data collection and storage in Africa need not be impeded by commitments to outmoded methods. As we are just beginning this task we have the opportunity to use from the outset the most modern and efficient techniques. We can agree on uniform systems for collecting and classifying data, employing perhaps a grid system covering Africa; we can establish several data centres throughout Africa where information can be stored on tape and analysed with the aid of modern computers. Indeed, this is one of the most obvious uses of modern technology in Africa because it can in this instance enable us to get a very important and basic job done in the shortest possible time.

The collection and storage of data is not an end in itself. The exercise pays off in the analysis and dissemination of information and in its use in the making of better decisions. I am thinking in this regard not only of governments, but also of decisions in the private sector, particularly investment decisions in the industrial field. The industrial sector is contributing very little to national incomes in Africa. Indeed industrial output in all of Africa except South Africa is less than that in Sweden alone, and contributes only 14 per cent to our national income as compared with 20 to 30 per cent in Latin America and 40 to 50 per cent in the advanced countries.

As I have already pointed out, an improved continental infrastructure will open up many opportunities for industrial development but we must also ensure that these opportunities are widely known and understood. In many advanced countries the identification and evaluation of industrial opportunities is readily and willingly performed by the private sector in the competitive race for profit. Indeed the initial approach to this problem in many African countries also, was to assume that private enterprise could be left to itself to accomplish this task. Experience now suggests, however, that reliance on private enterprise alone to discover industrial opportunities will not yield the rapid industrialisation necessary to make a noticeable impact on poverty and underdevelopment. In the first place, the very scarcity of indigenous entrepreneurs means that those people with the most intimate knowledge of African resources and aspirations are unable to recognise, appreciate or take advantage of the abundant opportunities in the industrial field. In the second place, many of the industrialists and financiers outside Africa have not yet acquired a first-hand knowledge of Africa, and must therefore spend substantially more time and money to investigate the feasibility of a projects in Africa than would be necessary in the familiar surroundings of their home country. In the African context, therefore, it has become absolutely necessary to increase our investment of time and money in surveying and evaluating industrial opportunities as a service to potential foreign and domestic investors.

Substantial work of this kind has already been undertaken by E.C.A. Numerous opportunities have been identified by sub-regions, the future demand for many products has been estimated, some raw material supplies have been identified and for some industries suitable sites have been suggested. Similar studies on a considerably smaller scale have also been undertaken by various development banks in the African countries and on occasion by outside consultants on specific contract.

What has been done is simply not enough. In the future rapid industrialisation will require a much more carefully organised approach to the identification and evaluation of industrial projects, primarily to overcome the sheer ignorance of both foreign and domestic investors with regard to opportunities in Africa.

I suggested last month at the Addis Ababa Conference of Industrialists and Financiers that serious consideration should be given to the establishment of several Feasibility Analysis Centres at strategic points throughout Africa. These centres would survey industrial opportunities and assess the feasibility of promising projects as a service to government and, as time permits, directly to private investors at cost. Specifically, each centre would:

(1) identify and survey industrial opportunities;

(2) perform feasibility studies covering—
(a) costs and methods of production;
(b) marketing and management problems;
(c) potential contribution to development;
(d) nature of sub-regional co-operation required, if pertinent;
(e) possible sources of finance and management, and
(f) identification of economic levels of protection or subsidy,

(3) assist in identifying and negotiating with interested foreign and domestic investors;

(4) perform follow-up evaluations as projects get under way.

Such centres could be established within or under the sponsorship of E.C.A., and indeed the Executive Secretary of E.C.A. has tabled at this conference a report which recommends the establishment of Industrial Information and Promotion Centres. This recommendation should be supported and the co-operation and active participation of national and international associations of commerce and industry should be enlisted in the endeavour. After all, private investors will profit as a result of the work of the centres and they should be willing to contribute, collectively if not individually, to their effective operation. Moreover, such associations should assist in identifying suitable staff and specialised consultants.

The third aspect of the programme to fill the information vacuum is the intensification of our research activities. There is a wide range of problems to be solved in Africa and only concerted, well-organised research efforts will yield the solutions we seek. Three problem areas in particular merit special attention — nutrition and food production, education and training, and the social and economic problems of development.

The need to find better foods and to increase the nutritive content of those we now produce is an urgent research matter if the diets of our people are to be improved and infant mortality reduced. We must also find and employ more efficient food varieties, methods of cultivation and means for storing and preserving food so that increasing quantities will be available. Research on the recovery and use of arid areas is particularly needed in Africa. Scientists must also help us to reduce insect, crop disease and rodent damage to crops which destroy more than a third of our food before it is harvested. Progress on these problems is not only basic to development it is basic to our very survival.

The methods now employed to develop our human resources are both archaic and unsuited to our needs. Rote learning and examination passing, frequently in irrelevant subject matters, have become almost an end in themselves. Research on the learning process, the identification of aptitudes, teaching methods, and curriculum should enable us to educate many more people, more suitably and faster for the same money. The waste in education is apparent in the advanced countries also, but they can afford waste — we can't. Research on informal means of human learning and development and on the acquisition of traits, such as integrity, imagination and initiative, is also urgently needed if we are to make full use of our human resources.

Finally, we need extensive inter-disciplinary research on the social and economic problems associated with development. How can we best adapt modern technologies to our needs? Can we find solutions to our growing unemployment problem? Are the fiscal policies and tax measures we have borrowed from advanced countries, which have abundant capital, a shortage of labour and no subsistence sectors, appropriate for us? Can we distribute incomes so that our food production is spread effectively to all our people? Should each of us aim at self-sufficiency in food production or are there advantages to be gained from specialisation and exchange? How can traditions antagonistic to development be modified? What is the impact of rapid change on the moral and cultural values of our people? All of you could add equally important questions to this list, but where is the massive research effort needed to find answers to these questions?

I suggest that in Africa we need at least one large-scale research institute dealing with each of these three sets of problems. The centre being started in Nigeria is a beginning on food research, but where are the others? We cannot depend on research abroad. While the problems I have mentioned have an international flavour, they have unique characteristics in Africa. Research on European agriculture is not directly applicable to tropical agriculture; educational systems in all advanced countries have obvious short-comings in Africa; and economic policies formulated in fully employed economies have little relevance for us. The research we need must be done here, not in Paris or London and not at Yale or Harvard. We have contributed, not always willingly, a number of our well-educated people whom we could ill-afford to lose to bolster professional ranks in the advanced countries. The institutes I propose may help to reverse this flow. The foundations could assist us tremendously in this aspect of the information programme, but it is also an investment that should qualify for financial support on a grant basis from the International Development Association.

The Food Programme

The information programme will have a critical impact on long-term development and will assist significantly in the shorter term as well — but it is not an action programme in the same sense as the other three. I return then to positive proposals for visible development on the ground in discussing the Food Programme.

A good programme for Africa must be intimately related to the needs of the rest of the world. Our aim is not self-sufficiency; it is to become a major net supplier to the rest of the world. No matter how successful our efforts are to industrialise, it remains a fact that Africa will be for many generations, primarily a producer of agricultural and other primary products. We must learn to do it well and on a rapidly growing scale. This will require a massive frontal attack, not only on the research needs to which I have already referred, but also on the practical problems of production, storage and marketing.

The most critical and immediate problem is the storage and preservation of food. In particular, we need in Africa capital for the construction of storage facilities and finance for the crops to be stored. Continuing famine conditions in many parts of the world and the rapid depletion of surplus food stocks in the United States could signal a major catastrophe for mankind. These factors may also foreshadow rising prices for basic food crops. It certainly means that major efforts must be made throughout the world to expand production. The matter is urgent and cannot await the slow response of production to prices which may, in fact, not rise until the catastrophe is upon us. Thought is being given, notably in the Kennedy Round discussions, to increasing production in advanced countries. It is important for production to be increased in developing nations as well, not only for domestic use but also to supply food to countries with shortages. The stimulation of production in advanced countries will help famine-stricken areas; similar efforts in the developing nations themselves will further development as well. Africa is well placed and endowed to assist in this gigantic task. It has the natural resources, and the areas of major world shortage lies just across the Indian Ocean from Eastern Africa. Unfortunately today Africa is a small net importer of grain. This is a situation that must be quickly corrected.

I suggest, therefore, that the United Nations make advance commitments to purchase essential stocks of basic goods at negotiated prices from those African nations who may be able to grow surpluses. The United Nations should also construct essential storage facilities in these countries. Both the storage facilities and the grains stored would remain the property of the United Nations, and the food could be drawn upon and shipped by the United Nations whenever and wherever the need arises. It is no longer sufficient for one or a few nations to assume the responsibility for supplying and otherwise arranging to meet the needs of famine areas. It is a world problem requiring a co-ordinated solution. The United Nations is an appropriate organisation; Africa can contribute and benefit by participating. I am aware that proposals of this kind have been the subject of discussion for many, many years. It is now time for constructive action.

A shortage and marketing programme along these lines should by itself lead to a substantial expansion of the production of staple foods. Other complementary measures are also necessary primarily to increase agricultural productivity, open up new lands, reclaim exhausted acres, and by these means expand output. The research efforts to which I have referred must be followed up by effective systems of well-manned extension services, the determination and implementation of sound land tenure policies, the development of transport and marketing facilities in the rural areas, and the provision of loan capital on a large scale to small farmers. None of these fundamental needs can qualify as a 'glamour project', but taken together and on the scale I am contemplating, they would have a profound impact on development, employment, and attitudes toward rural living. We must in Africa find means of expanding in a big way the flow of capital for rural and agricultural development. The seriousness of the situation can be indicated by noting that while perhaps 75 per cent of our economy is based on agriculture only 6 per cent of official aid to all countries and 15 per cent of technical assistance has been committed to agriculture in recent years.

The handling and marketing of food products today involves considerable waste and unnecessary expense. The rationalisation of this phase of food processing could save millions of dollars and at the same time serve as an impetus to development. My suggestion is that much of the processing of food that now takes place in advanced countries should be transferred to the developing countries where the basic crops are grown. It makes basic sense to transport food as cheaply as possible and to process it as quickly as possible if waste and spoilage can be reduced by so doing. The canning of various foods before shipment is an obvious example. It would also be more economic to make instant coffee and tea where the products are grown. The production of powdered milk and other dehydrated foods must also be encouraged in developing countries. What is needed here is not capital and technical assistance — private investors will supply these quickly enough. We need the elimination of those trade barriers in advanced nations that prevent these kinds of economies from being realised and at the same time make the development task so much harder.

The Human Resources Programme

Perhaps the most rewarding and fundamental task confronting us is the development of human resources. While it must be given the highest priority today for economic reasons, the benefits of success will extend well beyond material welfare alone. We are today, however, faced with a gigantic shortage of high and middle level manpower and a general illiteracy problem that hampers labour force efficiency and effective agricultural extension work. While 97 per cent of the people of fifteen years of age and over in many advanced countries are literate, in Africa probably less than 20 per cent in that age group can read and write. Literacy rates are considerably higher in most other developing countries being, for example, about 85 per cent in Argentina, 70 per cent in Thailand, 60 per cent in Mexico and Burma, and 50 per cent in Brazil. Our vast shortages of trained manpower are also not typical of the rest of the developing world. India today even has a problem finding employment for its university graduates. The problem in Africa is therefore a very special one and it demands special attention on a vast scale. As I conceive of it, our Human Resources Programme must in the near future concentrate on overcoming our manpower shortages.

Our need for high and middle level manpower will require a very rapid and large expansion of secondary school and university facilities. We do not, however, want monuments for universities, we want practical centres for effective study and learning. We cannot afford luxurious accommodation or exotic subjects and we must ensure that our facilities are fully utilised throughout each day, over a lengthy academic year and during vacation periods. We cannot afford the low student-teacher ratios or the élite pattern of education typical of some of the advanced countries. Our curriculum structure must be accommodated to our needs at both secondary and university levels and designed at every stage for those who will be leaving school for jobs or specialised training as well as for those who will be fortunate enough to continue.

Rapid expansion will not be effective, however, unless fundamental and related services are also increased. In particular, we must have curriculum materials prepared for African needs, including specialist training courses and pre-vocational work, as well as history, geography and social institutions courses. We must also have modern testing equipment and the means to design, prepare, interpret aptitude and achievement testing.

I have often felt that some who assist us in our development efforts have tried to discourage the rapid expansion of our educational facilities. The argument is that we may overproduce and create graduate unemployment. This danger exists but we must first attempt to circumvent it by expanding job opportunities, not by curtailing enrolments. A massive programme in education does require massive development efforts in other sectors. Moreover, some overproduction may stimulate enterprising people to create self-employment opportunities and may also enable many positions to be up-graded more rapidly than otherwise. In the final analysis and for obvious reasons we simply cannot treat overproduction in education with the methods appropriate to overproduction of coffee.

Many of our manpower requirements must be provided for outside the walls of our educational institutions. We need extension services and capital for fledgling entrepreneurs, the means to provide training and practice for potential managers, apprenticeship and training schemes in all major industries, and practical programmes for training farmers. Such costs cannot be assumed entirely by our industrialist and large farmers without harming their already precarious competitive position in international markets. The existing private sector, small as it is, also cannot provide training for new industries not yet established. Training and apprenticeship opportunities abroad are therefore needed for many middle level occupations as well as the expansion of university scholarships.

While manpower shortages are the dominant consideration in this programme we must also take positive steps to expand primary school enrolments and reduce illiteracy among our adult population. Primary education is the pedestal on which all further formal education must rest. Its quality must be high, based on a modern curriculum taught by well-trained teachers. Moreover, the failure to expand enrolments rapidly means a considerable extension into the future of the illiteracy problem.

Adult illiteracy is not simply a social and cultural problem. It must be stamped out in order to promote national unity and to lay a basis for an efficient labour force in both rural and urban areas. To be effective, however, adult literacy efforts must have a purpose that is meaningful, not only to the nation but to each participating adult. Too frequently in the past literacy has been taught for its own sake and quickly forgotten when meaningful follow-up materials were not available.

We need then strong educational programmes in all three of these areas — manpower, primary level, and adult literacy. The moulding of our nations and the development of our continent cannot be wholly successful until all of our people can participate effectively in both the effort and the benefits.

Policies and Procedures

The programme I have sketched will be expensive in both development capital and technical assistance. The earliest and most pressing need will be for technical assistance on a significantly greater scale than in the past. There is first of all the need to plan and design the infrastructure programme which will be a mammoth task if carried out properly. The preparation and co-ordination of projects in the other programmes will also demand more expert and professional manpower than we in Africa can supply. There is no question in my mind that all of us in recent years have greatly underestimated the time and manpower required, for project preparation. This is partly because the red tape and mass of detail involved have increased, often unnecessarily, partly because we are relatively new in this development business, and finally because the African situation is not a simple replica of situations in other developing areas and experience in those areas by people and institutions has not been readily transferable to Africa. The project formulation bottleneck, which has now reached serious proportions, must be broken.

We shall also require massive infusions of teachers, curriculum specialists, testing experts, agronomists, economists, architects, engineers, physical planners, data processors, statisticians, and researchers of all kinds. A truly massive influx over the next several years is the most effective way in which we can train our own manpower while simultaneously carrying out our ambitious development programme. The need is clear; the critical question is can these experts be found and furnished in the vast numbers that will be needed. Technical assistance is already flowing most heavily to Africa. To double that flow quickly would put a severe strain on existing recruiting methods and would require a substantial increase in grants to cover the costs involved. Moreover, unless our needs are carefully and clearly defined, much of the additional technical assistance may be inefficiently employed. These problems are serious but not insurmountable.

The most urgent need is for the substantial expansion of planning staff in E.C.A. and the African Development Bank so that meaningful estimates of our technical assistance needs can be formulated. Simultaneously, our main sources of bilateral and multilateral technical assistance should be devising methods for expanding the flow and widening the net to include more countries and to make fuller use of private as well as public channels. The use of longer contracts and expert groups or terms should also ease the recruitment problem. Indeed, the organisation of international management groups for major continental infrastructure projects might be considered as a means of ensuring continuity from the initiation of planning until completion.

If this African Technical Assistance Effort can be mounted and organised quickly and efficiently, it should within a decade be fading away. After all, a fundamental purpose of the effort is to make technical assistance unnecessary.

The organisation of a substantially larger flow of development capital is a more complex matter requiring a more imaginative use of the world's capital markets and the fullest co-operation of the advanced countries. It is time I think for Africa to draw on the world's capital markets on a much larger scale than in the past and the African Development Bank is an appropriate means for doing so. By pooling our efforts and credit standings we should be able to borrow larger amounts at more reasonable terms. Guarantees and interest subsidies by the advanced countries would make such flotations easier and reduce the costs to Africa at very little expense to the assisting nations. Projects financed in this way must of course, be economically viable within the maturity periods of the loans. Many aspects of the Food Programme might be financed in this way.

But the bulk of the Development Programme for Africa must be financed on a more liberal basis than we can manage through commercial capital markets. We must therefore seek a substantial expansion in the flow of official development capital and indeed considerable liberalisation of the terms on which it is now being received. Official bilateral loans in 1965 averaged 22·2 years in length and 3·6 per cent interest. But investments in information, education, continental infrastructure and even basic agricultural services are not likely to pay off quickly enough to be financed safely on such terms. On the other hand basic investments of the kind I have outlined will continue to pay off for centuries. These basic investments are absolutely necessary to our development; we need capital for them on terms that make sense.

The external development capital for the programme I have sketched should be largely in the form of grants or alternatively century loans at low interest rates with a 20-year moratorium on both principal and interest. The external capital needed should be expanded and distributed by the African Development Bank. It should be raised through an international consortium of advanced nations in the form of special subscriptions in order to avoid jeopardy to existing aid programmes. Clearly an appropriate balance must be maintained among continental, sub-regional and national projects. The crash programme I am proposing is not a substitute for what we are already doing; it is an important, basic and necessary addition.

I know that questions will be raised about the realism of the programme I have suggested and more particularly about the likelihood that the African countries can secure the substantial degree of economic co-operation necessary to initiate the programme and see it through to fruition. I have confidence that we in Africa can do our part. The needs of our various countries are uneven. Some have ample foreign exchange; others are short of it. Some have small surpluses of high-level manpower; most have serious shortages. Some have arid lands; others tropical rain forest. Some are land-locked; others are little more than coastal strips. Some have emphasised industrial development; others have concentrated on agricultural diversification. It follows that the various programmes of the Development Strategy for Africa will affect our several countries differently. It is, however, clearly to our mutual benefit to build a continental infrastructure, to generate basic information, to educate our people and to contribute what we can to the world's food supply.

Our differences are also a source of strength. They are a means by which we can help each other. Those countries in a position to do so can assist others with their manpower needs. Neighbouring countries can pool their resources to ensure more even development. They can also share markets so that large-scale enterprises have a reasonable chance of success. Foreign exchange problems too, can be alleviated through mutual effort. Much more can also be done to harmonise development plans and in this way to ensure a co-ordinated approach to common problems. The success of the programme I have outlined rests squarely on the degree of economic co-operation we in Africa can achieve.

I propose, therefore, that E.C.A. should be asked to convene a meeting soon of all economic and finance ministers in the developing countries of Africa for the purpose of agreeing on a unified and co-ordinated approach to the advanced nations along the lines I have indicated. In preparation for that meeting E.C.A., in consultation with the African Development Bank, should assemble appropriate materials and a more specific and detailed plan including rough estimates of capital and manpower requirements. Perhaps at the meeting I have proposed, a committee of ministers can be appointed to assist the Executive Secretary of E.C.A. in preliminary discussions with the advanced countries.

Our development is at stake. Nothing less than a major effort, both within Africa and by our friends overseas can produce the progress we seek and make our continent a mature contributor to the world economy. What is more it is only through the process that I have suggested that we can achieve real continental economic co-operation and create what may be termed the 'African economy'. Unless we do something a few of our countries may develop while others stagnate. But above all, I fear that our dependence on the countries outside Africa will never some to an end. We shall continue to be manipulated and expected to respond to the economic needs and pressures from outside. There will be the continuous danger of Africa being dominated economically by 'spheres of influence' projected by the different developed nations.

The initiative and decision to co-operate constructively must come from Africa and it is in this spirit that I invite all my colleagues to consider most critically but positively all that I have said here today.

THE EAST AFRICAN TREATY OF CO-OPERATION— HOW FAR IS IT A STEP TOWARDS AFRICAN UNITY?

Speech given before the University Students' Association of East Africa, Makerere University College, Kampala, Tuesday, 19th December, 1967

The opportunity to discuss with students of the University of East Africa our recently signed East African Treaty of Co-operation and the broader objective of African unity is a challenging one for two reasons. First, the student body of the University of East Africa represents one of the strongest intellectual forums in East Africa, and the views presented to it are certain to receive careful consideration and critical appraisal. It is of course a major function of our University to inculcate in our students an interest in today's important political and economic questions and the ability to consider these problems objectively, critically, and constructively. Second, but clearly related to the first, is the fact that the students of the University of East Africa are the future leaders of East African nations and many of the problems of the future will be left to you to solve. It is therefore significant that you have an interest in today's problems, policies, and decisions, because it is in these that you will find the roots of the challenges of tomorrow.

The extent of the dependence of African countries — not on each other — but on the rest of the world for trade is not always fully appreciated. Let me take East Africa as an example. In 1968 the three countries of East Africa exported goods and services worth £214 million to the rest of the world. You may be surprised to learn that of this amount only £15 million or about 7 per cent was exported to other African countries excluding South Africa and Rhodesia. Of the £15 million which East Africa sold to the rest of Africa, £11 million was sold to the seven neighbouring independent African countries. During the same year, 1968, East Africa imported nearly £220 million worth of goods and services from the rest of the world. Of this amount less than £3 million or barely more than 1 per cent, came from other independent African countries.

These figures give some idea of the enormous gap that is left for us to fill. It is inconceivable in my view to imagine that Africa can successfully develop without giving the highest priority to the generation of trade among the African nations themselves. It is indeed one of the major advantages that the large countries like the U.S., the U.S.S.R., and China have over the smaller nations. Trade within the borders of the large countries is generally free and unfettered. This freedom of trade has been and continues to be a major factor in the rapid growth these larger countries are able to engender. If we allow our development to remain so heavily dependent on markets on other continents, we cannot gain the control over our own destinies that we are all so urgently seeking. The goods we can sell in those markets depend not on our efficiency of production, but also on the tariffs and other artificial barriers which the industrialised countries may choose to place against our goods. If we wish to have more control over our own future in Africa we must be prepared as nations to sacrifice some of our national sovereignty for the benefit of Africa as a whole. The need to develop transportation and communication systems among our nations is great indeed. The need to find a means of gradually reducing the tariffs that form barriers to trade among ourselves is of even greater urgency.

There may be some who would maintain that the possibilities for promoting intra-African trade are negligible. Our experience in Africa suggests that such a position is wrong. Let me give you figures for 1966 on trade among the three East African countries. In 1966 these three countries exported to each other nearly £44 million worth of goods and services. This you will recall compares with total East African exports to other African countries of only £15 million. The substantial trade which has developed within East Africa is of course primarily due to the common market which was created among these three countries during the colonial period. The magnitude of this trade has contributed in no small way to the development of the three countries and to the rising *per capita* income our people enjoy. I suggest that this same pattern of success can be repeated on a larger scale and in other parts of Africa as a prelude to that greater African unity we may some day enjoy.

The advantages of the framework for co-operation which East Africa inherited from Britain are notable, but there were also many difficulties in the structure which the three independent countries had to re-examine. In a sense, I suppose, the colonial roots of the common market tended to taint the old structure in the minds of a few. The governments of the countries of East Africa, however, were determined to retain the advantages of economic co-operation, but to establish a framework for that co-operation more suitable to the needs and aspirations of independent nations. Some first steps were taken in the negotiations which resulted in the so called Kampala Agreement of 1964. It was clear, however, even before that agreement was concluded that the terms of reference given to the group which worked out the agreement were far too narrow to achieve the results that the three Governments desired. It was therefore decided to establish the Phillips Commission* with a view to examining all aspects of economic co-operation in East Africa and drafting a treaty which would lend legal status to the deep desires for co-operation that existed in all three countries.

The Treaty which came into force on December 1st of this year is a truly historic document which will guide economic relations among the three East Africa countries, and I hope others as well, for many years into the future. It will also, I am convinced, provide a basis for growing political ties among those who belong to the East African Community.

The Treaty provides for continuing economic co-operation among the three East African countries on a broad front. It establishes an East African Community, whose headquarters will be located in Arusha and as an integral part of that Community, the East African Common Market. The Community itself will operate a number of services on an East African basis. The principal common services will be administered by four corporations — the East African Railways Corporation the East Africa Harbours Corporation, the East Africa Posts and Telecommunications Corporation, and the East African Airways Corporation. The community will also undertake to co-ordinate the commercial laws, transport policies, and economic planning functions of the partner states. It will also develop in the long term a common agricultural policy, and will provide for the harmonisation of the monetary policies of the member countries. A common agency will collect income, customs and excise taxes for the partner states, and the

* See pp. 242–243.

Treaty provides for consultation on all tax matters as well. A number of important research activities will be conducted by the Community and the East African Industrial Court will hear disputes involving employees of the Community and the Corporations. The Treaty also guarantees the freedom of current account payments among the partner states and the freedom of capital account payments which are necessary to further the aims of the Community.

The Common Market itself provides for the establishment and maintenance of common customs and excise tariffs. At the same time artificial restrictions on trade among the three countries are abolished, but transfer taxes may be imposed in special cases against imports from other partner states. The provision for transfer taxes and the establishment of the East African Development Bank are widely regarded as the two major innovations designed to stimulate an equitable distribution of industrial development among the three countries.

Transfer taxes can be imposed only if a partner state is in deficit in its total trade in manufactured goods with the other partner states. At the present time therefore the Treaty permits both Uganda and Tanzania to impose transfer taxes, but Kenya does not now qualify for the privilege. Transfer taxes can be imposed only upon manufactured goods, and only if the goods on which a tax is levied are being manufactured in the state imposing the tax. The transfer tax itself cannot exceed 50 per cent of the rate of duty prescribed by the customs tariff and expires automatically unless earlier revoked, eight years, after the date it is first imposed. The purpose of the transfer tax is to give those partner states who are less developed industrially some protection against partner states that are relatively better off, without at the same time causing imports from partner states to be diverted to non East African sources. The limited protection thus provided should stimulate substantial industrial development in the less developed partner states, not only because the domestic market is given this protection, but also because exports to Kenya will not be subject to the same barrier. Thus many industries should find it profitable to locate in Uganda and Tanzania because such a location will make available to the firm a market of at least two countries and in most cases of all three.

The stimulus to industrial development in Uganda and Tanzania supplied by the transfer tax mechanism is supplemented in the Treaty by the establishment of the East African Development Bank. The East

African Development Bank is intended to assist industrial development throughout East Africa but with a bias in favour of Tanzania and Uganda by supplying capital for the financing of industrial projects. The treaty also provides that while every country contributes equally to the funds of the bank, only $22\frac{1}{2}$ per cent of the loans made by the bank will go to Kenya, while Uganda and Tanzania will receive $38\frac{3}{4}$ per cent apiece.* The bank therefore has been designed to channel more finance to Uganda and Tanzania, and this coupled with the transfer tax system should lead to substantially more rapid industrial development in Uganda and Tanzania than either country could manage alone.

The very considerable economic co-operation provided for in the Treaty is supplemented by provisions for administrative, judicial, and political co-operation as well. The Treaty establishes a Common Market Council and a Common Market Tribunal to administer the common market arrangements and to provide a means for settling disputes. The East African Community, of which the Common Market is a part, will be governed by the East African Authority which is the principal executive authority of the Community. The Authority consists of the Heads of the partner states. The day to day operation of the Authority will be managed by three East African Ministers, each appointed by the Authority upon the nomination of one of the partner states. The Common Market Council to which I have already referred will consist of the three East African Ministers together with nine other members, of whom three will be designated by each partner state from among its Ministers. In addition to the Common Market Council, four other councils are established by the Treaty, and these councils too have as members, the East African Ministers, plus other ministers designated in equal numbers by the partner states. These additional councils are: the Communications Council, the Economic Consultative and Planning Council, the Finance Council, and the Research and Social Council.

---

* The authorised capital of the Bank is £20m and the called in capital is £10m. The Partner States Kenya, Uganda and Tanzania each contribute £2m. The remaining £4m. is to be found from external countries and other institutions. The £2m. to be paid by each state is payable in four instalments. The first instalment is £200,000. The other three instalments £600,000 each. The first two instalments have already been paid by each country which means that the bank has now £2·4m.

In addition, an East African Legislative Assembly is established for the Community composed of the three East African Ministers and their deputies, and 27 appointed members — nine of these are appointed by each partner state. The Assembly has the power to pass Bills which become Acts upon the Assent of all the Heads of State of the partner states. These Acts will have the force of law in all partner states. Thus the Treaty gives substantial powers to the three East African Ministers and, the Assembly for initiating measures dealing with the Community within the very broad outlines specified by the Treaty.

The Treaty has been hailed throughout Africa and elsewhere in the world as a truly major achievement. I agree with that assessment, but at the same time we must not allow our present optimism to lead us to the conclusion that the Treaty is perfect. It is not. The Treaty has many weaknesses, but it is hoped that the governing machinery established will succeed in correcting these with the passage of time. Let me however note some of the weaknesses that are already generally recognised by those who worked closely with the Phillip Commission.

First, there is nothing in the Treaty which guarantees the free movement of labour among the three countries. In this sense therefore the Common Market is much more of a customs union than a common market. Second, the transfer tax is in effect an internal tariff and therefore violates the fundamental rule of an ideal common market, namely that there should be no internal restrictions on trade. Third, while the transfer tax and the Development Bank should assist in promoting a more equitable distribution of industrial development, the Treaty does not provide for any central means of industrial allocation or a common scheme of fiscal incentives, although the intention to seek a common scheme of fiscal incentives, is clearly stated in the Treaty. Fourth, the Treaty makes little progress towards achieving a common agricultural policy, although the intention to do so is again clearly stated. Fifth, while means for co-ordinating the tax systems of the three countries are established by the Treaty, there is nothing in the Treaty to prevent the three countries from having different tax systems with the exception of external tariff and excise taxes. Finally, the co-ordination of a number of matters are left to the Councils, frequently without specific instructions. As one example, the Economic Consultative and Planning Council is the national charged with assisting by consultative means the national planning efforts of the partner states, but is not given the specific task of co-ordinating these efforts or of preparing a development plan for East Africa as a whole!

On the political and administrative side there are also weaknesses which may cause difficulties in the future. First of all there is no injunction provision which might be used to prevent a transfer tax from being imposed if one of the partner states feel that the imposition is in violation of the Treaty. Second, the members of the Legislative Assembly are appointed rather than elected. This means that the members of the assembly are more likely to regard themselves as representatives of the partner states' Governments rather than as representatives of the people of East Africa. While this does reduce the amount of political unity that might otherwise have been achieved, it is in my view the only effective means of establishing the East African Legislative Assembly at the present time. Finally, it will be noted that the Head of each partner state in effect has a veto over any bill passed by the Legislative Assembly. The Treaty provides that if assent to a bill is not given by all Heads of State within nine months, the bill shall lapse.

Many of the weaknesses I have noted here will undoubtedly be corrected with the passage of time as confidence in the East African Community grows, as I am sure it will. Indeed, confidence in the Community has already been made manifest by the agreement of the three East African Governments to the Treaty, and by statements by a number of neighbouring countries including Zambia, Ethiopia and Somalia of their intention to apply for membership.*

The establishment of the East African Community and its warm reception by neighbouring countries suggests that we have at least resolved one of the problems that has retarded our progress towards unity in the past. While clear and strong hopes have been expressed by all independent African nations for greater co-operation both on a widening geographic basis and in the scope of social, economic and political policies to be co-ordinated, there have been differences in views as to how these related objectives were to be attained. There were those who felt that the possibility of achieving significant economic

* Burundi, Ethiopia, Somalia and Zambia have formally applied for membership.

co-operation must depend substantially on the prior achievement of political unity. There were others who felt that increasing economic co-operation must precede any significant steps towards political unity. There is, however, still another group which has felt that progressively greater economic co-operation must necessarily involve substantially increasing political affiliation as well so that in fact the promotion of the one is the promotion of the other. I think that the creation of the East African Community has demonstrated that genuine political unity must rest on substantial economic co-operation which in turn cannot be achieved without substantial political unity and growing sacrifice of national sovereignties which this implies.

There have also been differences in views with respect to the geographic areas that should first be involved in political and economic co-operation. There have been those who have felt that political unity on essentially a continental basis should be a first step rather than an ultimate objective. The approach which is emerging as the only practical one, however, is that symbolised by the East African Community, namely to develop economic and political co-operation among a few nations, and to expand its size by encouraging other nations to join. Once several larger units of this kind have been created throughout Africa, I am convinced that these several communities will find it to their advantage to promote closer political and economic ties among the communities themselves. This is in my view the only realistic way in which to make progress towards the ultimate objective of a united Africa. I think the successful establishment of the East African Community has demonstrated the wisdom of this approach.

In conclusion I would like to raise with you the degree to which political and economic unity within Africa may be dependent on policies formulated outside Africa. This dependence is not always fully understood or appreciated. There are first of all a number of forces that originate outside Africa which tend to make unity in Africa more difficult to achieve. No-one would deny that while we have achieved political independence, the spheres of interest of the former colonial powers have not entirely disappeared. These spheres of interest are promoted through the very substantial trade ties which continue to exist in many cases, and are given further support by the insistence of the advanced countries that aid should be given primarily on a bilateral basis tied to imports from the countries making the aid available. As the advanced countries are also selective in the countries to which they give aid, the strengthening of spheres of influence is almost a necessary conclusion.

Moreover, the nature of aid itself may tend to retard intra-African trade. I have already noted the fact that much aid is tied to imports from donor countries, which obviously makes it difficult for African nations to produce the products that must be imported from abroad. We also have as a recent example of the import of food and crops by African countries from overseas, when surpluses of similar food and produce exist in other countries in Africa. What we must recognise here is that while the African countries have the produce to supply, they are not in a position to finance the purchase on as favourable terms as say the U.S. The possibility of developing financial arrangements among a number of African nations as a means of stimulating the flow of intra-African trade is a matter that should be given priority.

But there are also forces that originate outside Africa which tend to stimulate the movement towards unity within Africa. The Kennedy Round discussions on the reduction of tariffs is a case in point. While it was announced at the outset that one of the major objectives would be to open up markets in the advanced countries for the products of the developing nations, this objective clearly disappeared in the concern of the principal negotiators with promoting the welfare of the advanced countries themselves. The developing nations clearly found themselves on the side lines in these discussions and emerged with very little of benefit to themselves. It is becoming increasingly clear that if advantages are to be obtained for the developing nations they must unite more closely than they have in the past, not only to secure a reduction in the barriers to trade among themselves. The need to unite in Africa is therefore in part due to the need to improve our bargaining position with the advanced countries.

The second example is the rapid development of the European Economic Community and the distinct possibility that over the next decade this community will be strengthened by the addition of both the United Kingdom and E.F.T.A. nations. If we in Africa are to deal with the European Economic Community on an equal basis we cannot do so by approaching the Community one by one. Indeed it is one of our great hopes that the establishment of the East African Community will considerably enhance our bargaining position with respect to the

European Economic Community. Our position can only be improved
if additional nations apply for membership in the East African Community. Clearly as Europe proceeds with its economic and political
integration, the need for Africa to achieve comparable successes
becomes increasingly important.

If the East African Community is a success, and I am convinced
this is so, it will be a major step toward the larger unity we all desire.
There is already little room to doubt that a number of other nations
will join the Community over the next few years until we have achieved
a community of Eastern and Central Africa. Similar progress will
undoubtedly be achieved in West and North Africa. There will be
trials and tribulations in the process but we have already demonstrated
in Africa that genuine progress always emerges from our apparent
difficulties. After all, our freedom of choice in the matter of unity is
considerably limited. We either grow slowly alone and stagnate in the
world economy or we grow rapidly together and assume our rightful
place in the councils of the world.

Part Three

AFRICA
AND THE WORLD

Robert Ruark, of *Something of Value* and *Uhuru* notoriety, writing from Nairobi in the Washington *Daily News* in 1960, quoted a high government official in Kenya as saying that 'Tom Mboya is two people. When he is abroad and sweetening it up for the press and public and the TV, he is Dr. Jekyll. When he gets back home to Africa he is Mr. Hyde.'

There is little doubt that between 1952 and 1960 Mboya was regarded as an extremist by the majority of non-Africans. But while abroad, Mr. Mboya's major contribution during the same period consisted in explaining to foreign audiences the African aspirations. In newspaper articles, in pamphlets, at public meetings and over the radio, he argued forcefully the case for African freedom. For thirteen months in 1955/56, for example, when he was supposed to be studying trade unionism at Ruskin College Oxford, Mboya became a crusader abroad. He spent much of his time and energy addressing British audiences at meetings organised by the Movement for Colonial Freedom, the Africa Bureau and the Fabian Bureau. Then he moved across to Hamburg and by August 1956 he was in America as guest of the American Committee on Africa.

Since those early days, Mboya has travelled extensively in Europe, the United States, Canada, South America, Russia, India and Australia interpreting Africa to the world. Dynamic and dedicated, urbane and articulate, Mboya has contributed as much as any African politician towards the establishment of a genuine and meaningful dialogue between Africans and non-Africans.

AFRICA AND AFRO-AMERICA

Tom Mboya was assassinated in Nairobi on 5th July, 1969. He completed this article for the New York Times, *the outgrowth of a visit to the U.S., shortly before his death*

Black Americans today are more concerned with their relationship to Africa than at any point in recent memory. The emergence of this concern at the present time is a phenomenon of great significance and a source of increasing controversy and confusion. The *nature* of the relationship between Africans and black Americans therefore merits extensive dialogue between the two groups, in the hope that issues can be clarified, illusions dispelled and a common understanding reached as to where our immediate objectives coincide and where they do not. Our struggle and goal are the same, and we need a common understanding on strategy so as not to cancel each other out.

It is precisely because communication and clarification are so important that I was deeply disturbed by an incident that occurred when I spoke in Harlem on 18th March. In my one-hour speech I explained the challenges of development in our new African nations. I discussed the difficult period of post-independence through which we are now passing. The economic and social problems we face are complex, and it is very important that those who are interested in our development understand the formidable task that now confronts us. I found the audience in Harlem highly receptive to my remarks on this subject. At the end of my speech, however, in response to some people who had approached me before the meeting, I decided to comment on the proposal for a mass movement of black Americans back to Africa. I began by rejecting the proposal, but before I had a chance to elaborate I was noisily interrupted by two or three people, one of whom projected four or five eggs in my direction. His aim was as bad as his manners.

Needless to say, I found this a rather curious and crude way of impressing African leaders with the genuine desire of black Americans to identify with Africa. By their deliberate and planned activities, a handful of people succeeded in disrupting a very important opportunity for dialogue between an African leader and black people who feel the need for closer relations with our new nations. Africans involved in the serious task of nation-building can hardly be expected to look kindly upon the discourteous and self-indulgent activities of these few individuals. They may also be led to doubt that black Americans in general have any appreciation of, or desire to understand, the problems that we must cope with. Apart from this, the enemies of the black man's struggle were given yet another excuse to justify their continued efforts to disorganise and divide and weaken us.

We must, however, be careful not to dramatise or generalise this incident. Indeed, I have received many letters from black people disassociating themselves from it. The only significance that I now attach to the incident is that it may, by underlining certain confusions, help clarify the relationship between Africans and Afro-Americans. Thus the disrupters, who wanted to obstruct dialogue, may unwittingly have helped to foster it.

In a fundamental way, Africans and Afro-Americans today find themselves in remarkably similar political and economic situations. As I have already indicated, the new nations in Africa have passed through one stage — that of the movement to independence from colonial rule — and are now engaged in the post-independence stage of nation-building. The first stage was primarily *political*, our objective being to achieve the political goal of self-determination.

We suffered during our struggle for independence, but in many ways it was a simpler period than today. It was one of mass mobilisation, dramatic demonstrations and profound nationalist emotions. The present period is less dramatic. Fewer headlines are being made; fewer heroes are emerging. Nationalist sentiment must remain powerful, but it can no longer be sustained by slogans and the excitement of independence. Rather, it must itself sustain the population during the long process of development. For development will not come immediately. It is a process that requires time, planning, sacrifice and work. Colonialism could be abolished by proclamation, but the abolition of poverty required the establishment of new institutions and the development of a modern technology and an enormously expanded educational system. We are engaged, therefore, in an economic and social revolution that must take us far beyond the condition we had achieved when we won our independence.

Our slogan during the independence struggle was 'Uhuru Sasa', and

I do not think it is a coincidence that its English translation, 'Freedom Now', was the slogan for the civil rights movement in America. For the black American struggle in the 1950s and early 60s was very similar to our own. The objective of both was political liberty for black people. In America, black people demanded the abolition of Jim Crow segregation and the right to vote, and they won their fight through courageous and inspiring political protest. But like their African cousins who must meet the challenge of development, they now confront the more difficult task of achieving economic equality.

I have seen black ghettos in America. I have seen individuals living under degrading conditions. Black poverty is more outrageous in America than in my own country because it is surrounded by unparalleled wealth. Thus, for black America the problem of equality looms larger than the problem of development; but they are similar in that the achievement of both requires massive institutional changes.

The struggles of black people in Africa and America are related on more concrete levels. Let us not forget that the independence movement in Africa has had a great impact on the civil rights movement in America, besides giving it a slogan. In addition, this movement for independence has posed many important questions for white America in regard to the race problem in the United States. For example, James Baldwin has quoted in *The Fire Next Time* that the 1954 Brown v. Topeka Board of Education decision concerning school desegregation was largely motivated by 'the competition of the cold war, and the fact that Africa was clearly liberating herself and therefore had, for political reasons, to be wooed by the descendants of her former masters'. In its supporting brief in the Brown case, the Justice Department explained that 'it is in the context of the present world struggle between freedom and [communist] tyranny that the problem of racial discrimination must be viewed'. In other words, the United States Government understood very well that it would have difficulty making friends in Africa so long as the black American remained subjugated. Africans are highly conscious of the plight of black America, and they will be suspicious of the intentions of American foreign policy until they are convinced that the goal of American domestic policy is social justice for all.

I believe, furthermore, that our independence movement has also influenced the thinking of black Americans towards Africa and toward themselves. I have returned to the United States many times since my first visit in 1956, and have observed a remarkable transformation in the black's attitude toward Africa. Thirteen years ago Africa was seen as a mere curiosity, a jungle country of primitive people. This is not surprising, since the image that *all* Americans had of Africa was created by sensational novels and Hollywood films that were far more indicative of American values than of actual life in Africa. Of course, there were some exceptions, like Dr. W. E. B. DuBois; but the majority of black Americans either were ashamed of their association with Africa or were entirely indifferent to her.

These attitudes changed rapidly as much of Africa gained independence. New states and leaders took their place in the world community. African flags flew high and the national anthems of the new nations were sung with dignity. Respected statesmen, scientists and professional men became visible representatives of Africa, thereby destroying the stereotypes that had existed for so long. Many black Americans observed these phenomena at first with disbelief, but soon their shame in their African heritage was transformed into great pride, and they began to identify with Africa with great intensity. Indeed, it can be said that some of them became, in a sense, more African than the Africans.

It is unimportant that this new identification be understood within its proper context. Most African leaders have emphasised the *universality* of the black man's struggle for freedom and equality. Thus, we see the gains made in Africa as representing battles won in a much bigger war that must continue until total victory is achieved. It is in this spirit that African states accept as their responsibility struggles that continue in parts of our continent not yet freed from colonialism and white racist domination. Thus, the new nations of Africa will not be entirely free until the black man is liberated in South Africa, Namibia,* Rhodesia, Angola and Mozambique.

The social movement of black people in the United States is also part of this universal struggle for equality and human dignity for all our people. We cannot survive as free nations if there is any part of the world in which people of African descent are degraded. This is the

* South West Africa.

context in which African interest and aspirations extend beyond the borders of our individual nations and of our continent. This is also the basis of the long-standing collaboration between African nationalists and black leaders from other lands. The heroes of the black man's struggle include those who fought in Africa as well as in America. A. Philip Randolph and Jomo Kenyatta are universal black spokesmen, as were the late Malcolm X and Dr. Martin Luther King Jr. Africa is the birthplace of the black man, but his home is the world. To us, this is the meaning of total independence. We refuse to think of being free in Africa but treated as inferiors the moment we step out of the continent.

In this decade the black man has made enormous progress, in Africa and elsewhere. It is our political decade. Particularly in America, the society has been forced to undergo a genuine social revolution in response to the black struggle. Special note must be taken of the role of young people in this cause. Their fearlessness, resourcefulness and resolve must be recognised and encouraged. My only regret is that many of our leaders and people in Africa have not had the opportunity to visit the United States and thus do not fully appreciate the new mood of militancy and self-assurance that prevails there among black people.

African nationalism is, by its very nature, integrationist, in that its primary objective is to mould numerous tribes into a single political entity. Tribalism, in fact, was one of the major obstacles in the way of independence, and it remains a problem today, as can be seen in the Nigerian-Biafran conflict. The European colonial powers tried for a long time to build up tribal antagonisms in order to weaken nationalist opposition to their rule. Local energies that were channeled into tribal hostilities obviously could not be used to oppose colonialism, and if one tribe became hostile to the Europeans, the latter would befriend another tribe, foment tribal conflict, and then watch the fighting from the sidelines as 'neutral' observers. This was the straightforward tactic of divide-and-rule.

This tactic is by no means unique either to Africa or to colonialism. In Northern Ireland, for example, conservative aristocrats have been able to maintain their power by playing on the religious hostilities between working-class Protestants and Catholics, and have thereby prevented the emergence of a broad-based opposition. A kind of religious tribalism is thus obstructing the formation of a unified and progressive political force there, and in the United States I would think that the same role is played by racial and ethnic tribalism.

Just as the African must reconcile the differences between his tribal and his national identity, so too must the black American realise to the fullest extent his potential as a black man and as an American. I find his task an extraordinarily difficult one, particularly because he has been part of an oppressed racial minority. His new assertiveness is important here. He has cast off the myth of racial inferiority, and he is demanding that he be treated with dignity. But the danger is that his racial pride may become a form of racialism that would be unfortunate not only from a moral point of view, but also from a political one, in that he would be separated from potential allies. From the African point of view, the black man's struggle in America must assert the right of equal treatment and opportunity. I have not found a single African who believes in a black demand for a separate state or for equality through isolation.

The contradiction between black nationalism and American nationalism can lead to much confusion, particularly when black nationalists, in search of a national base that they cannot find at home, turn to Africa. There is the possibility that they want to identify with Africans on a purely racial basis — which is unrealistic since they are citizens of different nations. I think it is this confusion that has led some black Americans to try to impose upon the American political situation concepts and ideologies that grew out of the African experience with colonialism and imperialism. Thus, writers like Frantz Fanon have become popular in certain black American circles, even though these very writers would be the last to want their ideas exported to other continents. Fanon, for example, wrote that 'the test cases of civil liberty whereby both whites and blacks in America try to drive back racial discrimination have very little in common in principles and objectives with the heroic fight of the Angolan people against the detestable Portuguese colonialism'.

Fanon, who advocated the use of violence by the oppressed, is popular among some black Americans because of their tremendous frustration with the conditions under which they must live. The fact that these black Americans would turn to an African for guidance may be an indication of why some of them are now thinking of expatriating to Africa. I think the reason is, again, their frustration, as well as their inability or unwillingness to resolve the tension between their racial and national identities.

At this point I should deal with the specific question of the Kenya Government's attitude toward a motion tabled in our Parliament last year. Reference was made to this motion at the Harlem meeting. Some of the Afro-Americans who spoke to me were angry that our Government had rejected a motion calling for automatic citizenship for any black American who wished to come to settle in Kenya. The point here is a legal one. The fact is that even Africans coming from neighbouring states cannot acquire automatic citizenship. The Constitution lays down the conditions that must be fulfilled by all persons who wish to become citizens. We could not discriminate in favour of any group without first having to amend the Constitution itself. The point must also be made that our Government has to retain the right to keep out undesirable individuals, i.e., people with criminal records, mental cases or others whose presence would create problems for our new nation.

I know that those who meet the conditions will be able to acquire citizenship as easily as have many foreigners since Kenya's independence. Kenya has a large body of non-black and non-African citizens. At the time of independence we gave all persons of non-African origin two years to become citizens by registration, and more than 40,000 Asians as well as thousands of Europeans took advantage of this. Since December, 1965, when the two-year period ended, many more have become citizens through the Naturalisation Act. This method is available to foreigners even today. What is more, we now have many more foreigners in Kenya who have come as businessmen, technicians, etc., since independence, and who enjoy protection under the law without actually being citizens.

Perhaps some of our critics do not realise that we, too, have the many problems confronting black people in America. We have our slums, our unemployed and other social shortcomings. Our first responsibility must be to our own citizens. Emotional crusades cannot change this hard fact.

Perhaps the desire to return to Africa is so unrealistic because it is based upon despair. I do *not* mean by this that African states should refuse black Americans who wish to expatriate. On the contrary, those who want to make a home in Africa are free to do so. There are many opportunities in the new nations, particularly for trained and skilled persons. They could help us enormously during our period of development, and we welcome our American cousins to come and work among us.

What is unrealistic about the proposal is the ease with which some black Americans think that they can throw off their American culture and become African. For example, some think that to identify with Africa one should wear a shaggy beard or a piece of cloth on one's head or a cheap garment on one's body. I find here a complete misunderstanding of what African culture really means. An African walks barefoot or wears sandals made of old tires not because it is his culture but because he lives in poverty. We live in mud and wattle huts and buy cheap Hong Kong fabrics not because it is part of our culture, but because these are conditions imposed on us today by poverty and by limitations in technical, educational and other resources. White people have often confused the symbols of our poverty with our culture. I would hope that black people would not make the same error.

Our culture is something much deeper. It is the sum of our personality and our attitude toward life. The basic qualities that distinguish it are our extended family ties and the codes governing relations between old and young, our concept of mutual social responsibility and communal activities, our sense of humour, our belief in a supreme being and our ceremonies for birth, marriage and death. These things have a deep meaning for us, and they pervade our culture, regardless of tribe or clan. They are qualities that shape our lives, and they will influence the new institutions that we are now establishing. I think that they are things worth preserving, defending and living for.

But I should point out that there is a great debate raging in Africa today over our culture. Certain customs and traditions are being challenged by our movement toward modernisation. People are asking what should be preserved and what should be left behind. They argue about the place universities should have in the society. African intellectuals and governments demand the teaching of African history, and efforts are being made to provide new school syllabuses and to encourage African writers. Some fear the breakdown of the extended family, others the emergence of a new élite removed from the people. We even argue about the use of cosmetics, hair-straighteners, miniskirts and national dress. Thus, black people who come to Africa will find many of their questions unanswered even by us.

Our new nations are in a transitional stage, and I think we can benefit greatly from contact with our American cousins. The African needs to understand and encourage the revolution of the black people in America, while the black people in America need to understand and encourage the effort of nation-building now taking place in Africa. Communication must be strengthened between us.

I have been impressed by new enterprises and economic and social institutions organised by black Americans. There is also a movement in the universities to establish programmes in African studies. These are areas in which we could co-operate and promote our joint interests. Of course, I do not share the view of those who demand black studies and then insist that white students be barred from them. Such an attitude reflects a contradiction, and conflicts with our search for recognition and equality.

Freedom for both Africans and black Americans is not an act of withdrawal, but a major step in asserting the rights of black people and their place as equals among nations and peoples of the world. Freedom involves the full realisation of our identities and potential. It is in this sense that the objective of the African must be the development of his nation and the preservation of his heritage. And the objective of the black American must be the achievement of full and unqualified equality within American society. The black American should look to Africa for guidance — and for a chance to give guidance — but not for escape. He must merge his blackness with his citizenship as an American, and the result will be dignity and liberation.

Black people in Africa and America have survived slavery, colonialism and imperialism. Today we can survive change. We have been oppressed as a people, and have been divided to the point of taking roots in different cultures. But as we struggle to achieve our full liberation, these differences should become less important. If and when we are all free and equal men, perhaps even those racial distinctions that now divide our societies and that separate one nation from the other will disappear in the face of our common humanity.

In conclusion, I note a similarity between the positions of the black American and our own people. In both cases there is impatience to see a promise kept — on the one hand is the promise of civil rights legislation, and on the other, the promise of independence. There is a crisis of confidence. The danger in America, as in Africa, is that such impatience can lead to confusion of priorities and failure to recognise the goals of the movement. Effective unity and committed national leaders are needed more now than ever before. If these elements are absent, the enthusiasm of the young people and the tremendous sympathy and support of other groups may be lost in despair.

This, in my view, is the challenge before the black people and their leaders in America. The struggle calls for even greater resolution and dedication if they are to translate past victories into a programme of action for the more difficult task of achieving actual equality — as against legal and constitutional proclamations.

Bayard Rustin has offered the best explanation I have yet read of the origins of the 'Back to Africa' movement among his people:

'There is a reason for this movement which has far less to do with the Negro's relation to Africa than to America. The "Back to Africa" and separatist tendencies are always strongest at the very time when the Negro is most intensely dissatisfied with his lot in America. It is when the Negro has lost hope in America — and has lost his identity *as* an American — that he seeks to re-establish his identity and his roots as an African.

'This period of despair has historically followed hard upon a period of hope and of efforts to become integrated — on the basis of full equality — into the economic, social and political life of the United States. The present separatist mood, as we know, has come after a decade in which the Negro achieved enormous and unprecedented gains through the civil rights struggle, and it has coincided with a right-wing reaction that has obstructed further measures toward equality. The combination of progress, aroused hopes, frustration and despair has caused many Negroes to withdraw into separatism and to yearn for Africa.'

Rustin goes on to observe that this syndrome has occurred three times in the past: in the early eighteen-hundreds, when the African Methodist Episcopal Church was formed; in the late nineteenth century, when Booker T. Washington became famous, and in the 1920s, during the heyday of Marcus Garvey.

I have accepted the opportunity to contribute this article, not as an apology for the Harlem incident, but because of my genuine concern about the relations between Africa and the black people in America. The achievement problems they face are of great interest to us in more than one way. In the first place, they are our cousins and we share together the black man's fate in the world. His complete liberation is our joint concern because, as I have said, black people cannot be fully free if there remains any part of the globe where a black man is denied his rights. Second, the complete emancipation of America's blacks will influence the country's policies in a way that can only lead to a better understanding of and sympathy for the cause of black people everywhere. And finally, a free and vigorous black community in the United States can, within its own organisation, play a much more effective and practical role in helping African and other black nations meet some of their challenges of development.

I have, since 1958, witnessed the true potential of the black American in this regard. People like Ralph Bunche, Jackie Robinson, Harry Belafonte, Sidney Poitier, Frank Montero, Bayard Rustin and the heads of such Negro institutions as Howard University, Tuskegee Institute and Morehouse, Morris Brown and Spelman Colleges in Atlanta played a decisive part in my campaign for a students' airlift to the United States. This programme helped to bring over 1,000 students from Kenya and other parts of East and Central Africa to study in America; today, many of these students are home, and are providing the backbone for our new public service.

A number of Afro-American leaders in church and community groups, like the Rev. James Robinson of New York, labour leaders like A. Philip Randolph and Maida Springer, and many black families across the United States took part in this unique experiment in people-to-people international co-operation. And there were, of course, many white Americans, like the late Senator Robert F. Kennedy and his brother, Senator Edward Kennedy; Theodore Kheel, the attorney and mediator; the distinguished statesman, Averell Harriman; Dr. Buell Gallagher, the educator; I. W. Abel, the labour leader; and white institutions and families who contributed to it.

The point I am making, however, is that black people have the scope and capacity to join in the challenge of development in Africa as free citizens in America. We need them there. I am not afraid of an exodus of black people from America to Africa because I know there will be no such exodus. I am, rather, concerned that the emotion and effort needed to promote such a movement would lead to sterile debate and confusion when there is an urgent need for unity and decisive leadership.

The challenge of the black American was stated with great beauty by W. E. B. DuBois over a half a century ago:

'One ever feels this twoness — an American, a Negro; two souls, two thoughts, two unreconciled strivings; two warring ideals in one dark body, whose dogged strength alone keeps it from being torn asunder.

'The history of the American Negro is the history of this strife — this longing to attain self-conscious manhood, to merge his double self into a better and truer self. In this merging he wishes neither of the older selves to be lost. He would not Africanise America, for America has too much to teach the world and Africa. He would not bleach his Negro soul in a flood of white Americanism, for he knows that Negro blood has a message for the world. He simply wishes to make it possible for a man to be both a Negro and an American, without being cursed and spit upon by his fellows, without having the doors of opportunity closed roughly in his face.'

SOME REFLECTIONS ON THE DEVELOPMENT OF A FOREIGN POLICY FOR AN AFRICAN STATE

Speech to the Diplomats Course at Makerere University College, Kampala, Monday, 17th August, 1964

You will note from the title given to my address — and you will observe in its delivery — that what I have to say is more in the nature of a dissertation, a thinking-aloud, than a fully extended thesis. I am not going to provide for you some handy panacea for the solution of all the diplomatic difficulties which face our countries and which you will have to cope with. However much time were available, such a task could never be completed. International affairs are the most fluid of operations. Not only are new issues continually arising, but old matters which one might consider settled require constant attention as cicrumstances alter. That is why I have preferred to speak of the development of foreign policy.

The growth of the art of diplomacy came about because nations sought alternative means to armed conflict for the settlement of their disputes. Military weapons have become increasingly destructive, increasingly complex. The practice of diplomacy has developed correspondingly in scope and complexity. Until now diplomacy has always been one jump behind and wars have continued. Let us hope that man's genius in the field of human relations may from henceforth be a match for the scientific creativeness which has given him weapons which can lead to his own destruction.

Nations born since Hiroshima in 1945 and since the successful testing of atomic weapons by the Soviet Union a few years later, have entered a totally different world to that which confronted young states before the Second World War.

Once nation states and empires replaced city states, the traditional pattern of international relations was for powers to rise and fall, and to be replaced by others. Earlier, such processes took place contemporaneously in different parts of the world but with technical advances, particularly in the communications and weapons field, the world became one.

The massive confrontation of empires and alliances progressed to a climax in the twentieth century, resulting in two world wars and we are now presented with the truly terrifying possibility of a nuclear holocaust.

Two major power blocs confront one another from behind their atomic stockades. A few years ago one might have used the description 'monolithic' of these two camps, but that is no longer true. Nevertheless, our new states come into existence in a world dominated by two strong power blocs, each having some ideological, economic and military unity.

How are we to face this situation? In the past some small states found the answer in a withdrawal into neutralism. They followed a policy of isolationism and non-involvement in world affairs. Strictly judged by the basic yardstick of diplomacy their policy was successful. They managed to exist and progress without becoming involved in wars.

But that is not our way. Nor, and this I need hardly mention, do we intend to let ourselves be drawn into one or other of the two antagonistic camps. We belong to the growing 'Third World' which believes in a policy of positive non-alignment.

Positive neutrality, President Modibo Keita of Mali has said, 'Is the refusal of a nation to lose its personality in a world where assimilation is the objective of every great power'.

President Nyerere summed it up like this: 'The poor countries of the world should be very careful not to allow themselves to be used as the tools of any of the rich countries — however much the rich countries may try to fool them that they are on their side. And don't forget, 'that the rich countries of the world today may be found on both sides of the division between capitalist and socialist countries'.

Non-alignment means that we are not going to take sides permanently and automatically with either the Western bloc or the Eastern bloc. If the West present a resolution at the United Nations, no African nation worthy of the name could be considered an automatic supporter. Nor should any Eastern resolution expect unthinking backing from Africa.

As we declared in the K.A.N.U. Manifesto upon which the Kenya Government was elected to power, 'Our policy is one of non-alignment, not of non-commitment. We fully commit ourselves to support what we believe to be right and just in international affairs. But each case will be judged on its merits'.

In the Manifesto we expressed our awareness that the African continent could be a force for good in world affairs as much by virtue of its moral strength as by any military might.

Speaking of the role of African states in world affairs, President Nkrumah of Ghana has said, 'They are able to operate their decisive influence because many of them adhere to a policy of non-commitment to either of the East-West blocs, a policy of neutral non-alignment but not of passivity. They exercise their right of free choice in supporting those acts which they consider will help to maintain the peace upon which their continuance as nations depends.'

At its inception the idea of positive neutrality was assailed both by the East and by the West. The late American Secretary of State, John Foster Dulles, said it had 'increasingly become an obsolete conception, and except under very special circumstances, it is an immoral and short-sighted conception'.

Equally vehement attacks came from communist states. Yet during the last few years we have seen some amazing changes in the attitude of the great powers. I think we can take it as a considerable victory that non-alignment has become a real force in world affairs and that the Cold War powers now consider it worth while to make allowance for such an idea instead of merely reliving it.

The late President Kennedy went so far as to say that 'We want for Africans what they want for themselves'. The Soviet Premier, Nikita Khrushchev, declared in 1960, 'Our stormy twentieth century has given a new meaning to the concept of neutrality. The following of a policy of neutrality by countries inhabited by a quarter of mankind, under present conditions restricts the field of activity of the aggressive military blocs. In effect, if formerly neutrality condemned a country to play a passive role in world affairs, today the situation has radically changed. The neutral countries play an active role by the very fact of their existence and by the example they provide.'

In the danger spots of the Far East, the big powers have insisted that the establishment of neutral states would be the solution and basis upon which to establish the peace. It would thus appear that the big powers have begun to learn that the world is no longer theirs to conquer. They have come to feel that the security of their own countries as well as world peace depends more and more in recognising the sovereign state of each nation however small or weak. One might even go as far as to suggest that the so called 'weak' nations may soon dictate the decision of the 'strong' nations.

Our policy does not only manifest itself in terms of voting records and declarations of support or opposition as the case may be. It finds expression in our economic dealings, in our ideological independence and in our military non-involvement.

Economically speaking, colonial Africa was merely an appendage of Europe. This is no time to get involved in considerations of whether imperialism brought economic advantages to the colonies. What I am saying is that a fundamental motive of colonialism was that an empire provided a source of cheap natural resources for the metropolitan power and an outlet for its manufactured goods.

In nearly every case, the achievement of political independence has not seen a correspondingly radical change in economic relationships. Many countries of Africa still belong to the franc zone, the sterling area or the dollar area. A glance at the trade figures for any African country will show how little the relationships with the former occupying power have changed in the economic field.

Yet it is difficult to disentangle economic ties and political strings. If we are dependent upon one country or group of countries as far as markets for our main crops are concerned; our diplomats, and hence our foreign policy, will be subjected to all sorts of pressures, both subtle and not so subtle. Similarly if those same countries supply us with a large proportion of our imports, the opportunities for pressure to be brought upon us in political matters will be so obvious.

If we trade with both the East and the West we shall be able to create for ourselves an economy which is not based entirely on the circumstances of one specific bloc. In the period of economic reconstruction we can avoid the situation of colonial days when we had to conform to one set of economic theories. We can build a structure of our own design, based on the principles of socialism, drawing what we consider appropriate both from the East and from the West.

Apart from the new economic structures needed, we need also to look at our political institutions. As we begin to develop these we are accused of moving too closely to the East. This is because the colonial period has left us with a structure of Western institutions and ideologies. As we abandon these for a way of our own choosing, those who see events only in their own blinkered Cold War terms will make allegations against us.

As the representatives of neutral nations, we must express our determination to devise such systems as we think fit without having them interpreted in terms of leaning Eastward or Westward.

Many African states are finding that the most appropriate form of political structure for their people at this time is a one-party state. It so happens that such a structure is also found in the communist state. It would be most short-sighted of the communist states if they rejoiced in this as a move by African states into their orbit and equally unobservant of western countries to see it as a move against them. It cannot be stressed too often that we are for Africa. These people must be made to realise that we want recognition that we are seeking our own way.

One way in which Africa can demonstrate its independence most clearly is by refusing to have a foreign military base of the major powers and their allies on its soil.

We in Kenya have taken steps to have the British base removed and it is already being dismantled. The speed with which this is being done and the alacrity with which British troops were withdrawn from Tanganyika after their brief assistance, indicates that the major powers have come to appreciate our feelings on this matter.

The question of military bases leads on to the general problem of nuclear disarmament. I think the Afro-Asian nations have made it quite clear that this is something which concerns them as much as it affects those powers which possess atomic weapons. If the horrors of a nuclear war were to occur we would all suffer. It might well mean the end of human life and our new nations would be denied the chance to show what they are capable of achieving. In fact our people would hardly have had the chance to start living as men. This explains the extent of our investment in world peace.

Yet so often when the major military powers discuss disarmament they are only interested in gaining tactical advantages and in scoring debating points over their opponents. They are so committed to the idea that world peace can only be maintained through nuclear deterrents that they have little room to look at disarmament from a dispassionate and non-involved point of view. The non-aligned states of Africa, Asia and elsewhere can desire for the lessening of world tension.

In their meeting, held at Belgrade, Yugoslavia, in 1961, representatives from twenty-three non-aligned countries declared that it was essential they should 'participate in solving outstanding international issues concerning peace and security in the world, as none of them can remain unaffected by, or indifferent to, these issues.'

An incidental benefit of disarmament would be that the skills, resources and manpower now wanted in preparing for destruction could be put to some positive use. Part of the efforts and resources could be diverted to succouring the sick and starving peoples of the under-developed countries.

It has been estimated by some people that one tenth of the expenditure involved in armaments would be enough to raise the whole of the less-developed world to the level of a self-sustaining economy.

I have already spoken of our intention of keeping foreign armies out of Africa. This is closely linked with the idea of establishing a nuclear-free zone throughout the continent. That is to say that Africa should not be used as a testing ground, as a store or as a base from which atomic attacks can be launched. In present terms we can achieve this by keeping our foreign bases. But with the development of nuclear weapons there is a terrible possibility that their ownership will spread. The more countries there are having atomic weapons, the more chance is there that they will be used and that a local conflict may spread into a world-wide nuclear war. The intention to declare Africa a nuclear-free zone is therefore a self-denying ordinance. It is something which the statesmen and diplomats of Africa will be concerned with in the immediate future. This question has been discussed by the O.A.U. and a resolution adopted accordingly.

But I am sure that Africa will need the use of nuclear power or energy for peaceful development. Our vast deserts and forests and some of our soil research and development could receive a real boost if we were able to share effectively in the peaceful use of atomic energy. Africa more than any other continent, needs to train scientists who can cope with our urgent development problems. I must therefore state very clearly that while we denounce and seek the control of nuclear weapons, we are anxious and must in fact insist on being able to benefit by this most precious of man's scientific achievements.

There is one fundamental aspect of foreign policy which I have not yet discussed, yet which is implicit in nearly all that I have said. This is the question of Pan-African unity. Those who belittle our achievements and mock our hopes should ponder how much constructive work has been done. Can any other continent claim to have realised such unity of purpose and of action?

I can tell you that in this, as in all other diplomatic activities, there will be difficulties. Consider how limited we are in resources, in facilities, in individual men and women of experience and in the traditions of diplomatic activity.

Most African countries can only afford to establish representation in half a dozen or a dozen states. The total staff of our Ministry of External Affairs, in Kenya and overseas, is smaller than that of just one embassy of some of the big powers. Our poverty means that we cannot afford the technical facilities — the libraries, the telecommunications systems and so forth — to the extent that we would like to have them.

The lack of trained personnel is something which is experienced throughout all professional fields. It is a particular indictment of colonialism that it failed to provide opportunities for the indigenous people to rise in such jobs as doctors, journalists, lawyers. It goes without saying that the training of diplomats was inconceivable under an imperialist regime. That is why all of our diplomats are having to start now right from the bottom, although they have to work with and against those who have many, many years of experience. Perhaps even more of a drawback than the paucity of individual experience is our lack of a diplomatic history and tradition in the international and modern sense.

As I remarked at the beginning, diplomacy is a developing and organic process. In the older nations, there is a great body of precedent to be referred to. Modifications can be made to meet new needs within the context of traditional policies. But with us so little of substance is given. True, we have our principles, but international affairs is not an intellectual, mathematical exercise in which a correct answer will logically be arrived at. There are too many variables and shifting circumstances. We have rejected the easy way out. We could have chosen to withdraw into passive neutrality, not committing ourselves on difficult issues. Alternatively, we could have adopted another simple path, by tying ourselves to the coat-tails of one or other of the great power blocs.

Instead we have decided to follow a course of positive and constructive non-alignment, judging each case on its merits, not allowing others — even our good friends — to make decisions for us. That is what makes our task so challenging.

Before I close, let me put forward one thought which may prove fruitful. Within Africa, through the O.A.U. we are developing a structural organisation for facing the problems of the continent. At the United Nations there is some organisational framework for the African Group. From these beginnings, in order to make up for our lack of facilities, personnel and experience, let us investigate how we can pool the diplomatic resources of Africa in our dealings throughout the world.*

---

* In his more recent statements Mr. Mboya has reflected even further on the international situation as it affects African states. He has discussed topics such as technical assistance and problems of aid and the Cold War. At a conference in Vienna, June 1968, he pointed out that aid had undergone a complete transformation, i.e. from the days when colonies received generous grants; the immediate post-war period when the big powers competed actively with each other for the support of smaller nations, building items such as stadiums plus foreign military bases; the troubled days of international economic and monetary problems — with the developed nations applying stringent conditions on aid using it more as a means of promoting their own trade. Lastly he envisaged the era of international co-operation through aid and trade and wanted African nations to concentrate on diversification of their economies and greater intra-African trade.

AID AND DEVELOPMENT IN THE COMMONWEALTH

Address to the Commonwealth Conference on Aid and Development in Nairobi, Kenya, 24th May, 1967

This Conference is yet another step made possible by the Commonwealth Secretariat, which has shown great foresight and imagination since it was established only a few years ago. The various points on the agenda for this meeting represent the most important aspects of the areas of co-operation within our Commonwealth association. The questions about aid, technical assistance and export promotion are of real interest to us all. In fact they are matters in which we can see genuine mutual interest and benefit. Exchange of experiences in problems of planning and planning techniques is an appropriate subject among countries who have so many historical ties.

The countries represented here come from different continents and represent the so-called old and new worlds, or developed and developing countries. This fact represents an opportunity if it is used realistically and based on recognition of our different interests as well as those common interests which we share. Your discussions will further be assisted by accepting the fact that our economies are faced with different problems and pressures and the techniques we use must reflect the local circumstances and conditions.

Against this background I think it is fair to ask 'Where does the Commonwealth go from here?'. What common interests can give it the purpose it so badly needs? How can this meeting contribute to those ends?

The emotional and traditional ties binding the Commonwealth countries together are the use of a common language, similar roots to our systems of Government, some trade preferences, and the reliance on sterling as a reserve for our currencies. These are not much with which to work, particularly if it is remembered that other countries use English, some more extensively than some of us; our governmental systems are departing rapidly from the British model; our trade preferences may diminish as Britain negotiates with the European

Economic Community and the use of sterling as a reserve can be replaced, though only with some inconvenience.

If in the past the Commonwealth has derived its strength from similarities among its members, it must find its purpose in the future among the existing and emerging differences. Our similarities are the basis for association and indeed a source of strength, but it is our differences that can lend purpose and meaning to our future joint endeavours. In brief, the Commonwealth must be transformed from a social club into a purposeful society for mutual aid and assistance.

The differences among Commonwealth nations that can lend purpose to our joint efforts are many, but four of them are, in my view, of special importance. These are differences with respect to continental location, economic structure, availability of manpower, and supply of capital.

Another factor that must also be taken into account in your discussions, although it is not on your formal agenda, is Britain's recent decision to seek entry into the European Economic Community. This decision was taken after this Conference was decided upon and its agenda prepared. If the decision had been taken earlier, I am sure your agenda would have provided for its discussion. We must appreciate, however, that the current British move is simply a part of the larger post-war trend towards continental trade accommodations, which in themselves pose serious questions about the future of multi-continental associations like the Commonwealth.

Those of you who have seen or heard my recent speech before the Economic Commission for Africa meeting in Lagos will know how very strongly we in Kenya feel about this trend towards regional and continental association. I think that for us in Africa our future success in development depends critically on our ability to co-operate closely on economic matters.

We feel that we are on the verge of significant success in those endeavours. The work of the Phillip Commission* and the Treaty

---

*The Membership was as follows:
    Chairman: *Kjeld Phillip*

Kenya members:
- *J. S. Gichuru*
- *T. J. Mboya*
- *B. R. McKenzie*

which will emerge from our recent discussions should put economic relations among the three countries of East Africa on a sound footing. Success at that level should contribute substantially to the creation of closer economic ties with our other neighbours.

Tanzania members: ⎰ A. H. Jamal
⎱ P. Bomani
   A. Z. N. Swai

Uganda members: ⎰ L. Kalule-Settala
⎱ L. Lubowa
   B. K. Bataringaya

The Terms of Reference were as follows:

'To examine existing arrangements in East Africa for co-operation between Kenya, Tanzania and Uganda on matters of mutual interest, and having due regard to the views of the respective Governments, to make agreed recommendations on the following matters:

(a) How the East African Common Market can be maintained and strengthened and the principles on which, and the manner in which, the Common Market can in future be controlled and regulated.

(b) The arrangements necessary for effective operation of the Common Market consequential upon the establishment of separate currencies.

(c) The extent to which services at present maintained in common between the three countries can be continued, and the form which such services should take.

(d) The extent to which (if at all) new services can be provided in common between the three countries, and the form which such services should take.

(e) The manner in which the common services should be financed.

(f) The extent to which the management of different services can be located in different parts of East Africa.

(g) The legal, administrative and constitutional arrangements most likely to promote effective co-operation between the East African countries in the light of the recommendations made under paragraphs (a) (b) (c) (d) (e) and (f).

To submit their final report to the Governments not later than 1st May, 1966.'

The decision to establish the Commission was made by the President of Kenya, the President of Tanzania and the Prime Minister of Uganda at a meeting held in Mombasa on 1st September, 1965. The Commission held its first meeting on 24th November, 1965 and its last meeting on 14th May, 1966. The report was signed on 13th May, 1966.

The need to consolidate our markets in Africa rests on the nature of modern technology and the economies of production associated with large markets. We cannot in Africa afford to forego these advantages and opportunities and our ties with the Commonwealth must not conflict with our objectives of closer co-operation on a geographical basis.

Like Britain, we in East Africa are also seeking closer ties with the European Economic Community, and Nigeria and the eighteen French-speaking African countries already enjoy the status of Associate Members. There is no question that we in Africa need readier access to the European market. We are also concerned, however, that relations with the European Economic Community should not distract our attention from the equally urgent need to develop Africa as a market for our own goods. But Britain is not alone in its endeavours. We in East Africa, for example, have also been hard at work to develop stronger common market ties among ourselves, and indeed to create a basis for closer economic association on the wider geographic basis of the sub-region of Eastern Africa.

The movement toward stronger geographic associations among nations is important and significant but it must not be regarded as being in conflict with the inter-continental ties like those represented by the Commonwealth. Regional groupings will for a long time to come be able to cater for only part of our interests. Indeed, such groupings must be regarded as an attempt to create a better and more positive basis for our contribution and participation in inter-continental economic and trade relations. We all know that any continental association conceived with a view to the isolation of a continent from the rest of the world is doomed to failure. Rather, such association must have as one of its main objectives an attempt to ensure more effective development of the world economy.

The fact that our membership spans many continents gives us the opportunity to initiate constructive measures for promoting freer trade on a world-wide basis. The advantages to be found in common market arrangements could be multiplied many times if similar arrangements could be concluded on a global basis. The recently concluded Kennedy Round negotiations among developed nations are an important step in the right direction, but those negotiations should signal redoubled efforts to open up markets for the developing countries.

The close trade ties existing among Commonwealth countries provide a basis for even more effective co-operation in the future. Differences in geographic location mean that the knowledge of markets inherent in the Commonwealth extends to every corner of the globe. But it is to be asked whether in fact we are sharing that knowledge effectively. I think the answer is a resounding NO. The scope for helping each other to identify market opportunities is great indeed. It extends beyond markets in Commonwealth countries themselves to those geographic markets with which Commonwealth countries are associated. Let us, therefore, find an effective mechanism for organising and sharing our wealth of market information.

We must also do a great deal more to reduce trade barriers among ourselves, and among those geographic associations to which we also belong. Commonwealth exports as a percentage of world exports have declined from over 25 per cent in 1959 to less than 20 per cent in 1965. Moreover, trade among ourselves has declined relative to our trade with other countries. These developments reflect in part the growing independence of economic decision-making that has followed political independence. It also reflects, however, a lethargy with regard to needed modifications of tariffs and the possibility of making mutually advantageous adjustments in trading arrangements.

I am not only concerned, however, with explicit barriers such as tariffs and quotas but also with restrictions and outright prohibitions that travel under the guise of health measures and quality control. Whatever their original purpose and justification, these kinds of restrictions should be thoroughly re-examined and thereafter kept under continuous review.

Differences in the economic structures of our economies offer another opportunity and indeed a challenge for constructive and co-operative efforts. Some of us are relatively advanced economically, with high *per capita* incomes; others of us are just beginning the enormous task of development. Some of us have economies that are well balanced as between industrial and primary productions; others of us are still mainly producers of primary products. Our domestic economies are of all types and the range of products produced, and production methods used, is vast indeed.

On the other hand, many of us are now beginning economic activities which, though new to us, are long-standing and efficient operations to others. This wealth of technological knowledge and production and marketing know-how could be of great value if it could be more effectively shared. In a narrow sense, the sharing of this kind of information means assisting a potential competitor. In the broader perspective which we in Government must take, it means increasing efficiency so that all of us can compete more effectively not only with each other but with producers outside the Commonwealth as well.

Differences in the availability of manpower can also lend purpose to our continuing association. This is too obvious a point to merit extensive discussion. All of us, whether developed or developing, have some manpower and knowledge that could be of assistance to others, either in central bodies conducting studies or organising and disseminating information or on location furnishing practical advice and assistance. We need a mechanism and the financial arrangements for bringing qualified people and important tasks together quickly and efficiently.

Differences in the availability of capital in our different countries provide another opportunity for associated effort. There is, of course, the obvious value to those of us who are short of capital of an expansion in the amount of aid forthcoming from those who are more fortunate. But I would also like to see the Commonwealth do something more constructive about the terms on which aid is arranged. In particular, as most of us are in the sterling area and rely on sterling as a reserve, it should be possible to find a way to arrange aid so that it can be used to finance imports anywhere within the Commonwealth rather than tying aid to imports from any one country. All of us who receive aid would prefer it to be untied, but we can all agree that Commonwealth ties would be far superior to bilateral ties.

There are two possibilities that may merit exploration in this regard. One is to channel more aid through a Commonwealth Loan Fund which would serve as a clearing house between donors and aid recipients. Its aid would be tied to imports from member nations, thus assisting in increasing the exports of member nations while at the same time assisting developing members with capital aid.

The second possibility, which I personally do not like very much but which may be mentioned, is certainly less attractive than the first. Aid in sterling could be ear-marked for expenditure within the Commonwealth. Such credits would not be convertible into non-sterling currencies, either by the initial or secondary recipients. Commonwealth nations who received such loans could use them only for purchases from other sterling reserve countries. Moreover, countries receiving these ear-marked funds in payment for goods would also be restricted to using them within the Commonwealth. These special credits would be non-convertible at every successive spending stage, the amount so ear-marked being reduced, however, as the loans are repaid. There are a number of technical problems associated with this device and the non-convertibility feature has undesirable connotations. Perhaps you at this Conference can identify more effective ways of reducing import restrictions on aid.

We must be equally concerned, however, with liberalising the flow of private capital and ensuring that opportunities for investment are identified, analysed and made known to those with the capital to implement them. I have discussed this matter in the specific context of the needs of Africa in a recent speech at Lagos. A major barrier to the flow of private capital is ignorance — ignorance about the climate for investment and ignorance about the specific opportunities that exist throughout the developing countries. Perhaps the Commonwealth can become a major means of overcoming that ignorance.

The line of thought I have been pursuing has obviously been paralleled to some extent in the serious consideration that has been devoted to these matters in the preparation of the agenda for this Conference. In particular, you have before you for discussion at this meeting three matters which are directly related to the thesis I have developed, namely, trade promotion and a Commonwealth Market Development Fund, Commonwealth Development Projects and technical assistance and a Commonwealth Planners Service.

Many of us in the Commonwealth are too small, both as nations and as producers of particular commodities, to undertake effective and extensive trade promotion campaigns. Moreover, we cannot each gather and digest all of the necessary information on marketing and production opportunities without substantial, and in my view unnecessary, duplication of effort. The proposal before you to remedy these difficulties through a co-ordinated and common effort is a sensible and commendable one. You may, however, wish to consider if it may not be too modest in resources to accomplish its important objectives. I should also like to see included in the activities of the proposed Market Development Fund the identification and alleviation of the many barriers to trade which restrict our access to many profitable markets.

The scope for joint development projects, in particular those in one country financed and otherwise assisted by two or more countries, is considerable. I would hope that the magnitude of the programme would be increased as soon as its success has been demonstrated. It should also be considered if the programme would not have a better chance of success of it were operated as a genuine Commonwealth programme rather than within existing bilateral programmes, as the discussion paper suggests. There are some obvious and time-consuming administrative difficulties if each project must be arranged and agreed by three or more countries.

The proposed technical assistance programme can be of substantial help to all of the developing countries in the Commonwealth. In particular, it could assist in recruiting high-level technical advisers by compiling a Commonwealth list of interested people, with dates and periods of availability. Serious attempts should be made to reduce the currently very long lag between request and fulfilment. The proposal recognises that developing countries have experts in many fields, but usually cannot afford to lend them to others without charge. Finance is therefore necessary to cover essential costs if the developing nations are also to contribute to the needs of others. This is an area that requires urgent action if we are to take advantage of the manpower surpluses in some of the developing countries within the Commonwealth.

Your discussions during this Conference can do much to lend point and purpose to the Commonwealth association, and to find in our differences the scope for positive, constructive and co-operative effort. There is, however, a pressing and immediate problem to which I hope you can give some very serious attention, although it is not on your formal agenda. I am again referring to Britain's decision to seek entry into the European Community and to press forward this matter as quickly as possible. The importance of this move for the other Commonwealth countries varies widely but all of us have intimate stakes in the outcome of Britain's effort. All of us have protected markets in Britain, to one extent or another, as a result of the system of Commonwealth tariff preferences. Britain's entry into the Community will mean in principle the removal of tariffs between Britain and the Six and the erection of common Community tariffs against outsiders. Some of the goods we have been selling to Britain may then be purchased by Britain from her new European partners instead. There is, therefore, the very real threat to some of us that a major market for certain of our goods will shrink.

But when Britain enters the Community there is also the possibility that some Community tariffs may be reduced, possibly even on a preferential basis to Commonwealth countries. This opens up the possibility that some of us may gain access to the larger European market for some of our goods that we are not now able to sell there. The nature and extent of our possible access to the European market is complicated by the special arrangements the eighteen French-speaking African countries now enjoy with the Community. It is also Community policy to demand reciprocal tariff benefits which could be costly if the demands are extensive. It may also be possible, in cases where permanent and favourable tariff adjustments cannot be negotiated, to arrange for temporary transitional preferences.

The point is that all of these fundamental matters will be the subject of negotiations in which we cannot directly participate. Britain has expressed a willingness to discuss, mainly on an individual basis, the concerns and desires of her Commonwealth partners. But is this likely to be enough or will it have the effect of dividing our interests and conquering our resistance to proposed British concessions to the Community?

I am concerned that the smaller members of the Commonwealth in particular will be unable to find the experts, or spare them if they have some, for the enormous but delicate task of assessing the economic costs and benefits of the intricate negotiations that will be taking place, but in which we will have no direct participation. Moreover, will each of us be able to undertake the careful analysis needed to ensure that all consequences are being considered, and to make imaginative and constructive proposals? Finally, does it make sense for each of us to attempt the major effort necessary when substantial economies and better results might be achieved by pooling our efforts, if only on the most basic analysis?

Britain suggests that our problems are so diverse that they can best be dealt with individually. But those problems have both a cause and a common care. I suggest that the Commonwealth countries should give immediate consideration to two independent measures for improving the representation of our interests in the forthcoming discussions.

First, a Commonwealth meeting of economic Ministers should be arranged before negotiations begin in earnest to ensure that the views of member countries are based on complete information and are fully considered. Second, and independent of the decision on the first, the Commonwealth Secretariat should be strengthened for the duration of the negotiations to undertake basic and continuing analysis of the problems arising and to keep all member nations fully informed of the state of the negotiations, and in particular of the scheduling of matters for discussion which are of special interest to any country. Britain's decision is a matter of great importance to all of us. We cannot afford to neglect it or to depend on Britain or the European Community to give full consideration to our interests unless we ourselves ensure that those interests have been properly identified and adequately and persuasively presented.

If these two steps could be taken, I for one would have considerably greater confidence in the outcome of the forthcoming negotiations. After all, in addition to finding future purposes for the Commonwealth association we have a great stake in preserving those beneficial arrangements which have served us so well in the past.

But before I sit down I should like to refer to the need for consultations on some of the subjects that will be discussed at the next United Nations Conference on Trade and Development meeting. I know it is assumed that when we get there we shall operate as two groups; the Developed Countries and the Developing Countries. But I feel there is scope for some exchanges. I hope there can be such consultations among those who will lead delegations from the different Commonwealth countries.

In conclusion I would like to remind you again about the wide diversity of interest represented in this room to-day. We represent poor countries and rich countries, primary producers and highly industrialised economies, nations that are sea-faring and some that are land-locked, and governments from every part of the globe. These differences are a challenge. They are also a cross-section of the differences that exist among all nations. We in the Commonwealth have the opportunity to demonstrate to the world how nations can co-operate to alleviate poverty, reduce discriminatory practices and ease world tensions. If we in the Commonwealth cannot contribute effectively to these objectives, there is little hope from more heterogenous organisations.

I am aware that there are some in the older Commonwealth countries who have become disenchanted and look at the Commonwealth as a burden. In fact, some people tend to think that the developing countries need the Commonwealth more than the older ones. This is not true. In terms of trade, the developing countries make a substantial contribution as a market for the older nations. In some cases we have substantial trade deficits in favour of the older members of the Commonwealth. We are in this association, free and sovereign states, but we also know that it is to our mutual advantage to co-operate in a world which is becoming increasingly complex and difficult for many nations. There is today no place for inward-looking policies.

This conference on Aid and Development was one of the most important organised by the Commonwealth Secretariat. It was opened by Mr. Mboya.

The main objectives of the meeting were to discuss, review and recommend measures appropriate for enhancing (1) Co-operation in planning, (2) Technical assistance, and (3) Trade Promotion among the Commonwealth members.

The following was the result of the meeting:

(1) *Co-operation In Planning*. The meeting recommended that the Commonwealth Secretariat should prepare an analytical report in consultation with the Chairman of the Planning committee taking into consideration:

(a) Basic Development problems and objectives;
(b) The choice of strategies and plan construction;
(c) Practical problems of Development Planning, and
(d) Regional Co-operation in planning; and with particular concentration on implementation problems, administrative changes and external technical assistance. On co np etion of the Report it should be submitted to the member Governments for approval.

(2) *Technical Assistance*. Since the meeting was of the view that there is sufficient room for more co-ordinated links between Commonwealth countries, a new programme in technical assistance to be co-ordinated through the Commonwealth Secretariat was recommended, i.e. a 'Headquarters Group of Experts' would be established in London for assisting the member countries in this field at their request.

(3) *Trade Promotion*. The creation of the Commonwealth Development Fund was welcomed by all members to assist in various fields of trade promotion.

(4) Another proposal which had been implemented was for Third Country Financing. Technical assistance from one Commonwealth country may be financed by a third member. One donor provides the personnel or facilities and another the finance.

THE FUTURE OF AGRICULTURE IN DEVELOPING COUNTRIES

Address to the Young World Food and Development Conference, Toronto, 12th September, 1967

This address is particularly interesting in the light of the Pope's Encyclical on Family Planning. The Kenya Government is firmly committed to supporting access to information and facilities for birth control to those who wish it. The policy is enunciated in Sessional Paper No. 10. Mr. Mboya, who is himself a Catholic, has said more recently that he sees no conflict between the Pope's ruling and the Kenya Government's policy.

There have always been in every generation some parents who conjure up devils and ogres in order to coerce their children into performing tasks which they might not have undertaken on logical grounds alone. I do not condone this practice and am equally grieved when mature adults employ it with their peers. Yet the literature on food supply and population growth abounds with examples of this approach, apparently on the presumption that a less flamboyant argument will not induce constructive action before the force of necessity takes its grim hand in the matter. Only last month I read an article by a very learned economist in which he pointed out that in 850 years at its present rate of growth the population of the world will not have standing room. Clearly some of us must learn to swim by the year 2818!

I do not intend today to be a prophet of doom. Nor do I intend to depreciate the gravity of the Malthusian problem. But we must, I think, have confidence that our people and their governments will invent and adopt social policies which are as imaginative and effective with respect to population growth as the technological achievements of our scientific and business organisations, must be in increasing world population. We will need both social and technological change in the decades and centuries ahead if a reasonable balance is to be maintained between a growing population with rising living standards and an increasing supply of better food.

In the long term the total economic demand for food, as opposed to the social need for it, is likely to grow at a faster rate than population itself. The need for food at any time depends on the size of the population, its age distribution and its activity. With this information our specialists in nutrition can estimate with considerable accuracy the amounts of food needed to maintain the population in a state of good health.

But the economic demand for food depends also on the incomes which people must have if they are to satisfy their needs in the market places of the world. Thus, as the developing nations of the world succeed in raising the incomes of their people, the total effective demand for food will increase even if population were to remain stationary.

Indeed, it is this overwhelming desire throughout the world for a high and rising standard of living that will in the long term turn out to be the effective check on excessive rates of population growth. The mechanism by which the check will be exercised will depend on research, dissemination of information, the desire of parents for a better life for their children, and the policies advanced by governments and supported by the people. This has happened and is happening in the higher income countries. To assume, as some pessimists do, that it will not happen in the developing nations of the world is to assume that people are only biological animals or that the developing nations will fail in their quest for higher incomes. I refuse to accept either of these assumptions.

But our efforts to raise living standards must not be limited to efforts to moderate population growth. We must also strive to increase world production. I accept the need for the former and indeed Kenya has taken the lead in sub-Sahara Africa with a positive programme of family planning education. But what is being done to increase world production? Very little and certainly not enough. Indeed many who could assist with that problem hide behind the spectre of population growth and allege that efforts to increase production are futile. These people attempt to blind us to technological change and agricultural potential. They conjure up images of a growing population requiring more and more land for living space and demanding increasing amounts of food from a steadily diminishing agricultural area.

Let us not be haunted by spectres such as this. The world's agricultural potential is far from being exhausted. While the United

Kingdom produces nearly sixty bushels of wheat to the acre, countries in need of food, like Pakistan and India, produce less than fifteen bushels per acre; while Japan and the United States produce about 4,000 pounds of rice per acre, yields in Pakistan, Burma, Brazil, Thailand, India, the Philippines and Cambodia hover around 1,500 pounds per acre. Future advances in technology will make possible even greater yields per acre than those we now regard as exceptional. Moreover, perhaps 50 per cent of what we now grow is lost to pests, insects and spoilage during storage, transport and marketing. Finally, in many parts of the world substantial amounts of arable land remain untilled and much land that is not now arable could be conditioned for use. It would be conservative in my view to suggest that, with what we know now and when we come to know more, world food output could be multiplied five times.

If we consider sources of food other than land, our estimates of food potential would have to be increased many times over. Already, advances in chemical technology are contributing to our food supply through additives derived from such sources as coal and petroleum. Indeed, petroleum shows promise of becoming a major and inexpensive source of protein. Moreover, food yeast can be produced from by-products of sugar and wood pulp, contributing significantly to world food supplies. Finally, the promise of the sea as a source of food is becoming stronger daily. Indeed, this promise has recently prompted Malta to introduce a motion before the United Nations designed to secure an orderly development of this resource for the benefit of all mankind. Even these limited examples are sufficient to suggest that the expansion of our food supply is primarily a function of our ability as human beings to overcome the limitations of nature. It is not necessary to look far into the future to see the possibility that agricultural sources of food may have to give ground to cheaper alternative sources. Then we in the agricultural countries will have to find more and more industrial uses for our growing agricultural output.

I will not speculate further on the course of events which may yet make swimming an unnecessary skill 850 years hence, because even with rapid advances in medical knowledge most of the youth present here will be old men and women by then. The solutions we seek for today's problems may be coloured by the potential of that distant future, but they must be selected with a view to a somewhat earlier impact. The plain fact is that the optimism with which we can view the far distant future cannot be applied so easily to the next decade and the next generation. Perhaps two-thirds of the world's population *is* undernourished; millions of people are struggling to stay alive on starvation diets; and our ability to cope with these problems on a world-wide basis seems to be deteriorating.

Why are we unable to utilise the world potential for food production? Why can't we find an effective mechanism for transferring food from countries of actual or potential surplus to those in deficit? Why can't we concoct techniques for helping the needy while preserving production incentives? Why can't we assist the poor in the developing countries to increase their output and by so doing to raise their incomes? What holds us back?

Is the problem so big that no solution is possible? Let us examine its magnitude in its largest conceivable sense. By how much must we increase production? What is the gap between need and supply? This gap between social need and food supply can best be considered in two parts, one of which is largely a matter of social conscience while the other is primarily an economic consideration. Each poses for us a somewhat different problem although the two must be considered together if our world food shortage is to be considered realistically. The first is the large gap between social need — the food required to provide necessary calories and nutrients — and effective demand — the amounts of food people can afford to buy. The second is the gap between effective demand at reasonable prices — again what people can afford — and actual or likely production. The first is a 'social gap'; the second an 'economic gap'.

The magnitude of these gaps was recently estimated in a report by the U.N.F.A.O.'s Committee on Commodity Problems. Over and above the food needed to meet effective demand, this report estimates that about another 64 million metric tons of cereal equivalents were needed in 1962 to provide enough calories for an adequate level of consumption for the world's population. In addition another 3·4 million metric tons of skim milk equivalents were required to overcome protein deficiencies. Similar estimates are made for 1975, which take into account probable changes in both effective demand and social need. They suggest that even in 1975 the gap for cereal equivalent foods will be 62·5 million metric tons and for skim milk equivalent over 4·0 million metric tons.

These estimates imply that both today and in 1975 the cost of a food aid programme to close the gap between social need and effective demand and to meet emergency needs is about 6·5 billion dollars or eight times the size of the present effort.

In addition to the social gap we must also consider deficiencies of production in relation to effective demand — what people could afford to buy, let us say at 1962 prices. The seriousness of production deficiencies in the developing nations on economic account alone is shocking. The report to which I have already referred suggests that in 1975, in addition to being unable to meet the gap between social need and effective demand, developing countries are likely to require imports worth 4·8 billion dollars to satisfy effective demand alone, and this shortage in adverse circumstances could be as high as 8·5 billion dollars. The projected deficit is only the more shocking if it is considered that Africa, Asia, and Latin America together exported 11 million tons of grain to other countries, principally to Western Europe, only thirty years ago, a flow that was reversed during the decade of the '40s. In 1966 these same areas had to import 31 million tons.

The total world deficit of food is the sum of these estimates. We must produce enough to fill the social gap and to overcome the shortfall of production on economic grounds alone. In order to satisfy both effective demand and social need, the value of food imports in the developing countries could easily be 11·3 billion dollars in 1975, and might under especially adverse circumstances reach 15 billion dollars, nearly eighteen times the size of actual food aid in 1962. Compared with actual food aid in 1962, the projected shortage in 1975 is large indeed. I have not attempted to minimise it. I have taken the higher of F.A.O.'s range of estimates. In terms of actual world production in recent years these additional needs are not so large. What is 60 million tons of cereals when in 1964 the world produced well over 800 million tons ? What is 15 billion dollars worth of food, when the world produced goods and services worth perhaps 150 times that figure in 1965. And in terms of the vast productive potential of the world to which I referred earlier our needs are truly insignificant.

Nevertheless, any request to finance imports of this magnitude through an international programme would be laughed out of court. On the other hand, the developing countries cannot conceivably finance imports of this magnitude without very substantial assistance. We must, think more on two fronts; make every effort to increase the size of international food aid programmes and at the same time undertake massive efforts to increase food production in the developing countries. The latter is, of course, the most desirable approach. Increasing output in the developing nations reduces their need for imports and by raising the incomes of the poor the gap between social need and effective demand is reduced.

But we have something of an enigma here. How can we satisfy the social need for food without at the same time discouraging the rapid expansion of agricultural production and rural incomes in the developing countries? Now at first glance that problem may appear to be no enigma at all. To satisfy the world-wide need for food, more must be produced and this is certainly consistent with increasing agricultural production in the developing countries. But let us delve beneath the apparent simplicity of the problem. If people cannot afford to buy food and for humanitarian reasons food is given to them at prices below the cost of production, is it really such a simple matter to stimulate the production of the food that is so urgently required? Moreover, if the richer countries are more efficient in producing food or can afford to subsidise its production at home, is it a simple matter to expand food output in the poorer countries? Finally, without storage and transport facilities, organised domestic markets and access to foreign markets, is it even a sensible proposition to encourage surplus production in the developing countries? I think you will agree that this problem is indeed an enigma. As the youth of the world is known to cherish riddles, I would like to examine this one with you in more detail.

There are people who are inadequately fed in every country of the world, but by far the largest number live in the developing countries themselves. It has been estimated that 60 per cent of the population in developing countries suffers from under-nutrition, malnutrition, or both. These are the people whose incomes are so low that they can't afford the food they need and can't produce it for themselves under existing circumstances. These are also the people whose incomes we want to raise, in large part by increasing their production of agricultural commodities.

How can we span this gap between the effective demand and the social need for food? In the longer term there is only one effective and acceptable solution — to raise the incomes and the production of those who cannot now afford to buy the food they so desperately need.

I would not suggest, however, that higher incomes will automatically result in adequate diets. People will then be able to eat what they like, but a balanced diet may be something quite different. Two complementary programmes are also necessary. First, education and information must be widely disseminated so that the tastes of people can be modified in favour of a more varied and nourishing diet. Second, our scientists must continue their efforts to increase the nutrition content of those foods that now make up the basic but limited diets of so many people.

The potential of these two programmes for the alleviation of nutritional deficiencies should not be discounted because so much of it can be realised even in the absence of successful efforts to raise incomes. I am convinced, for example, that many of our subsistence families in Kenya would have fewer nutritional deficiencies if they only wanted the more varied diet which they could grow. Our schools, the 4K clubs, adult education classes, and extension services have a very critical role to play in this endeavour.

But we cannot sit idly by until higher incomes improve tastes and more nutritious foods have given us a healthy world population. Shorter term measures, which may nevertheless have to span generations, are needed to reduce the gap between social need and economic demand. The measure we employ must at the same time avoid disincentive effects in agricultural production, particularly in the developing countries themselves. Prices to those in need must be within their ability to pay; prices to farmers must be high enough to stimulate even larger outputs. We must find a way of doing on a world-wide scale what has been done so successfully in a few advanced countries — establish support prices for farmers in developing countries which will induce there the spectacular increases in output and productivity that have characterised agricultural development in the advanced countries.

The developing countries are themselves too poor to finance a significant gap between incentive prices to farmers and subsidised prices to needy consumers. Nor do I believe it feasible on a world-wide scale to finance a significant gap between farmers' and consumers' prices for the total production of all major crops. What we must do is find an international method of financing such a gap for these farm surpluses intended for needy consumers and grown in the developing countries themselves.

The programme I would propose and which I first outlined in February of this year at the Eighth Session of the Economic Commission for Africa at Lagos would reduce the costs even further by eliminating from world-wide financing all surpluses intended for eventual domestic consumption. This leaves for consideration those surpluses which enter international trade. If we also eliminate from our special programme all regular commercial transactions in international trade, the finance required quickly diminishes.

I have proposed that the United Nations should be prepared to buy in the developing countries surpluses of basic crops at negotiated prices and to dispose of them as necessary in countries where food shortages cannot be met through regular commercial channels. Until we involve the developing countries in the supply as well as the need of these crops, we will make little discernible progress towards eliminating the problem. Increasingly, the surpluses of food for the needy must be found in the developing countries themselves. Advance commitments to purchase surpluses at guaranteed incentive prices from those developing nations with the potential to produce them would, in my view be a very effective way of getting strong, constructive agricultural programmes moving in those countries. This programme should also reduce considerably the present heavy dependence on supplies from a few countries. Administration of the programme under United Nations auspices should achieve a desirable separation between famine relief and political controversy.

In disposing of its purchases the United Nations would have to employ a flexible policy. Some could be sold to governments at world market prices possibly on a deferred payment basis, leaving to those governments the problem of subsidising the poor who need grain. Some would have to be sold at reduced prices to governments which themselves cannot afford to subsidise prices. In either case stern measures will be necessary, as now, to ensure that leakages of subsidised grain into regular commercial channels do not undermine incentives for domestic production.

A purchase programme of this kind will add considerable incentive to production in developing countries but will not in itself ensure that the required output will be forthcoming. More aid must be channelled to agriculture. In recent years only 6 per cent of financial aid and 15 per cent of technical assistance has been devoted to a sector of the economy on which perhaps 75 per cent of the people in the developing nations depend directly for a living. These discouraging figures are already in the process of increasing, but even more must be done.

Aid alone is not, of course, the answer. We in the developing countries must examine, modify and in some cases revolutionise our land tenure policies. We must make more rational decisions on land use. We must enhance the status of rural living. We must initiate co-ordinated and comprehensive rural development programmes instead of relying on extension service advice alone. We must expand research and adapt technology to our needs and circumstances. In the last analysis, however, there must be a joint effort to solve what is truly a world-wide problem. Aid and self-help combined in appropriate proportions and on an imaginative and massive scale can make substantial progress toward raising both production and incomes where both are most needed.

But higher production without considerable improvement in the distribution of the incomes generated may still leave us far short of social objectives. Indeed, the composition of production is heavily determined by income distribution and often in ways which may magnify the gap between social need and effective demand. The efforts of developing nations to raise incomes requires that land be devoted to the most profitable uses and these are not necessarily the most desirable from the social point of view. To seek the most profitable use of land, or of any other resource for that matter, means that production must be directed to those goods for which people can and will pay. Profit seeking production follows money demand indiscriminately; social need is determined by our concern for people, regardless of their incomes. The two can be reconciled through the market mechanism alone only if income distribution is such that every one who needs food has the income to exercise our demand for it.

Today, the world's use of land is distorted in favour of the higher income groups. The world's land area today is used only in part for the organic raw materials. Much of the rest is used for living space, industrial plant sites, tourism, etc. — uses which yield a high economic return because the services are demanded by people with incomes, but which do not add directly to food supply. Moreover, much of the land used to produce organic raw material is used for non-food purposes such as forests, tobacco and cotton. Finally, much of the edible production is bought by industrial users or used to produce alcoholic beverages or as feed for more exotic foods which higher income groups can afford to buy. Clearly, some of the inadequacy of today's food production, as measured against social need, can be traced to the very inequalities in income distribution from which the social need arises.

One final complicating factors in our enigma deserves note. The technical ability to produce does not mean an ability to sell. The isolated subsistence farmer may be able to produce much more than he and his family can consume. Indeed, if we observe him working only a few hours a day we may be tempted to call him a lazy good-for-nothing. It is clearly ridiculous for him to produce surpluses which will only rot in the field for lack of transport, storage and marketing facilities. It is my own feeling that while agricultural aid has been clearly deficient in total, we have allocated far too little of the aid available to the improvement of transport, storage and marketing facilities.

An effective international food programme cannot limit its functions to the purchase of surpluses wherever they can be found and to disposing of them where need exists. This approach will tend to perpetuate surplus production in the advanced countries with all the risks attendant on isolated and unplanned sources of supply and political preferences. The programme must, therefore, allocate more of its effort to stimulating production in developing nations and in particular to assisting with storage and marketing facilities and carrying costs in those countries having the potential to produce surpluses. It is patently unrealistic to attempt a solution to the growing food problem which relies in its essence on surplus production in the advanced countries without at the same time stimulating production and incomes in the developing nations.

What then is the future of agricultural production in the developing world? In the longer term I can visualise these areas becoming major suppliers of essential food crops. Beyond that as marine and chemical food supplies grow more and more agricultural produce may be intended for industrial uses. Indeed, chemistry may eventually be the science which will make many agriculturally based economies viable in the long term.

In the shorter term, it is in our hands to make or break many of the agriculturally based developing nations. It would be the height of insanity to establish a food programme intended to meet immediate social needs which at the same time undercut the potential of the developing countries to increase their own production and thereby raise their incomes and effective demand. The ultimate solution must be to close the gap by raising effective demand, incomes, and domestic food production not by undertaking steps which widen the gap in the very process of filling it. I am not unaware of the cries of the needy or of the urgency to respond to their entreaties quickly and effectively. Let us at the same time strive to give them the opportunity to help themselves, and each other.

I have raised this problem of food production with you tonight because it is the heart of the larger problem of economic development, because it is appropriate at a conference under F.A.O. auspices, and particularly because it is in need of a youthful search for solutions. It is the youth of the world who look to the future, who are willing to see new and imaginative ways to forge ahead, who can make large programmes possible and impossible tasks tractable. Your teachers and elders are too often steeped in the past, committed to the old ways and bound to magnitudes that with growth have already faded into insignificance. It is the youth of the world who must make the transition from the past knowledge to future needs. The youth must not be swayed by the petty jealousies, economic self-interest and political intrigues that have warped the thinking of the older generation. You are right to rebel against such things, and we will all be better off for it. But above all the Young World Food and Development appeal comes at a time when the world is in dire need of vigorous national policies as well as an imaginative world approach to this problem. In developing nations we face the danger of an exodus from the land thereby reducing production and creating unemployment at the same time. Youth has to be taught to enjoy living and working on the land. In the developed countries youth is in a rebellious mood, but often they seem concerned with the more sophisticated problems of the world. What we need is the greater concern with the world's oldest and most basic problem — food. I am sure the F.A.O. effort to mobilise the youth of the world to face this challenge is well timed. My hope is that all countries will give this programme the support that it deserves. I wish your Conference every success.

Conclusion

THE CHALLENGE OF DEVELOPMENT

THE CHALLENGE OF DEVELOPMENT

In June 1967 an important conference was held in Nairobi covering the whole spectrum of Human Development, from the framework of economic planning to the tremendous movements of social and cultural change sweeping the continent. Contributions were made by experts from Tunisia, Tanzania, Malagasy, Nigeria, Uganda, Zambia and Kenya. Mr. Mboya prepared the paper which is reproduced here and the title of which has been used for this book. Mr. Mboya's paper was also used for the title of monograph No. 7 put out later by the East African Publishing House and the sponsors of the conference.

I would like to observe that there are two questions implicit in 'The Challenge of Development'. The first question is: What is the challenge? The second is: Why is it a challenge?

In my view the challenge is that of rapid economic and social progress of the underdeveloped nations for the benefit of their populations. Fortunately, it is not necessary to explain why these countries must develop. The misery, poverty, unemployment and insecurity of life which characterise the underdeveloped countries are now being recognised. The people of these countries recognise that their hardships are not inevitable. In the developed countries, the poverty and misery of the underdeveloped countries are now being recognised, albeit gradually. However, in many of the developed countries the majority of the people have no idea as to the seriousness and the size of the problem. What is perhaps more serious is that where the problem is recognised, there is a tendency for the people in the developed countries to assume a distant attitude, while they should be, instead, thoroughly concerned. I will return to this point later.

The second question is: Why is rapid economic and social development a challenge? It has now become quite clear that despite efforts the underdeveloped countries are making in the field of development, the gap between them and the rich nations is increasing. This is happening not really because of insufficient effort on their part but because of certain forces which are in operation. In the last decade or so, some of the so-called developing countries have not been developing.

In fact, in some cases *per capita* incomes have fallen, while for very many of them *per capita* incomes have either remained constant or have risen at negligible rates. In short, the five per cent target rate of growth for the underdeveloped countries set by the United Nations General Assembly for the development decade (1960s) will not be achieved although major strides towards it could be made given international dedication to the cause. On the other hand, rapid growth rates have been recorded in the industrially developed nations. As a matter of irony, it is the developed nations which are the developing nations. The lot of the underdeveloped countries has been stagnation, although there are a number of notable exceptions. Consequently, it is only euphemistic to refer to them as the developing countries.

The widening gap between the rich and the poor nations must be seen against the background of the so-called revolution of rising expectations in the developing countries which is gathering considerable momentum. This is the problem. It is an international problem, not only because world peace will never be fully achieved in a world of 'haves' and 'have-nots', but also because material progress of the world as a whole will be held down if the poor countries do not develop rapidly. Moreover, the problem is likely to get worse unless full attention is turned towards its solution. There are those prophets of doom in the rich nations who try to give the impression that this problem is impossible of solution. On the other hand there are those people in the developing countries who tend to over-simplify the problem and say that if only more aid were given the problem would disappear.

These two views are wrong. The problem can be solved, certainly not overnight, but within a much shorter period of time than frequently mentioned in academic discussions if the world as a whole turned full, sustained and positive attention to it. I will now present some thoughts very briefly on the possible ways of solving this problem. Needless to say, my discussion on this is not exhaustive, if only because of the complexity of the problem and the fact that each of the points I will make below could benefit from infinitely more detailed discussion and analysis. My purpose then will be to indicate, not to put forward final suggestions.

Achievement of rapid development in the developing countries requires simultaneous and complementary action by the developed countries on the one hand, and the underdeveloped countries on the other. As a starting point, we should perhaps mention some of the requirements for more rapid development in the developing countries. Here, I must seek indulgence for gross over-simplification in that, in this discussion, I will regard all developing countries as forming one identifiable group with similar problems. This is not, of course, true. There are those countries, especially in Latin America, where *per capita* incomes are several times those of the African countries. There also are differences in the stage of industrialisation reached, the available stock of high-level manpower, diversity of exports, development of infrastructure, and so on. There are, however, broadly similar problems in all these countries. Some of these common attributes are, for example, dependence on agriculture for both foreign exchange earnings and employment; fluctuations in export earnings; deterioration in terms of trade; difficulties of selling manufactured goods in the industrial nations; rapidly increasing populations; unemployment and underemployment and existence of large subsistence sectors. At any rate there have been enough similar problems and difficulties in the field of economic development, especially as regards international trade and foreign aid, for these countries to come together and form a group in the first U.N. Conference on Trade and Development.

One way of identifying the requirements of more rapid development in the developing countries is to look at the constraints in their development. This can be further reduced to examining shortages in key resources. In these countries there are severe shortages of high-level manpower, domestic savings, foreign exchange and government revenues. There are obviously other shortages, for example land and water, in some of these countries. But by and large the ones listed here are the most common. The solution to the under-development of the developing countries must be based on attempts to ease these shortages.

I will start by making proposals regarding what is expected from the developed countries. My proposals fall into four categories: the international power struggle, financial aid, technical assistance, and trade.

It is most unfortunate that while the world should be concerned with the development of all its resources for the benefit of all its people, a lot of emotional energy and material output are being spent on an international power struggle and ideological warfare. What is perhaps more unfortunate is the fact that the big powers are doing all they can to draw the developing countries into this conflict. It appears to me that the world needs a new objective which should be the development of all its resources for more and more equitably distributed benefits. At present, expenditure on war preparations is substantially well over one-twelfth of all output. Further more, valuable technical resources, including scientists and engineers, which could be used for development are, from the point of view of the world as a whole, being wasted. Without international peace and good will, the development of the poor nations will always take second place.

The other field where thorough re-examination is needed concerns financial aid to the developing nations. Several observations can be made here. Firstly, the aid being given is not enough. In fact, the volume of aid is far short of the 1 per cent of the developed countries' Gross Domestic Products which has been generally regarded to be the minimum target. Moreover, net aid given is even smaller than the figures frequently published by the donor countries because of repayments and interest charges. This poor performance must be compared with the expenditure on war preparations which, as I have already indicated, amounts to several times more than the amount of aid being given.

Secondly, financial aid is becoming more and more tied to the imports and professional services of the donor countries. This has several consequences. For example, the donor country may not be the cheapest market for the goods and services concerned, in which case the aid given will not go so far as it would otherwise do. It forces the recipient countries to distort their priorities and embark upon, say, industrial projects instead of agricultural extension. Since aid tied to imports does not cover local costs, aid tying makes it difficult, and in some cases impossible, to use the aid promised. It leads to diversity of capital equipment in the developing country with resultant increases in maintenance costs.

The increasing tendency today is not only tying financial aid to imports and services from the donors but also to particular projects as well. This has, at times, very unfortunate and serious consequences in the developing countries. For instance, it encourages these countries to think in terms of big and mainly industrial projects which ultimately do not do well because, among other things, the development of other sectors does not keep pace.

There is another new development which is worth noting. Some countries seem keen on using aid for export promotion purposes as well as redirecting the trade of the recipient countries. What happens is that a developing country is given goods on credit to sell in her domestic market to generate the financial resources required for a given aid project. While such a procedure may work in a few cases because it generates resources for the local costs required, the usual thing is that it depresses the recipient country's existing industries whose products are displaced by the goods obtained on credit. Consequently, this kind of aid has very limited value and is one explanation why many developing countries have not actually made us of aid promised by certain donors.

Thirdly, the flow of aid is irregular, which means, that the developing countries cannot plan ahead effectively. This is very important because the developing countries will not achieve much unless they plan on a continuous and long-term basis. Furthermore, aid is given on an annual basis. For most donor countries, the amount of aid to be given is determined annually in the national budget. This way of giving aid means that politics come into play if only in the sense that aid can be cut off because of political differences between the donor and the recipient. Aid has actually been cut off in some cases for such trivial reasons as the recipient recognising another country not on good terms with the donor. This tends to build up hostile pressures against aid and is one strong reason (there are others, of course) why multilateral aid should be increased. Unfortunately, the developed countries are giving little support to multilateral aid and the trend is for bilateral aid to become more and more dominant.

Fourthly, aid is being given increasingly on a short-term basis, while what is needed is long-term loans or grants. In fact short-term capital is abundant, but its use for development purposes is restricted because a poor country soon finds herself with an impossible debt burden. In trying to move out of such a situation, a developing country is often forced to cut down expenditures as a condition for more assistance. As a result, development is interrupted. This problem is made worse by encouragement given by the developed countries to their private entrepreneurs to establish 'turn-key' projects for the developing countries. With regard to 'turn-key' projects, it must be realised that what a developing country needs is not only, say, a sugar factory but also assistance for growing sugar-cane, building roads for the project, training extension officers, and so on. All these problems need to be clearly recognised, for they seriously restrict the effectiveness and contribution of the aid actually given.

By and large aid from international organisations such as the International Bank for Reconstruction and Development and the International Development Association is much better, although the World Bank itself still seems to insist on financing those projects which are considered profitable. The point, however, is that if aid is going to be aid for development and not an instrument of foreign political policies and export promotion, it must be increased, given more regularly and be united to imports and services from the donors. Another thing which needs to be done is to reduce the complexity regarding foreign aid. There are so many different procedures, preferences as regards projects and conditions on their aid, that unless a country has someone working fully on how to get aid, it will not get as much aid as those countries with such experts. This is yet another reason why multilateral aid should be given support.

Another field where action by the developed nation is required concerns technical assistance. It has now been realised that rapid development requires not only capital but also skills. In the countries of Africa there are very serious shortages of high-level and medium-level manpower, mainly because the colonial masters did not provide for the education of the African people. In fact, the policy of colonialism was not to develop the indigenous people but the resources available for the benefits of the immigrant communities and the metropolitan power. The African countries are now making every effort to educate their people. But this takes time. For instance it takes about fifteen years to produce a university graduate, and a few more years for doctors, veterinarians and engineers. Consequently, if these countries were to depend on their own people, development will be intolerably slow. It is therefore obvious that the developing countries require not only financial aid but also technical assistance in the form of high-level manpower. The greater the volume of technical assistance the sooner will be the time when the developing countries can be reasonably self-sufficient in this field. I should also point out that the argument often put forward that the capital-absorptive capacities of the developing countries are limited and therefore there is no sense of giving them more financial aid, holds little water if technical assistance programmes are stepped up.

Finally, and as far as the developed nations are concerned, I come to the problem of trade. The seriousness of the trade problems facing the developing countries were considered at great length at the first U.N. Trade and Development Conference in Geneva. One major problem is the deterioration in the terms of trade of the poor nations. There are some economists who argue that there are no indications of a long-term downward trend in these countries' terms of trade. This may be true if one examines the last half century or so, but it is cold comfort. Certainly in the last decade and a half the terms of trade facing these countries have deteriorated. At the moment there are no signs of this trend reversing itself. The result of this has been that the losses incurred by these countries through falling prices of their exports and rising prices of their imports have been greater than all the aid given. Moreover, the fluctuations in these countries' foreign exchange earnings have created enormous problems, including interruptions in their development efforts.

There are several other trade problems in which appropriate action by the industrial countries is needed. First, almost without exception, developed countries heavily protect their farmers by quantitative measures, tariffs, internal fiscal charges which limit demand for imports from underdeveloped countries, and the so-called health regulations against livestock products. Incidentally, and as regards health regulations on livestock products, the developing countries realise the need to protect the livestock industry in the developed countries from such diseases as foot and mouth and rinderpest. But the appropriate action is to give all the assistance necessary to the developing countries to overcome the animal diseases involved. This is the positive approach: the present practices of just barring imports are essentially negative.

Because of all these restrictions, underdeveloped countries are finding it difficult to increase their export earnings. It should be realised that these countries prefer to earn their foreign exchange instead of being given aid on an essentially charity basis. As it is, the industrial countries are slowly edging out the developing countries in the total world exports of primary products because the industrial nations are increasing their share in total world exports of these products.

Trade restrictions are not only applied on primary products. In fact, tariffs are higher for manufactured and semi-manufactured goods. This does not make sense because industrialisation is necessary if the developing countries are to raise incomes and provide employment to their increasing populations. If the developed countries opened their markets to the manufactured products of the developing countries, they could help enormously in the industrialisation process of these countries.

Over and above all this, there is the serious problem of the increasing production of synthetics which makes the future of primary exports to the industrial nations even more bleak. One comes to the conclusion that definite measures to remove trade obstacles in the way of the developing countries' exports must be taken by the developed countries. The developing countries will not grow rapidly unless they can exploit their natural resources. This requires access to the markets of the industrial nations. I do not have to point out that financial aid and technical assistance will achieve little unless the developing countries can sell the products produced on the basis of this assistance. Trade and aid must go together: to deal with only one and forget the other is not enough.

The achievement of rapid economic and social development of the developing countries will also depend on these countries' own efforts. The major burden in this task is, and should be, on their shoulders. Unless these countries make the maximum possible effort and sacrifice for the attainment of their own economic independence, they have neither a moral claim to outside assistance nor is foreign aid likely to do them much good in the long run. Moreover, they cannot expect foreigners to do this work. If this happens, not only will the developing countries be disappointed in most cases, but the foreigners will try to get the maximum they can through young nations' natural resources. In short, resources of these countries will be developed for the benefit of the foreigners, instead of the indigenous people. Furthermore, these countries will never achieve economic independence: neo-colonialism will be the order of the day.

There are several things which the developing nations must do. Firstly, they must avoid being involved in the power struggle and ideological warfare which is raging on an ever-increasing scale. To be involved in this struggle means to relegate the objective of rapid development to second place. This must not happen.

Secondly, the developing countries must be committed to, and believe in, rapid development. Such commitment is a precondition for sustained and maximum effort and sacrifice. To assume a fatalistic attitude will be disastrous. It will be like an army going to war already convinced that it will be defeated.

Perhaps I should mention here what the term 'effort and sacrifice' means. Earlier I indicated critical shortages facing the developing countries in certain key resources. The developing countries should do all they can to overcome this. Education and training programmes, with the short-term and long-term manpower needs of the country in mind, must be mounted to over-come shortages of high-level and medium-level manpower. Savings campaigns, including establishment of appropriate institutions, must be mounted, followed by measures to ensure that the savings are retained in the country and invested in those areas where they can be of maximum benefit to the country. The need to inculcate savings habits at early stages of development should be recognised, so that savings can increase rapidly as *per capita* incomes rise. Unless deliberate steps are taken, increases in incomes are likely to go into conspicuous consumption and more demands for imports. Here I am not·suggesting that living standards should not be allowed to rise. On the contrary; the living standards of the mass of the people in the developing nations are so low that, of necessity, they must be raised as rapidly as possible. However, one must also recognise the connection between more savings now, and improved living standards in the future. It is our experience in Kenya that for every pound we save and invest, we can get £3 to £4 from·abroad. Domestic savings are therefore important in attracting foreign capital into the country. I need not point out that investment of domestic savings ensures that benefits are retained in the country, instead of being remitted abroad. These are only some of the reasons why every effort must be made to increase domestic savings. Savings campaigns are only one measure. Other measures include taxation, wage policies and exchange controls. In particular it should be observed that formulation of appropriate wage policies presents a real challenge in the developing countries. Unless care is taken, wage increases as a result of union demands may make it more difficult to provide adequate employment, besides making the products produced uncompetitive in price. One way out of this difficulty is to have the trade unions thoroughly involved in the development effort, so they can be guided by national objectives and needs, instead of narrow views and interests. Trade Unions must realise that if we were to distribute all the benefits of our economic activities to wage earners, we would have only served a small but privileged minority of our population.

As regards the shortages of foreign exchange, I have already outlined areas in which the developed countries can enormously help. The developing countries themselves can do a lot to ease this problem if they recognise that policies of import substitution must not obscure the need for export promotion. This means, *inter alia*, that agriculture should not be neglected in the development programme. It means that such industries as tourism should be given the attention they deserve.

Our country, Kenya, has a great tourist potential and so have many other African countries. But there are two quick observations I feel I must make at this point. Development of tourism should not be restricted only to the attraction of overseas visitors. As our peoples' incomes increase, they too should be encouraged to enjoy our tourist attractions. This alone can help development in some areas which may not immediately attract foreign visitors. At the same time we must not restrict tourism to showing wild life, scenic beauty and historic sights. It should include a tour of major development areas. These are projects which can be of great attraction to foreign visitors. Such an approach will help in efforts to sell our products abroad. If one takes the developing countries as a group, the success in earning more foreign exchange from the developed nations will depend on the necessary actions being taken by the latter group of countries.

Another shortage, not so universal as the former three, is that of government revenue. In the developing nations there are great pressures on the governments to provide certain welfare services, and to participate on an increasing scale in all sectors of the economy. Moreover, it is becoming common for foreign firms to insist on government participation in projects — mainly as an assurance against nationalisation, although joint participation is also insisted on for other reasons, e.g. since the government has a stake in the project, it will be committed to its profitability and thus will not, for instance, allow competitors to come in. Furthermore, with efforts to stimulate development of the economy, recurrent costs tend to rise fairly rapidly, especially where social services, including education, are given emphasis. From all this, it will be clear that government revenues must rise rapidly as development takes place. This is easily said but difficult to achieve. There are such problems as the *per capita* incomes, lack of experienced tax administrators and difficulties of reaching agricultural incomes which make it difficult to obtain significant revenue from conventional taxes. Over and above this, there is the fact that taxation must be consistent with rapid development, i.e. it must not kill the goose that lays the golden egg. For all these reasons, it is obvious that measures to increase government revenue will differ from country to country. There are, however, several areas in which the developing countries could co-operate. One such area is the inducements given to private investors. At the moment, developing countries are competing for private foreign capital by offering more inducements than those offered by their neighbours. This only works to their mutual disadvantage and to the benefit of the private investors. In terms of potential tax revenues, this competition is very costly.

I now come to a most important action which developing countries can take, not only to accelerate rates of development already attained, or promote efficiency of economic co-operation among the developed nations, but to establish the necessary conditions for development to take place. This point must be grasped, for it means the matter is that much more urgent.

Economic co-operation among developing countries must include effective measures to increase trade among themselves. When one examines trade statistics of developing countries, one notices their trade is mainly with the industrial nations. Trade among them is only a small proportion of their total trade. Intra-trade is a source of growth which so far has been little exploited. In particular, if these countries are to industrialise on the basis of import substitution, it must be realised that the larger the domestic market the easier and more rapid will industrialisation be. This also applies to some sectors of the agricultural industry. It is not unusual these days to see agricultural products in a developing country rotting away while her neighbours continue to import similar products from the industrial nations.

What perhaps is not fully realised is that economic co-operation does not only mean tariff preferences. Indeed, tariff preferences are only a permissive measure. To be effective, tariff preferences must be accompanied by co-operation in other sectors, for example in co-ordinated industrial programmes. It must be accompanied by measures to improve transportation and means of communications among these countries. This is particularly important in Africa. In this continent, transportation facilities are often straight lines from the interior to the sea outlets, for this suited the interests of the colonial powers who developed them. If the African countries are to benefit from trade with each other, every effort must be made to link these nations together through roads and, in some cases, railways.

Economic co-operation among the developing countries presents not only a real opportunity for more rapid development but a challenge: in the sense that most political problems are also economic ones. Some countries fear that economic co-operation might dilute their recently gained sovereignty. My view is that this sovereignty will be an empty possession (and indeed it will be hard to maintain it!) unless we also attain economic sovereignty. To achieve economic sovereignty requires economic co-operation on the widest scale possible. The longer we wait the more difficult and costly will it be to co-operate effectively.

Another aspect of co-operation which receives little attention is in the field of technical assistance and manpower development. It is common to look to Western Europe, America, Eastern Europe and even Asia when we people in Africa seek training opportunities for our own people. We do this when we wish to recruit staff for our services or projects, and again when we wish to appoint a commission to study our economic or social institutions! In short, we have forgotten the roses in our garden. This outlook is the result of many years of dependence on overseas countries. But I suggest that already within Africa there is increasing scope for technical assistance — backed by the United Nations where necessary — between our own countries. This trend can be accelerated if we press more and more for experts from other African countries. It has the advantage that such experts will be more familiar with our problems. We should press multilateral agencies to support this approach even more than we have done in the past. In manpower training we could save on capital expenditure and personnel by more intensive use of already existing facilities to cater for the sub-regions of Africa.

Africa must make her contribution to the U.N. and other international agencies. But the draining of our nations to serve on such bodies must be reviewed. We need a formula that will reconcile the need to take a more active part in U.N. organisations and the need for trained manpower in our countries. This will enable our promising young people to be employed to serve in their own countries or sub-regions for at least a period of time. Otherwise, the moment we train a person, he leaves the country because he is offered a fat salary and great opportunities by an international organisation.

I would like to conclude by going back to the seriousness of the problem of the wide and widening gap between the rich nations and the poor nations. A visitor from another planet would be appalled by what he sees on Earth. He would see people in rich nations suffering from diseases of affluence, while millions of people in the poor nations are suffering from abject poverty and lack of the most basic needs. He would see in some countries farmers being persuaded not to produce, while in some continents people are dying of hunger. He would see vast resources being wasted in preparing for war against fellow Earthmen. He would see relatively empty countries with stringent immigration controls while in other countries population density is reaching a critical stage.

It so happens that there is nothing which unites a people as strongly as a common enemy. What we need is a common enemy. The point, however, is that we have such an enemy — not in another planet but here on Earth, namely, the poverty of the so-called developing nations.

POSTSCRIPT
BY MRS. PAMELA MBOYA

This volume is proof that while a man's life can be tragically and wastefully cut short, the ideals and principles for which he stood can live on. For me and my children and our family as a whole, Tom's love is a permanent inspiration. It is my sincere hope, therefore, that what Tom stood for, as seen in this book and his other writings, will continue to inspire the future generations in Kenya, Africa, and the whole world.

Apart from the horror, shock and personal grief and loss which I felt at my husband's murder, I was also stricken at the thought of how much he had hoped to achieve and how much will now remain undone. Many friends have generously pointed out the range and value of what he had already undertaken and accomplished in so many fields. As a wife I was more specially and constantly aware of all his hopes for the future of our country and its people.

This book was one project among scores which he was involved in at the time of his death. It was one which was particularly dear to him and it is for this reason that I took the decision that publication should go ahead as quickly as possible. Fortunately, its preparation was almost completed at the time of his death, and a number of friends who had been closely involved in its planning, particularly Philip Ndegwa and Tony Hughes, were able to continue their work and see it through to fulfilment in the way my husband would have wished. I am grateful to them and to the publishers for their help and understanding. I hope that its publication will make some contribution to the frank and open discussion of the problems facing our country, our continent and our world. For, as Tom believed, action based on principle, not force and violence, will solve these problems. Force and violence can only increase them.